THE SOUTH PARK
EPISODE GUIDE

VOLUME 1   SEASONS 1 - 5

Creative Direction and Design by Christopher "Crispy" Brion
Art Direction by Brandon Levin
Licensing Artists: Erick Thorpe, Jeff Delgado
Layouts by Matthew Goodman
Edited by Greg Jones
Special Thanks to Anne Garefino

Typography: South Park and Arial

Running Press Book Publishers
2300 Chestnut Street
Philadelphia, PA 19103-4371

Visit us on the web!
www.runningpress.com
Visit South Park on the Web at:
www.southparkstudios.com

THE SOUTH PARK EPISODE GUIDE
Volume 1 - Seasons 1-5

Created by Trey Parker and Matt Stone

Text by Sam Stall

Additional material by James Siciliano

TOM'S RHINOPLASTY

Post Office

RUNNING PRESS
PHILADELPHIA • LONDON

CONTENTS

INTRO (P.7)

By Sam Stall

SEASON 1 (P.9)

SEASON 2 (P.36)

INTRODUCTION

Ever since the first *South Park* episode aired on August 13, 1997, the world has been waiting patiently for an in-depth, truly authoritative analysis of the show's cultural and social impact.

Well, keep waiting.

Instead, what you will find inside is an almost obsessively comprehensive recap of the first five seasons, from the Season 1 premier, "Cartman Gets An Anal Probe," all the way to the Season 5 capstone, "Butters' Very Own Episode," which originally aired on December 12, 2001.

In addition to fanatically thorough plot summaries, this episode guide tells you what fucked-up things inspired the creators to write it. You get body counts and graphic descriptions of the grossest deaths. Classic lines are highlighted next to details about every celebrity take-down. All that and more fun facts that even the most hardcore fans haven't figured out yet.

So if you want to know how many times the word "shit" was deployed during "It Hits the Fan," or who uttered the immortal phrase, "Get out of my ass you stupid rainbows!" during "Weight Gain 4000," then this is your book. Hell, this is your Bible.

—Sam Stall

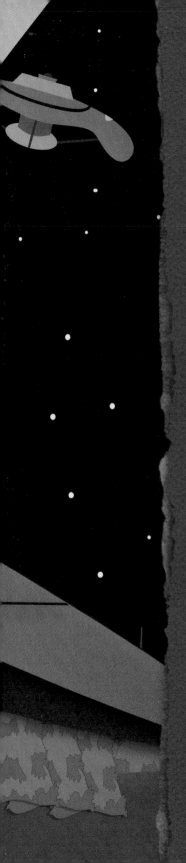

SEASON 1

CARTMAN GETS AN ANAL PROBE

Original Air Date: August 13, 1997
Episode No. 101

THE STORY: One morning at the bus stop, Cartman tells Kyle, Stan and Kenny that he dreamed he was abducted by aliens and given an anal probe. The boys think it actually happened, but Cartman refuses to believe. After they board the school bus Kyle looks out the rear window and is horrified to see his baby brother Ike taken away by aliens.

During lunch in the cafeteria, Stan is confronted by his secret love, Wendy Testaburger, and gets so nervous he vomits on her. In spite of the fact that he always pukes in her presence, the two decide to meet later. Cartman emits a flaming fart, followed by a long metal stalk with a giant mechanical eye on its tip. It takes a quick look around before retreating back inside its host.

Though Cartman—in spite of ample evidence to the contrary—still doesn't believe in the "visitors," Chef does. He pulls the cafeteria's fire alarm so the boys can escape and head for the woods to look for Ike. En route Cartman gets zapped by a mysterious ray that causes him to perform a 1930s ditty called "I Love to Singa." When a UFO passes overhead, Kyle hits it with a rock. The ship retaliates by firing a death ray that, inevitably, strikes Kenny.

In an inaugural death scene that's only slightly less protracted than the one in Brian's Song, Kenny is first singed by the ray, then crushed by stampeding cattle, then run over by a police car.

Shortly thereafter Cartman abandons the quest. Stan also bails in order to keep his rendezvous with Wendy.

Kyle, dejected, tags along with Stan. Wendy suggests using "the fat kid" to lure the aliens. Cartman is rounded up and tethered to a tree, and an 80-foot satellite dish promptly emerges from his anus. The aliens arrive and a hatch on the side of their mother ship opens, revealing Ike. He jumps down into a snow bank. Meanwhile, the aliens begin a long conversation with a herd of local cattle. Via subtitles, we learn that of all Earth's life forms, they respect cows most of all. They give them a strange-looking device, then return to their ship and depart—but not before beaming up Cartman. As the ship flies off he's heard screaming, "Heeeeeeelp! Sons a bitcheeees! Diiiiiillldooos!"

Stan repeatedly vomits on Wendy. Kyle and Ike go home.

The next day Stan and Kyle wait for the school bus as usual. Suddenly Cartman falls out of the sky. He says he had another bizarre abduction "dream," during which Scott Baio, who was aboard the alien ship, gave him pinkeye.

Stan and Kyle point out that Cartman does, indeed, now have pinkeye.

Finally, Officer Barbrady corners the runaway cows that met with the visitors. They promptly zap him with the alien device, which causes Barbrady to perform "I Love to Singa," just like Cartman did.

Where'd The Idea Come From? Trey and Matt are fascinated with alien "visitors"—specifically the tall, big-headed, black-eyed ones featured in everything from *Close Encounters of the Third Kind* to *The X Files*. They surface regularly in later South Park episodes, and appeared (in the background) during numerous scenes in *Cannibal! The Musical*.

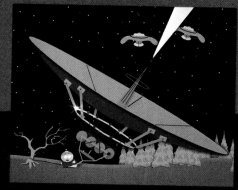

MEMORABLE LINES:

"Screw you guys, I'm going home!"
—*Cartman*

"Ow, my ass!"
—*Cartman*

"Yeah, I want Cheesy Poofs!"
—*Cartman*

"Oh my God! They killed Kenny!"
—*Stan*

"You bastards!"
—*Kyle*

"No Kitty, this is MY pot pie!!!"
—*Cartman*

"I'm not fat, I'm big boned."
—*Cartman*

"Kick the baby!"
—*Kyle*

BODY COUNT

Just Kenny and a couple of cows. Cartman causes potentially life-threatening injuries with his flaming farts, setting both Pip (the annoying English kid) and his own cat, Kitty, on fire

CHARACTER DEBUTS

Stan, Kyle, Cartman, and Kenny, plus Chef, Wendy, Mr. Garrison, Ike, Pip, Cartman's mom, Ms. Crabtree, Officer Barbrady, Farmer Denkins, Visitors, Mr. Hat, Kitty.

ORIGINAL SONGS

The episode opens with the boys singing "School Days" at the bus stop, and they also break into song after ditching school with "We Got Out of School. . . ." But the real iconic tune from this episode is Chef's first song, "I'm Gonna Make Love To Ya Woman." It's the first of many, many sexual lessons that Chef teaches the boys through the magic of song.

POINTLESS OBSERVATION

"Cartman Gets an Anal Probe," along with "Damien" (page 28) are the only two South Park episodes to get a TV-14-DLV rating, instead of the show's customary TV-MA.

POP-CULTURE REFERENCES

The tune "I Love to Singa" is lifted from a 1936 Tex Avery cartoon. Weirdly, it also served as one of the inspirations for the movie Happy Feet. And when the local cattle, fearing they'll be mutilated by the aliens, try to escape on a train, the conductor tells them he can't allow "cows on a people train." It's an absurdly obscure reference to the children's book In a People House, which was written by Dr. Seuss under the pseudonym Theo LeSeig.

While waiting for first contact with the aliens, Chef mentions that there's only 20 minutes before Sanford & Son is on. Apparently, Chef was a big fan of the 70's show starring Red Foxx.

BEHIND THE SCENES

This is the only South Park episode that Matt and Trey animated themselves, using bits of cutout paper to create every . . . single . . . frame.

It took three months to animate the entire 28 minute pilot in "stop motion." Yet, the pilot episode as you see it does have a few brief scenes in which computer animation was added—most notably, the scene where the 80-foot satellite comes out of Cartman's ass. After this episode, South Park switched entirely to computer animation. Otherwise they'd probably still be working on the first season.

CELEBRITIES IMPUGNED

When Kyle pleads with Ike to take a gigantic swan dive off the alien ship, he tells him to "Do your impersonation of David Caruso's career." At the time Caruso had made the extremely unwise decision to ditch the TV show NYPD Blue and pursue movie roles.

When watching a news report about local UFO sightings, Cartman observes that a crop circle, when seen from overhead, "kinda looks like Tom Selleck." The crop circle is actually a picture of Cartman.

Although he's not seen in the episode, Scott Baio (star of Who's the Boss and Joanie Loves Chachi) is reportedly responsible for giving Cartman pinkeye while aboard the alien space ship.

WHAT KYLE LEARNED

"This morning you took my brother, Ike. He's the little freckled kid that looks like a football. At first I was happy you took him away. But I've learned something today: that having a little brother is a pretty special thing."

WEIGHT GAIN 4000

Original Air Date: August 27, 1997
Episode No. 102

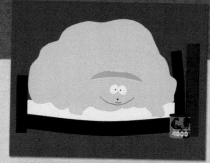

THE STORY: Cartman wins a "Save Our Fragile Planet" essay contest, for which he's to receive a trophy from Kathie Lee Gifford on national TV. To "get in shape" for his big moment he gorges on a high-calorie body-building product called Weight Gain 4000. Soon he's packing on pounds of extra fat.

The entire town goes berserk over Gifford—except for Mr. Garrison. Decades earlier Gifford crushed and humiliated him during a children's talent show. Mr. Garrison—and, more importantly, Mr. Hat—never forgave her.

On the day of the award ceremony Mr. Garrison takes a rifle up to the second floor of the town's book depository and waits for his chance. Wendy, who gets wind of his plan, enlists Stan to help her stop it.

Kathie Lee Gifford finally arrives, encased in a bullet-proof plastic bubble. Mr. Garrison, figuring she'll have to expose herself to give Cartman

his trophy, bides his time. Suddenly Wendy and Stan burst in and try to talk him out of it. He hears them out, then goes ahead and squeezes off a shot at Gifford. But the stage collapses under the strain of Cartman's Jabba-esque bulk, launching Gifford out of harm's way. The bullet instead hits Kenny, who is blasted high into the air and impaled through the head by a flagpole.

Gifford is hustled out of town. Wendy announces to the crowd that Cartman's "winning" essay is really a copy of *Walden* with Henry David Thoreau's name scratched out and Cartman's written in. No one cares. Mr. Hat is arrested and sent to a mental hospital to recover. Of course Mr. Garrison, for obvious reasons, has to go too.

There's a happy ending of sorts. Chef has sex with Kathie Lee Gifford, and Cartman finally gets on TV—specifically a *Geraldo* episode about the morbidly obese.

BEEFCAKE

MEMORABLE LINES:

"Follow your dreams. You can reach your goals. I'm living proof. Beefcake. BEEFCAKE!"
—*Cartman*

"Screw you, hippie!"
—*Cartman*

"How are my little crackers today?"
—*Chef*

"Get out of my ass you stupid rainbows!"
—*Cartman*

"C'mon people! We've got to turn this place around! Hang up the lights, string up the banners, castrate the cows!"
—*Mayor McDaniels*

"Beefcake! BEEFCAKE!"
—*Cartman*

"God damnit, that's a big fat ass!"
—*Kyle to Cartman*

BODY COUNT

When Mr. Garrison's class is rehearsing their "Pioneers and Indians" play, one of the students (Casey) is killed during the violent pioneer take over. Kenny is also crushed by the teepee during the rehearsal, but isn't killed. At least, not yet. During Garrison's assassination attempt on Kathie Lee, his gunshot mistakenly hits Kenny—who is then launched onto the flagpole, where he is speared through the head and killed.

POINTLESS OBSERVATION

In his talent show flashback, the 8-year-old Mr. Garrison is shown already bald on top, with gray on the sides. Yet in a flashback during "Cartman's Mom Is a Dirty Slut" (page 34), he possesses a full head of hair.

This show also contains the first reference to *Jesus and Pals*, a public access TV show hosted by no other than Jesus himself. Although we only see a commercial for it here, *Jesus and Pals* can actually be seen in the next episode "Big Gay Al's Big Gay Boat Ride." The rest is history.

POP CULTURE REFERENCES

When Wendy pleads with Mr. Garrison not to kill Kathie Lee Gifford, he responds by saying, "It is too late for me . . . young Wendy." The line is a lift from *Star Wars: Return of the Jedi*. Also, Gifford's talent show song, "If They Could See Me Now," is the same tune she sang when shilling for Carnival Cruise Lines during the early '90s.

When Mr. Hat is arrested by Officer Barbrady at the end of the episode, he says "I would have gotten away with it if it weren't for those meddling kids." This is a reference to a popular line used in *Scooby Doo*, usually uttered by villains after their plans were thwarted.

After becoming so obese on the Beefcake diet that he can't even leave his house, Cartman makes an appearance on the skeevy daytime show *Geraldo* . . . as a "Fat Ass."

CHARACTER DEBUTS

Wendy's friend Bebe Stevens. Although he's not named officially, Clyde has his first lines of dialogue.

CELEBRITIES IMPUGNED

Singer, hostess, and actress Kathie Lee Gifford, who at the time was the co-host of the daytime show *Live with Regis and Kathie Lee*. In the course of the episode, Chef professes his love for her while Garrison confronts his hatred for her.

Kathie Lee's husband Frank Gifford also gets a nod, as Chef tells the boys that he's "three times bigger" than him. Chef's talking about his chocolate salty balls, of course.

Mr. Garrison's hatred for Kathie Lee was foreshadowed in "Cartman Gets an Anal Probe" (page 10), where the sentence, "I'm not positive, but I think that Cathy (sic) Lee Gifford is much older than she claims to be," can be seen on his classroom's chalkboard.

ORIGINAL SONGS

Chef serenades Kathie Lee with "Kathie Lee, You're My Sexual Fantasy," much to the horror of Mayor McDaniels. He gets cut off before the climax of the song, but Kathie Lee had already heard enough (as we see at the end of the episode).

WHAT WENDY LEARNED

"You can't win all the time. And if you don't win, you certainly can't hold it against the person who did, because that's the only way you ever really lose."

VOLCANO

Original Air Date: August 20, 1997
Episode No. 103

THE STORY: Kyle, Stan, Kenny and Cartman go hunting with Stan's Uncle Jimbo and his one-armed Vietnam War buddy, Ned. Unfortunately, Jimbo's idea of "hunting" is blasting anything that moves. He always shouts, "It's coming right for us!" before firing, because a legal loophole allows the killing of any animal in self-defense.

Kyle tries to follow suit, but discovers he can't shoot innocent creatures.

The mountain the boys have camped on begins to rumble—a fact soon noted at the South Park Center for Seismic Activity. It's really a volcano, and it's about to erupt.

That evening around the campfire, Cartman tells the story of Scuzzlebutt, a hideous mutant with a piece of celery for a right hand and Patrick Duffy for a left leg. The creature likes to weave wicker baskets, and to slaughter anyone trespassing on its territory—which happens to be this very mountain.

Not surprisingly, no one believes him. Infuriated, Cartman puts on a Scuzzlebutt costume and

tries to scare his friends. Instead they try to kill him. Stan hopes to redeem himself by shooting the cornered Scuzzlebutt/Cartman, but once again hesitates. His indecision gives Cartman just enough time to squeeze out of his costume and wave off the attack.

Back in town, the South Park citizenry dig a huge trench to divert the lava. Suddenly the mountain erupts. The hunting party flees, only to be stopped at the trench. Suddenly the real Scuzzlebutt appears. He weaves a giant wicker basket and uses it to hoist the group to safety. The lava trench does indeed divert the magma flow—onto Denver, which is incinerated.

Stan, still trying to impress his uncle, then guns down the obviously peace-loving Scuzzlebutt. Baffled when the adults react with horror, he and the other boys decide hunting sucks and go home to watch TV.

Ned, disgusted by the carnage, vows never to use a gun again and throws down his rifle. It misfires, killing Kenny.

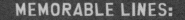

BODY COUNT

Kenny, Scuzzlebutt, and various woodland creatures (Rocky Mountain Black Bear, deer, ram, bald eagle, and every fish in South Park's lake). After the volcano erupts, several South Park citizens are killed by the lava, as well as the entire population of Denver.

POINTLESS OBSERVATIONS

In the second-season episode, "City on the Edge of Forever" (page 50), an alternate-universe version of Scuzzlebutt uses sports announcer Brent Musburger for a leg. In the Spanish-language version of "Volcano," Duffy is replaced by Ricky Martin. Finally, the Happy Tarts snacks mentioned in this episode are also discussed in the Trey Parker movie *Orgazmo*.

Uncle Jimbo makes Kenny his "honorary nephew," much to the dismay of Stan. The title is short-lived, as Kenny is killed minutes later.

POP CULTURE REFERENCES

South Park's residents view an "educational" film called *Lava and You,* which tells anyone caught in the path of red-hot molten rock to "duck and cover." This is an obvious reference to the 1951 civil defense film *Duck and Cover.*

When Mayor McDaniels finds out South Park is "totally screwed" by the impending volcanic eruption, she doesn't panic. She puts the warning message out to the right people—*Inside Edition, Rescue 911,* and *Entertainment Tonight*—as well as her stylist.

Ned sings "Koom By Ya" around the campfire.

This episode played upon the boom of volcanic disaster movies that came out in 1997, as it was made only months after feature films *Volcano* and *Dante's Peak* were in theaters.

CHARACTER DEBUTS

Uncle Jimbo, Ned, Mayor McDaniels, and Stan's dad Randy Marsh (the geologist who reports the impending eruption). His relationship to Stan isn't actually revealed until "An Elephant Makes Love to a Pig" (page 18). He's based on Trey's father, who's also named Randy and also a geologist.

We also meet Scuzzlebutt, a mythical woodland creature.

CELEBRITIES IMPUGNED

Is it insulting to imply that Patrick Duffy, star of TV's *Dallas* and *Step by Step,* might be employed as an appendage by a hideous mutant? If so, then consider him impugned.

WHAT THE FUCK HAPPENED TO NED?

A hand grenade took off his arm in 'Nam. He lost his voice to throat cancer.

OBSCENITY REPORT

This is the first (and so far only) episode that contains no "bleeps."

ORIGINAL SONGS

After the lava is safely diverted away from the town, Chef breaks into a funky jam "Hot Lava," surrounded by a plethora of dancing women.

WHAT NED LEARNED

"Only now in this late hour do I see the folly of guns. I'll never use a gun again." However Ned soon takes up arms again during the bloody battle against mutant turkeys in "Starvin' Marvin" (page 24).

BIG GAY AL'S BIG GAY BOAT RIDE

Original Air Date: September 3, 1997
Episode No. 104

THE STORY: Stan gets a new dog named Sparky, who turns out to be gay. Frustrated, he wishes out loud for a butch pet. Sparky overhears and runs away.

The distraction couldn't come at a worse time, because Stan quarterbacks the school football team, the South Park Cows, who are about to play the Middle Park Cowboys. Jimbo bets that the boys can beat the game's absurd 72-point spread, and everyone in the town follows suit. They vow to make Jimbo pay if he steers them wrong.

Jimbo and Ned decide to improve the odds. Learning that John Stamos' brother, Richard, will sing "Lovin' You" at halftime, they wire the opposing team's mascot, a horse named Enrique, with a bomb that's set to explode when Richard hits the song's high F note.

Stan ditches the game to look for Sparky. On the edge of town he meets Big Gay Al, proprietor of Big Gay Al's Big Gay Animal Sanctuary, where Sparky now lives. Big Gay Al takes Stan for a voy-

age on Big Gay Al's Big Gay Boat Ride—an excursion into the history of gayness. Stan accepts Sparky just as he is, and they return to town together.

Meanwhile, back at the game, South Park is getting pummeled. At halftime Richard Stamos sings, but he fails to hit the fateful high F note and the bomb on Enrique doesn't detonate. Suddenly Stan and Sparky appear. Stan takes the field and lofts the ball to Kyle, who scores a touchdown as the clock runs out. The final score is 73 to 6—South Park beats the spread.

Stan leads the townspeople to Big Gay Al's Big Gay Animal Sanctuary, only to find it gone. However the pets are still there, and they joyously reunite with their former owners. Stan finally spots Big Gay Al, who thanks him for helping find homes for his charges. Then he steps into a suitcase, closes it and rockets off into space. Then Enrique finally explodes.

MEMORABLE LINES:

"I'm super, thanks for asking!"
—*Big Gay Al*

"Stan's dog's a homo!"
—*Cartman*

"Football is like making love to a really beautiful woman. You can't always score, but when you do, it makes all the trying worthwhile."
—*Chef*

"We treat star athletes better because they're better people."
—*Mr. Garrison*

"You know what they say . . . you can't teach a gay dog straight tricks."
—*Chef*

"Oh my! I haven't seen a Jew run like that since Poland, 1938!"
—*Sports Announcer*

BODY COUNT

Kenny dies on the football field, after being decapitated and torn to pieces while making a run for the end zone. Also, Middle Park's horse mascot, Enrique, gets killed in explosive fashion. Interestingly, after he's killed, Kenny suddenly reappears in a shot of the football team.

POINTLESS OBSERVATION

Two alien "visitors" can be seen in the bleacher crowd as the Middle Park team gets off its bus.

Mr. Garrison is called out for being gay for the first time in this episode. Chef mentions how "he, of all people, should be accepting towards gays," sighting his overt gay tendencies. Garrison denies it, as he will continue to do, until he finally confronts his gay side in "Fourth Grade" (page 132).

CHARACTER DEBUTS

Big Gay Al. Though he comes off as some sort of magical Willy Wonka-type being, in later episodes he'll morph into just another South Park citizen. Albeit a South Park citizen with a penchant for flashing his nips. Also Sparky, who returns sporadically in future seasons. As everyone in the entire universe already knows, George Clooney provided his "voice."

While they aren't mentioned by name, two of the boys' 3rd grade classmates have their first lines of dialogue: Fosse, characterized by his scraggly, Charlie-Brown-like hair, and Bob, a brown-haired boy with thick eyebrows. They can be seen in many future episodes, mostly as background characters laughing at gay jokes.

Jesus also makes his official television debut as the host of the public access show *Jesus and Pals.* Jesus played a large role in the animated "South Park" short Parker and Stone created before the television show ("The Spirit of Christmas"), and they re-introduce him here for the first time.

POP CULTURE REFERENCES

Big Gay Al's peculiar departure at the end of the episode is an homage to a scene from the movie *Seven Faces of Dr. Lao.* Even though the assignment was on "Asian Cultures," Cartman gives a presentation on the 1980s detective show *Simon and Simon,* saying, "And so you see, Simon and Simon weren't brothers in real life. Only on television." He gets a D-.

ORIGINAL SONGS

The happy, gay-friendly "We're All Gay and It's OK!" plays during Big Gay Al's boat ride. Also, the hard-rocking ballad "Now You're a Man" by DVDA plays during the credits.

CELEBRITIES IMPUGNED

John Stamos' older brother, Richard. Though he probably doesn't count, because Matt and Trey made him up. Also Hugh Grant. When Pip (who isn't equipped with a helmet) gets pummeled during the game, one of the announcers says, "I haven't seen an Englishman take a blow like that since Hugh Grant."

Brian Boitano can be seen gaily ice-skate-dancing during the "We're All Gay and It's OK!" song on Big Gal Al's boat ride.

PUBLIC REACTION

Nominated for an Emmy Award for Outstanding Animated Program. Also nominated in the Outstanding TV-Individual Episode category for the 1998 GLAAD (Gay & Lesbian Alliance Against Defamation) Media Awards.

WHAT STAN LEARNED

"It's OK to be gay! Being gay is just a part of nature, and a beautiful thing!"

AN ELEPHANT MAKES LOVE TO A PIG

Original Air Date: September 10, 1997
Episode No. 105

THE STORY: During a class discussion on genetic engineering, Kyle hits upon the idea of combining an elephant with a pig. He already owns an elephant (which he got via mail order), and Cartman has a potbellied pig named Fluffy. A classmate named Terrance (no relation to Terrance and Phillip) bets he can clone an entire human being before Kyle can produce his elephant/pig. And the race is on.

The boys visit a "genetic engineering ranch" on the edge of town, where they meet the mysterious Dr. Mephesto. He tells them it's impossible to splice elephant and pig DNA. So Chef suggests a different tactic—get the animals drunk. The boys tank up their pets on beer, and they finally make sweet love.

Meanwhile, Mephesto (whose son turns out to be Terrance) creates a gigantic, misshapen clone of Stan. The monster escapes and goes on a rampage through South Park.

Stan catches up with the creature, calms him and lures him to his house. He wants it to beat up his sister, Shelly, who regularly stomps the crap out of him. But the plan fails when Big Stan goes berserk, hurling Kenny into a microwave and cooking him to death. Only the timely intervention of Shelly, who drops the clone with one punch, restores order. Mephesto arrives and shoots Big Stan in the head, killing him.

The school's science fair suddenly becomes much less interesting. Terrance, deprived of his human clone, displays a five-assed monkey instead.

At the last moment, word comes that Cartman's pig has given birth. Its offspring is brought to class, where the kids notice it looks a lot like Mr. Garrison.

"Oh, gee," Mr. Garrison says. "Isn't that an amazing coincidence? What are the odds of that?"

He gives the boys first prize.

MEMORABLE LINES

" I would NEVER let a woman kick my ass! If she tried anything, I'd be like 'HEY! You get your bitch ass back in the kitchen and make me some pie!!!'"
—*Cartman*

Kyle: "When does Mother Nature go from beautiful to ugly?"
Chef: "Usually about 9:30 in the morning, children."

"I'll kick you in the nuts!"
—*Cartman*

"Tonight is right for love. Love gravy. . . ."
—*Chef*

"Well, spank my ass and call me Charlie. Isn't this exciting, two A+ students in a cloning war!"
—*Mr. Garrison*

BODY COUNT

Kenny, as well as a number of townspeople, are killed in the wake of Big Clone Stan's rampage. Clone Stan is ultimately shot in the head and killed by Dr. Mephesto, bringing an end to his reign of terror.

CHARACTER DEBUTS

Dr. Mephesto, Stan's sister Shelly, Stan's mom Sharon Marsh, Kyle's pet elephant, Terrance Mephesto (a fellow 3rd grader and Dr. Mephesto's son), Kevin (Dr. Mephesto's small, silent assistant), Cartman's pig Fluffy andvvarious 4-assed animals that Dr. Mephesto has genetically engineered.

ORIGINAL SONGS

Chef's duet with Elton John on their slow jam "Love Gravy."

CELEBRITIES IMPUGNED

Elton John, who sings a love song to help the pig and elephant get "in the mood."

WHERE DID THE IDEA COME FROM?

The character of Shelly is based on Trey's sister (also named Shelly). When they were kids, she regularly beat him senseless, once even tossing him down a flight of stairs.

POINTLESS OBSERVATION

Originally Shelly was supposed to douse Stan with an accelerant and set him on fire. Because the network feared this might encourage copycat behavior among children, the scene was deleted. So now there's a moment where Stan is seen inexplicably lying in a puddle of liquid. It's the lighter fluid or gasoline or whatever it was that Shelley would have used to set him ablaze.

This is the first time that we see Stan's family. While we've met Randy before in "Volcano," here he's presented as Stan's father. The addition of Randy, Sharon, and Shelly Marsh marks the first exploration into the home life of the boys.

POP CULTURE REFERENCES

Dr. Mephesto is an homage to Marlon Brando's portrayal of Dr. Moreau in the 1996 version of *The Island of Dr. Moreau*. Also, both Mephesto and Chef state that the lyrics of a particular Loverboy song explain that you can't splice elephant and pig DNA. The line goes, "Da'n Do-A, Pig and Elephant D-N-A Just Won't Splice."

The plot of this episode has great parallels to the classic tale *Frankenstein*. When the boys go to Officer Barbrady for help finding the mutant clone, he tells the kids they've "been watching the '*X-Files*' too much."

The last line of the episode, "That'll do, pig" is a reference to the 1995 movie *Babe*, about a gallant pig who wants to be a sheep dog.

BEHIND THE SCENES

Matt and Trey originally wanted to call this episode "An Elephant Fucks A Pig." Not surprisingly the network brass didn't go for it. The cafeteria scene with the boys and Pip was originally in the pilot episode "Cartman Gets An Anal Probe" (page 10), but was cut for time. It appears here, and if you look closely, you can notice the animation is a bit more crude.

WHAT DR. MEPHESTO LEARNED

"All I've ever wanted was to genetically engineer something useful. But I've failed. Perhaps we shouldn't be toying with God's creations. Perhaps we should just leave nature alone to its simple one-assed schematics."

DEATH

Original Air Date: September 17, 1997
Episode No. 106

THE STORY: Stan's grandfather celebrates his 102nd birthday. When asked what he wants, he says he wishes someone would kill him. He tries to talk Stan into helping, first offering him a dollar and then telling him that "I killed *my* grandpa when I was your age!"

Kyle's mom catches him watching Terrance and Phillip and is horrified by the fart jokes. She starts a campaign against the show. The boys watch an episode in secret, and become so engrossed that they don't notice when Grandpa uses a rope that Stan's holding to try to hang himself.

The case becomes a national scandal, with Terrance and Phillip getting the blame. Soon the entire adult population of South Park protests at Cartoon Central headquarters, demanding an end to the show. Kyle's mom uses a giant catapult to fire people at the network's building, splattering their bodies across the façade.

Back in South Park, the boys finally agree to help Grandpa kill himself. But just as they're about to drop a cow on his head, Death suddenly appears. "It's about time you late ass lazy son of a whore!" Grandpa shouts.

But Death pursues the boys instead. They dash through a TV store, where Terrance and Phillip plays on every set. Death watches and laughs. The boys stop running and join in.

At the same moment, Cartoon Central finally agrees to dump Terrance and Phillip. Back in South Park the show suddenly vanishes from the TVs. Death goes berserk and touches (surprise) Kenny, who dies instantly. Grandpa is furious. But then the ghost of his own grandfather tells him that he must wait until he dies of natural causes.

With Terrance and Phillip gone, the boys wonder how they'll kill time. Perhaps by smoking crack. Or inhaling gas fumes. Or watching porn.

MEMORABLE LINES

"What, What, WHAT??!"
—*Mrs. Broflovski*

"What has America's youth come to? Kids won't even kill their own grandparents!"
—*Grandpa Marsh*

"I think I've caught a touch of the flu from little Kenny this morning. I've got the green apple splatters."
—*Mr. Garrision*

"If there are any questions, you may direct them to that brick wall over there."
—*Cartoon Central President John Warsog*

"Now get away from here and take your diarrhea with you!"
—*Cartoon Central President John Warsog*

BODY COUNT

Kenny, plus every South Park resident catapulted into the side of the Cartoon Central building. Grandpa, however, does not fulfill his wish for death.

POINTLESS OBSERVATION

Mr. McCormick, although he's not actually identified as Kenny's father here, is introduced to us as a "martyr" right before he is catapulted against the side of the Cartoon Central building. He's re-introduced later for "Starvin' Marvin" (page 24).

This is the only time that there is a bathroom inside Mr. Garrison's classroom.

This is the first time we see "Snacky Cakes," one of Cartman's favorite junk foods.

CHARACTER DEBUTS

Terrance and Phillip, Grandpa Marsh, Kyle's mom Sheila Broflovski, and Death. The Ghost of Grandpa's Grandpa also makes a cameo.

POP CULTURE REFERENCES

Jack Kevorkian (whom Cartman calls "Jack Leborkian") is held up as an example of someone who can go around murdering people and not get in trouble.

While leading the charge against Terrance and Phillip, Mrs. Broflovski demands "more quality television . . . like *Full House*."

CELEBRITIES IMPUGNED

Suzanne Summers, whose sitcom *She's the Sheriff* replaces Terrance and Phillip. Also the pop star Enya, whose music is used by Grandpa to give Stan some sense of what it feels like to be in constant agony and long for death's sweet release.

WHAT KYLE LEARNED

"I think that parents only get so offended by television because they rely on it as a babysitter and the sole educator of their kids."

PINKEYE

Original Air Date: October 29, 1997
Episode No. 107

THE STORY: Kenny is killed by the falling Mir space station while waiting at the bus stop with Stan, Kyle and Cartman. The boys quickly shake off the incident and debate who has the most ass-kicking Halloween costume. Kenny's body is trucked off to the morgue, where his embalming fluid is contaminated with Worcestershire sauce. This causes him to reanimate as a flesh-eating zombie. He escapes, mauls the mortician and his assistant, and heads into town.

Next day the boys are back at the bus stop, each wearing a costume. Kyle is dressed as Chewbacca and Stan (because his girlfriend Wendy told him she was coming as Raggedy Ann) is dressed as Raggedy Andy. Cartman wears a Hitler costume. As Kyle tries to understand what possessed his friends to make such poor choices, zombie Kenny staggers up and joins them.

At school, nearly everyone is dressed in identical Chewbacca outfits. Even Wendy. When Stan asks what happened to their Raggedy Ann/Raggedy Andy pact, she says, "I guess I just realized how stupid we would look."

That evening's trick-or-treating doesn't go well, because Kenny attacks everyone who answers their door. They visit Chef's house, who greets them with a chainsaw in each hand. He's aware of the zombie invasion and leads Stan, Kyle and Cartman to the mortuary to try to find out what happened. They're attacked by a mob of undead and Chef, bitten, joins their ranks. The boys flee into the night.

Kyle manages to find a pay phone and call the Worcestershire help line while Stan and Cartman, in a bloody chainsaw fight, hold off the zombies. He's informed that once the original zombie is neutralized, everyone else will revert to normal.

Stan encounters a zombified Wendy and can't bring himself to kill her. Just then, Kyle appears and cuts Kenny (the original zombie) in half. Suddenly everyone (that is, everyone the boys haven't slaughtered) returns to life.

MEMORABLE LINES

"You're probably wondering why we're standing here with a pile of money and no pants on."
—*Officer Barbrady*

"Let's all point at Stan and laugh, children."
—*Mr. Garrison*

"You scared me you communist bastard!"
—*Mir Cosmonaut*

"I'm gonna make love, even when I'm dead."
—*Zombie Chef*

"Too bad drinking scotch isn't a paying job or else Kenny's dad would be a millionaire!"
—*Cartman*

"At least my mom's not on the cover of Crack Whore Magazine!"
—*Stan*

"Oh my God I killed Kenny!"
—*Kyle*

"Remember kids . . . dressing up like Hitler in school isn't cool"
—*from "That Hitler Guy" PSA*

"You know, I think death is least funny when it happens to a child."
—*Mortician*

BODY COUNT

Kenny, three times. The first time he died only 24 seconds into the episode. The second time he was cut in half (the long way) by Kyle. Finally he was crushed by a funerary statue while trying to rise from his grave, and then a plane crashes on top of that.

The zombies who were diced up by Stan and Cartman's chainsaws stayed dead, even after they killed the master zombie (Kenny). Also Mr. Torres, who was in the doctor's office for a routine checkup when Chef mistook him for a zombie and ripped his arm off.

WHERE DID THE IDEA COME FROM?

The episode is a salute to the flesh-eating zombie movie genre, but mostly to the 1985 flick *The Return of the Living Dead*.

POINTLESS OBSERVATIONS

A poster of Isaac Hayes is seen hanging in Chef's house.

The theme song, as well as opening animation, was totally redone for this Halloween-themed episode. Also, in a reference to *The Shining*, the school bus in these credits has "Redrum" (murder, backwards) scrawled on it. This modified theme song will be re-used in two later Halloween episodes.

Uncle Jimbo and Ned can been seen on the rooftop of South Park Avenue with guns, shooting zombies.

Cartman's mom actually IS on the cover of *Crack Whore Magazine*, with the subtitle reading "Back do' ho . . . Five on one action!"

CHARACTER DEBUTS

Principal Victoria, the frizzy-haired matriarch of South Park Elementary.

POP CULTURE REFERENCE

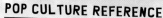

When Chef gets bitten, he immediately breaks into the song "I'm Gonna Make Love, Even When I'm Dead." The song, as well as the accompanying dance number with the zombies, is a takeoff on Michael Jackson's "Thriller."

Mr. Garrison is dressed as Marilyn Monroe (in her iconic white dress) for Halloween. This is not the last time that he will wear a dress. Chef is dressed as Evel Knievel, the legendary stunt man. After Principal Victoria makes Cartman change his Hitler costume into a "ghost" costume, he looks like a member of the Ku Klux Klan. In "Here Comes The Neighborhood" (page 170), townspeople also dress up like "ghosts" in order to scare the rich African American people out of town.

GERMANIC CULTURE REFERENCE

Cartman isn't finished dressing up like Hitler. He does it again in "The Passion of the Jew."

CELEBRITIES IMPUGNED

Author Jackie Collins, whom Mr. Garrison discusses in class on Halloween eve because she's a "great horror writer." Also, Tina Yothers from *Family Ties* judges the school's costume contest. Kyle responds by saying, "Dude, I thought she was dead." Finally, during the costume contest the horrifically decomposing Kenny wins second place for what Yothers mistakes to be an Edward James Olmos costume.

WHAT-THE-FUCK MOMENT

When Chef bursts into Mayor McDaniels' office to tell her about the zombie threat, he finds her with Officer Barbrady, who's wearing women's underwear. There's also a gigantic stack of money on her desk. "I can assure you that it has absolutely nothing to do with the Japanese mafia," McDaniels tells Chef.

WHAT STAN LEARNED

"Halloween isn't about costumes or candy. It's about being good to one another and giving and loving." Kyle states that his friend is thinking about Christmas, and that Halloween really is just about costumes and candy.

23

STARVIN' MARVIN

Original Air Date: November 19, 1997
Episode No. 109

THE STORY: After seeing a commercial in which Sally Struthers begs for money to help starving African children, the boys decide to pitch in—mostly because they get a free digital sports watch for their trouble. But due to a clerical error they receive not a watch but an actual Ethiopian child. Cartman names him Starvin' Marvin.

They bring him to school, to the delight of the kids and horror of the teachers. Mr. Garrison and Principal Victoria contact the Red Cross to have him taken home. The boys are pissed off, except for Cartman, who isn't too troubled about sending their "friend" back to poverty.

"You better watch what you say Cartman," Kyle warns. "You might be poor and hungry someday."

He has no idea how soon. That evening government agents show up at his house and, mistaking him for the African child, bundle him off to Ethiopia. The agents give Marvin a sports watch as they depart.

Meanwhile, a pack of evil, mutant turkeys developed by Dr. Mephesto is on the loose. Chef tells a crowd gathered in the town square that they have to destroy them before they conquer the world. A hideous, bloody battle ensues, with the humans finally annihilating the turkeys. But not before the birds peck out Kenny's eyes, killing him.

Meanwhile, back in Africa, Cartman is at the end of his rope. Suddenly he spots a small building that contains mountains of food, plus a big-screen TV and elegant furniture. Also, a grotesquely obese Sally Struthers. Cartman, angry as hell, tells the Ethiopians that Struthers is hoarding food.

Marvin is returned to Ethiopia and Cartman comes back to South Park. The plane that brings Marvin home is also stuffed with the dead, evil, but totally edible turkeys. The villagers hoist Marvin on their shoulders and march him through town—right past Sally Struthers, who's bound to a pole.

MEMORABLE LINES

"There are no stupid questions, just stupid people."
—*Mr. Garrison*

"I think I hear the flower children calling."
—*Cartman*

"Something went wrong. And the turkeys broke free. And the worst part is . . . they're really pissed off."
—*Dr. Mephesto*

"Wow, those are some pissed off turkeys!"
—*Chef*

"No, Starvin' Marvin that's my pot pie!"
—*Cartman*

"Every turkey dies, not every turkey truly lives."
—*Chef*

"OK, people, move along! Nothing to see here, you lookie loos!"
—*Officer Barbrady*

"These fudged up turkeys from the crustaceous era can take our lives, but they can never take our FREEDOM!"
—*Chef*

"We want to adopt an Ethernopian."
—*Stan*

"We're not gonna let our Thanksgiving be ruined by a bunch of turkeys!"
—*Chef*

BODY COUNT

Kenny, plus a large number of townspeople who are brutally pecked to death by the evil mutant turkeys.

POINTLESS OBSERVATIONS

Cartman's mother calls Kyle's mother "Carol," even though in "Mr. Hankey, The Christmas Poo" (page 26) she's called Sheila. Also, a couple slaughtered by turkeys at Stark's Pond is inexplicably resurrected for the final battle. Finally, Jerry Seinfeld expressed interested in voicing a character for the show, but his "people" turned down the proffered role—one of the turkeys in the climactic battle scene. Specifically, turkey No. 4.

The episode aired a week before Thanksgiving, hence the overt Turkey Day theme and the "Terrance and Phillip Thanksgiving Special."

This is the first time we see Kenny's family and their home.

CHARACTER DEBUTS

Starvin' Marvin. Also Kenny's entire family (Mr. and Mrs. McCormick, as well as Kenny's brother Kevin), who cheer him on while he tries to grab charity canned goods from inside a diabolical "can grab" machine. His father was briefly seen (but not identified as Kenny's dad) in "Death" (page 20).

POP CULTURE REFERENCES

Before the battle, Chef, his face painted blue and white, rallies the townspeople with a speech out of the movie *Braveheart*. At the same time the leader of the turkeys, his face also painted blue and white, gives a similar pep talk to his fellow birds.

When they first see Sally Struthers on TV, Kyle tells Stan that she used to be on *Full House*. This is the second time *Full House* has been mentioned, the first being in "Death" (page 20). It's also not true.

Garrison tells the kids that Englebert Humperdink was the "first person on the moon." He is an internationally known singer, but no Neil Armstrong.

CELEBRITIES IMPUGNED

Sally Struthers, who's introduced to us as a cake-eating, help-the-children spokeswoman. When Dr. Mephesto asks Chef to look into his microscope, Chef says he sees "an extreme close-up of Vanessa Redgrave's private parts." She's a famous British actress.

HIGH CULTURE REFERENCES

Wendy and Cartman, while debating the usefulness of a canned food drive for the poor, lapse into dialogue from Dickens' *A Christmas Carol*. Mr. Garrison ends their bickering by saying, "Okay kids, that's enough Dickens for one day."

Cartman calls Stan a "vas deferens," which is actually a scientific term for a sperm-carrying duct in the reproductive system. However, it doesn't appear that Cartman knows what he's talking about.

WHAT STAN LEARNED

"It's really easy not to think of images on TV as real people, but they are. That's why it's easy to ignore those commercials. But people on TV are just as real as you or I." Kyle points out that, using this line of logic, MacGyver is a real person, too.

MR. HANKEY, THE CHRISTMAS POO

Original Air Date: December 17, 1997
Episode No. 110

THE STORY: The South Park kids are rehearsing their Christmas pageant. Being a Mr. Garrison production, it includes a graphic birth-of-Jesus scene, complete with screaming and panting. Garrison tells Wendy (who plays Mary), "I'm still not believing the labor pains."

Rehearsal is interrupted when Kyle's mom shows up, furious at the show's overt Christian themes, and that her son, a Jew, is playing Joseph. When Garrison and Kyle's mom ask if there's something non-denominational he can do for the play, Kyle offers to sing "The Mr. Hankey Song," concerning Mr. Hankey, the Christmas Poo. Mr. Garrison remarks that that's what you get for raising a child a pagan, which sends Kyle's mom off to see the mayor.

Later, on the playground, Kyle tries to explain the Christmas poo concept. Apparently Mr. Hankey is a turd that comes out of the toilet bowl each holiday season to give presents to everybody who has lots of fiber in their diet.

At a town meeting, various factions complain about various aspects of the school's production. The mayor buckles and promises to ". . . the most non-offensive Christmas ever to any religious or minority group of any kind."

That evening before bed, Kyle is instructed by his parents to stop talking about Mr. Hankey. He agrees, but as he brushes his teeth a turd wearing a Christmas hat leaps out of the toilet. It's none other than Mr. Hankey. He sings a jolly holiday song, leaping around the room and leaving bits of poo wherever he lands. Kyle grabs him in mid-flight, just as his parents burst in. All they see is a room covered in poop smears, with their son clutching what looks like common garden-variety feces.

Kyle, in a not-very-well-thought-out plan, puts Mr. Hankey in a box and takes him to school,

where the set for the play is being dismantled. Mr. Garrison, at a loss, asks the kids if they know any non-denominational, non-offensive holiday songs. Cartman recommends they sing "Kyle's Mom Is a Stupid Bitch" in D-minor. He then launches into a looooong rendition of the tune. Offended, Mr. Hankey leaps out of his box and hurls himself at Cartman.

This lands Kyle in the school counselor's office, where we meet Mr. Mackey for the first time. Mr. Hankey decides to take a bath in Mackey's cup of coffee, earning Kyle a ticket to the South Park Mental Institution.

That evening the kids put on their new play, now called the *South Park Elementary Holiday Experience*. Music and lyrics are provided by minimalist composer Phillip Glass. The show is terrible, and a full-scale riot breaks out in the audience.

In the midst of it, Chef asks what happened to Kyle. The boys tell him about his obsession with Mr. Hankey, and Chef, to their amazement, tells them the talking turd is real. Stan and Wendy say that they believe, and Mr. Hankey leaps out of his shoebox and comes to life. He talks to the crowd about the meaning of Christmas, and they stop fighting—mostly out of sheer amazement.

The entire town, led by Mr. Hankey, heads for the South Park Mental Institution to release Kyle, who discovers to his relief that he's not crazy. Mr. Hankey hands out presents, then flies off into the night to spread Christmas cheer.

Yet something feels . . . unfinished. Stan, Cartman and Kyle look at Kenny, still alive and well only seconds from the closing credits. The words THE END appear onscreen, and Kenny jumps up and down in triumph.

MEMORABLE LINES

"Oh good, Kyle's mom is here to ruin Christmas."
—*Cartman*

"I'm not fat, I'm festively plump."
—*Cartman*

"Right now, you're nuttier than Chinese chicken salad."
—*Mr. Mackey*

"Dude, this is pretty fucked up right here."
—*Stan*

"Howwwwdyyy Ho!"
—*Mr. Hankey*

BODY COUNT

No one. This was the first—and for a very long time, only—episode in which Kenny wasn't killed.

CHARACTER DEBUTS

Mr. Hankey, the Christmas Poo.

Santa Claus can be seen briefly during Kyle's song "A Lonely Jew on Christmas," with a line of children waiting to sit on his lap. He will eventually become a main character.

Kyle's dad Gerald Broflovski, who wears a customary yarmulke. Up to this point, we have only seen Kyle's mother Sheila and his brother Ike.

Mr. Mackey, the school counselor, is seen for the first time as he chats with Kyle about being Jewish at Christmastime. Trey says Mackey was modeled after his own junior high school counselor.

Priest Maxi, the town's resident Catholic pastor, also makes his debut.

CELEBRITIES IMPUGNED

Minimalist composer Phillip Glass, whose music for the *South Park Elementary Holiday Experience* triggers a riot.

WHERE DID THE IDEA COME FROM?

Reportedly inspired by the fact that Trey often forgot to flush the toilet as a child. His father told him that if he did not flush, the turd would escape and eat him.

POINTLESS OBSERVATIONS

There's a picture of Kyle and his pet elephant (from "An Elephant Makes Love to a Pig" (page 18)) on the dresser in his room. Craig can be seen sitting outside Mr. Mackey's office. Although he hasn't been introduced officially yet, he can be seen frequently outside the counselor's office. We learn later he has a bad habit of giving people the finger.

Stan says he's getting the "John Elway football helmet" he wanted for Christmas. This is the first of many times Elway and the Denver Broncos will be mentioned.

POP CULTURE REFERENCES

Stan's Biblical reading at the beginning of the school play is lifted directly from a similar scene in *A Charlie Brown Christmas*. So is the snowflake-eating scene. There's also a live-action "commercial" for the Mr. Hankey Construction Set that's an homage to Mr. Potato Head. Only instead of putting eyes and lips and ears on a potato, you stick them on a piece of poo.

ORIGINAL SONGS

The show's three songs—"Mr. Hankey, the Christmas Poo," "Kyle's Mom Is a Stupid Bitch," and "The Lonely Jew on Christmas"—are all heard again in later episodes. "Kyle's Mom Is a Stupid Bitch" even made it into the theatrical film *South Park: Bigger, Longer & Uncut*.

Also, Chef opens up the school play with his non-offensive, non-denominational song "I'm Gonna Lay You Down by the Yule Log."

WHAT-THE-FUCK MOMENT

At the end of the closing credits there's a short scene of Jesus, alone on the set of Jesus and Friends, singing Happy Birthday to himself and blowing out the candles on a forlorn-looking cake.

WHAT STAN LEARNED

"I learned that Jewish people are okay, and that Hanukkah can be cool too."

DAMIEN

Original Air Date: February 4, 1998
Episode No. 108

THE STORY: At school, Cartman passes out invitations to his birthday party—a celebration of legendary proportions. He's interrupted when Mr. Garrison introduces a new student—a sullen-looking kid named Damien. He's very up-front about the fact that he's the son of Satan. During lunch he turns Kenny into a duckbilled platypus, then causes a windstorm in the lunchroom.

"Bring me Jesus!" he shouts. "My wrath shall continue until I speak with Jesus!"

The boys fetch the Savior. Damien tells him his father, Satan, wants to battle him for control of the world—right in South Park.

The locals, oblivious to the broader metaphysical implications of such a conflict, haul ass to the local bookie to bet on Jesus. The fight is scheduled for Saturday at the South Park Forum.

But Saturday is also Cartman's birthday. The kids are torn about which even to attend. At the pre-fight weigh-in, they're also appalled to see that Satan clocks in at seven-foot-two, 320 pounds, while Jesus weighs only 135 pounds. This causes the townspeople to change their bets en

masse from Jesus to Satan.

The big day for the fight—and Cartman's birthday—arrives. Most of the town's kids elect to go to the party—including Damien, even though he wasn't invited. He wins over the other children by first torturing and then (apparently) murdering Pip in a highly inventive way.

The scheduling conflict with the Jesus/Satan bout is resolved when Kyle, instead of bringing Cartman a robot action figure as he was told to, gives him an "Ants in the Pants" game. Furious, Cartman throws everyone out and ends the party.

The kids head for the South Park Forum, where Jesus is taking a tremendous beating. Between rounds Stan gives him a furious pep talk. When the bell rings, Jesus strikes his first blow—an inconsequential tap on the arm. To everyone's surprise, Satan crashes to the mat and is counted out. As he explains before returning to Hell, he was the only person who bet on Jesus—and now he'll take the towns' hard-earned savings with him to the infernal regions.

MEMORABLE LINES

"God dammit Jesus, snap out of it!"
—*Stan*

"Wow, that kid has some real emotional problems."
—*Damien re: Cartman*

"That is one fudged-up little cracker!"
—*Chef*

"I can't hit Jesus Christ. My mother would never speak to me again."
—*Chef*

"I bet I can spit the most on him."
—*Clyde to Pip*

"Who cut your hair? Stevie Wonder?!"
—*Cartman*

"Holy crap dude, Satan's huge!"
—*Stan*

"Holy poop on a stick!"
—*Mr. Garrison*

BODY COUNT

Kenny, in his platypus state, is gunned down by Jimbo right after the Jesus/Satan fight. Jimbo uses the line "It's coming right for us!" before he shoots. We learn in "Volcano" (page 14) that you can shoot anything, as long as you yell that first.

POINTLESS OBSERVATIONS

The evil, demonic chorus that plays when Damien summons up his evil powers can also be similarly heard twelve seasons later in "Britney's New Look."

We get our first glimpse of South Park's bar, called "Bar."

POP CULTURE REFERENCES

The boys tell Damien that his mom is a "real dog"—a reference to *The Omen*, in which the Antichrist's mother was a jackal. Also, when Stan tries to buck up Jesus during the fight, he tells him, "Don't try to be a great man; just be a man." The line was lifted word-for-word from the 1996 film *Star Trek: First Contact*.

For his birthday, Cartman wants the set of green, yellow, and red Megaman. This toy is based on the legendary video game from the late 80s.

The Jesus vs. Satan "Boutin' at the Mountain" Pay-Per-View is an obvious take-off on HBO's premium pay-to-watch boxing events. Furthermore, the announcer screams "Let's get ready to rumble!!!" This phrase is trademarked by professional announcer Michael Buffer, who actually voiced it for this episode.

CHARACTER DEBUTS

Satan. In later episodes he's portrayed as thoughtful, sensitive and deeply conflicted. Here he's just an asshole.

Damien, Satan's twisted son. Just when he gains acceptance among the boys, he must return to Hell with his Dark Lord father.

CELEBRITIES IMPUGNED

Olympic skater Nancy Kerrigan. When Stan holds Kerrigan up to Jesus as someone who wouldn't let adversity keep her from becoming No. 1, Kyle reminds him that she only took home a silver medal. "Never mind, Jesus," Stan says. "Nancy Kerrigan sucks." Also boxing promoter Don King, who represents Satan during a pre-fight press conference. He admonishes reporters who ask if the Prince of Darkness had a hand in the Gulf War to "just let everything be decided in the ring."

After Garrison continues his lecture on "great singers of the baroque era," he goes on to say that "Nancy Sinatra was quite a choice piece of ass."

ORIGINAL SONGS

When the boys are being mean to the new kid Damien, Chef sings "We're All Special in Our Own Way." It starts off about accepting new people for who they are, and slowly turns into a smooth song about love making.

WHAT STAN LEARNED:

"Parents can be so cruel. Don't they realize that what a child needs more than anything is security?"

TOM'S RHINOPLASTY

Original Air Date: February 11, 1998
Episode No. 111

THE STORY: When Mr. Garrison has surgery, he's replaced by a substitute, the beautiful Ms. Ellen. Stan (and the rest of the boys) fall in love. Wendy is horrified. She takes matters into her own hands during an after-class heart-to-heart with Ms. Ellen. She tells her, among a great many other things, that if she messes with Stan she'll whoop her "sorry ho ass back to last year."

The next day Ms. Ellen announces that whomever gets the highest score on the next spelling test wins dinner with her. Later, in the cafeteria, Chef tells the boys that he's learned their teacher is a lesbian. They have no idea what that is, but if Ms. Ellen likes them, that's what they want to be. Told by Cartman's mom that lesbians like to "lick carpet," they spend hours on the floor, doing just that.

Wendy tries to win Stan back by dressing like a tiny, eight-year-old version of the slutted-out Sandy from *Grease.* But her plan derails when Ms. Ellen shows up wearing leather pants.

Even worse, Mr. Garrison returns to announce that he's quitting teaching to "hang out and screw hot chicks." It seems his surgery—a nose job—worked out better than expected. When the bandages came off he looked exactly like David Hasselhoff.

Ms. Ellen will replace him. Also, Stan got the high score on the spelling test and gets to have dinner with her. Finally, Principal Victoria tells Wendy that her grandma just died.

But then, just as suddenly, things turn around. Mr. Garrison tires of being pursued by horny women and has his surgery reversed. Then a group of Iraqi soldiers burst into the school and grab Ms. Ellen, whom they say is a war criminal. She's taken back to Iraq, packed into a missile and shot into the sun.

Wendy monitors her teacher's execution with great satisfaction during a pool party at her house. The attendees are a suspicious mix of the women who drove Mr. Garrison to reverse his operation, and the Iraqis responsible for capturing and killing Ms. Ellen.

"I told her," Wendy says, laughing insanely. "Don't fuck with Wendy Testaburger!"

MEMORABLE LINES

"I can't wait for Ms. Ellen to see what a raging lesbian I am!"
—Stan

"Are we making love yet?"
—Stan

"Oh thank you very much, Kenny. This is a very scrumptious looking sausage."
—Ms. Ellen

"When someone gets as old as you, do they have to wear Depends under-garments?"
—Wendy

"Alright ,Wendy, seriously, you need to stop with this whole jealousy thing."
—Cartman

"Oh boy, I'm gonna need some more smack."
—Mr. Garrison

"Wow! That's a pretty good nosejob!"
—Mr. Garrison

"Damn man, somebody's got to pull that monkey out of Wendy's ass."
—Cartman

"I've been licking this carpet for three hours and I still don't feel like a lesbian!"
—Cartman

BODY COUNT

Ms. Ellen. And of course Kenny, who is impaled on a sword that flies out of Ms. Ellen's hand as she tries to resist the Iraqis.

Wendy gives Ms. Ellen a dead animal as a present.

PROFANITY REPORT

Wendy becomes the first female character to drop an F-bomb on the show.

POINTLESS OBSERVATIONS

Stan (if you count flashbacks) pukes 19 times in this episode.

This is the first of three episodes in which Mr. Garrison will get major cosmetic surgery.

In an effort to meet Ms. Ellen, Chef comes into the classroom saying Kyle left his detergent on the playground. He gives Kyle a box of "Whitey's Washing Detergent."

Bebe goes to Wendy's house to give her a make-over. This is the first time they're seen hanging out together outside of school, and the first hint that they're friends.

When the Iraqis arrive, one of the alien "drawings" on the back wall has blinking eyes.

CELEBRITIES IMPUGNED

When Wendy shows up for class in her raunchy makeup and outfit, Cartman says "Wow, Wendy looks just like that chick from *Grease*, Elton John."

David Hasselhoff, famous star of *Baywatch* and *Knight Rider*. After Garrison's plastic surgery, pictures of his actual face are used.

In their desperate attempt to become lesbians, Stan buys an Indigo Girls CD, which they listen to while licking the carpet.

POP CULTURE REFERENCES

After his nose job, Mr. Garrison vomits when the movie *Contact* is mentioned. Also, the Andy Gibb song "Shadow Dancing" plays whenever Hasselhoff/Garrison appears.

When trying to gauge Ms. Ellen's looks, Chef uses a scale of celebrities: "Is she like, Vanessa Williams beautiful or Toni Braxton beautiful? . . . Or Pamela Anderson beautiful?" It's finally decided that she is ". . . Erin Grey in the second season of *Buck Rodgers* beautiful."

When Ms. Ellen asks where Mr. Garrison left off, Cartman responds, "We were learning about how Yasmine Bleeth was going out with that Richard Greico guy that used to be on *21 Jump Street*, but then he got his own show for just a while." According to this, he stopped teaching right before he got to the show *Booker*.

During the opening credits guest star Natasha Henstridge, who voices Ms. Ellen, is referred to simply as "the chick from *Species*."

ORIGINAL SONGS

Chef croons to Ms. Ellen with his funky jam "No Substitute." It secures him a dinner date but no love making.

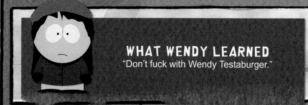

WHAT WENDY LEARNED

"Don't fuck with Wendy Testaburger."

MECHA-STREISAND

Original Air Date: February 18, 1998
Episode No. 112

THE STORY: During a school field trip to an archae-ological dig Cartman discovers a strange-looking stone triangle. The find attracts the attention of film critic Leonard Maltin, who asks Chef if he's seen singer/actress Barbara Streisand lurking around. He says that if Streisand knows about the triangle, the boys could be in terrible danger.

Soon Streisand does indeed turn up, landing her helicopter at the boys' bus stop and demand-ing the "Triangle of Zinthar." They enrage her by (1) not giving her what she wants, and (2) having no idea who she is. She returns in disguise, con-vinces them that the artifact belongs to her, offers a cash reward, and takes them to her mountain condo to collect it.

At the same time Maltin is driving Chef to Streisand's lair to confront her. He says she wants to conquer the world with the aid of the Diamond of Pantheos, which was split in half and its two pieces carefully hidden. Streisand found the first piece during the filming of *My Fair Lady*. The sec-ond was unearthed by Cartman. Possessing both pieces will transform her into a loathsome and all-powerful being.

Once at her mountain hideout, Streisand tor-ments the boys using both traditional torture as well as her singing voice. Finally they surrender the triangle, which she combines with the one she already possesses, creating the dreaded Diamond of Pantheos. She changes into a giant robot mon-ster intent on conquering the world—starting with South Park.

The boys are freed by Leonard Maltin and Chef and head back to town, where Maltin at-tempts to stop Mecha-Streisand by transforming into a giant robot. But he's no match and quick-ly defeated—as is actor Sidney Poitier, who transforms himself into a giant turtle.

South Park seems doomed. That is, until the timely arrival of Robert Smith, lead vocalist of The Cure. Changing into a giant moth, he punches Mecha-Streisand in her vulnerable nose, knock-ing the Diamond of Pantheos free. He then hurls the defeated monster into outer space.

The boys toss the two halves of the diamond into the trash. But Kyle's little brother Ike fishes them out and transforms into a gigantic Mecha-Ike.

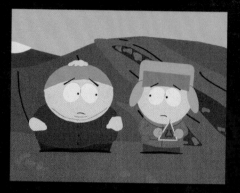

MEMORABLE LINES

"Well, I guess we'll have to Roshambo for it."
—*Cartman*

"Damn your black heart, Barbara Streisand!"
—*Cartman*

"Damnit Cartman, don't you ever learn anything?"
—*Kyle*

"Robert Smith is the greatest person who ever lived."
—*Stan*

Kyle: "Isn't there some rule about not getting into cars with strangers?"

Cartman: "Not when money's involved, stupid."

BODY COUNT

Kenny is strangled during a freak tetherball accident. Many South Park townspeople meet their fate in the wake of Mecha-Streisand's wrath.

WHERE DID THE IDEA COME FROM?

The show is a massive homage to Japanese monster movies. Mecha-Streisand is a takeoff on Godzilla; Leonard Maltin's robot is a thinly disguised Jet Jaguar; Sidney Poitier portrays a fire-breathing turtle very similar to Gamera; and Robert Smith morphs into a giant moth suspiciously like Mothra.

WHAT-THE-FUCK MOMENT

Leonard Maltin says Streisand found the first half of the Diamond of Pantheos during the filming of *My Fair Lady*. Streisand wasn't in that film.

POINTLESS OBSERVATIONS

Leonard Maltin chants "Kitte, Kitte, chuurippu," just before transforming into a giant robot. According to Trey, this is something the Japanese commonly say after farting. It means, roughly, "Listen, listen, a tulip." Also, inside Streisand's mountain hideout is a picture of her with Satan.

The term "Roshambo"—the process of settling a debate by kicking one another in the nuts until only one man is left standing—is introduced by Cartman here. The nut-kick will be used frequently to settle arguments between the boys.

When Chef and Leonard Maltin are driving to Streisand's condo, animators used greenscreen to place video of a snowy road in the background, a technique frequently employed in TV and movies. This is the first time they use actual video footage in the show.

BEHIND THE SCENES

Robert Smith wasn't told the context of any of his lines. Matt and Trey thought it would be funnier that way.

POP CULTURE REFERENCES

The entire program salutes Japanese kaiju (strange creature) movies. Also, Stan says, "My mother told me there are no real monsters, but there are." It's a line from the movie *Aliens*.

Officer Barbrady says to Barbara Streisand, "Well, you ain't Fiona Apple. And if you ain't Fiona Apple, I don't give a rats ass!"

As Robert Smith is walking into the sunset, Kyle yells "*Disintegration* is the best album ever!" This is a nod to The Cure's iconic 1989 album, a personal favorite of Parker and Stone.

CELEBRITIES IMPUGNED

Barbara Streisand, big time. She made the incredibly poor decision to criticize South Park, saying it was bad for kids because it promoted cynicism. She got blasted again in the episode "Spookyfish" (page 66).

Sally Struthers is shown doing a scene on set with Sidney Poitier. Just like in "Starvin' Marvin" (page 24), she is seen shoving large amounts of cake into her mouth.

CELEBRITIES EXALTED

Both Leonard Maltin and Sidney Poitier are portrayed as courageous defenders of the earth. And Robert Smith becomes the savior of the human race and gets a shameless album plug to boot. Not surprisingly, Matt and Trey are big fans of The Cure.

WHAT KYLE LEARNED

"I've learned that people who want power, a lot of power, always end up dead."

CARTMAN'S MOM IS A DIRTY SLUT

Original Air Date: February 25, 1998
Episode No. 113

THE STORY: When Cartman doesn't show up for school for several days, Stan, Kyle and Kenny ditch class and visit his house to see what's wrong. They find him in his backyard, holding a tea party with dolls and stuffed animals. The boys are so disturbed that, instead of making fun of Cartman, they consult Mr. Mackey about what to do. He tells the boys to videotape a tea party so he can study it. The boys happily comply.

Later, Cartman asks his mom who his father is. She says she "met" him eight years earlier at the Twelfth Annual Drunken Barn Dance. The problem, as Cartman soon discovers, is that his mother seems to have slept with quite a few people, including Chef and Mr. Garrison.

Cartman, furious, confronts Mr. Garrison at a local watering hole. His teacher admits he might have had sex with his mother, but so did a lot of other people. He challenges anyone in the packed bar who hadn't had sex with Cartman's mom to fess up. Nobody—not even Jesus—does so.

Dr. Mephesto says he can do a DNA test to find out who among the many, many candidates

is Cartman's real dad. But it will cost $3,000. Dejected, Cartman tells Stan and Kyle about the search for his father, and despairs as to how he'll raise the money for the test. Stan and Kyle, against their better judgment, tell him they sent in a tape to the TV show *America's Stupidest Home Videos*, which has made the finals for a $10,000 best-video prize. They offer to cut him in.

Cartman is at first grateful. He's less grateful when he sees they've sent in footage of one of his tea parties. The video loses to a tape shot by Stan's grandpa of Kenny being run over by a train.

However it does get a $3,000 runner-up prize, which is enough for the DNA test. Dr. Mephesto reveals the results at his lab, which is packed with all the potential dads, including Officer Barbrady, Chef, Jimbo, Mr. Garrison, Ned, Chief Running Water, Gerald Brovlofski (Kyle's dad), Dr. Mephesto and his "friend," Kevin, and the entire 1989 Denver Broncos.

The show then ends with a teaser, saying the answer will come in the next episode.

"What? Son of a bitch!" Cartman rails.

BODY COUNT

Just Kenny, who's dragged onto the railroad tracks by a runaway go-kart and then run over by a train.

CELEBRITIES IMPUGNED

Bob Saget, who's portrayed as the smarmy, unfunny host of a lame video clip show.

CHARACTER DEBUTS

Chief Running Water, a Native American man who's one of Cartman's many potential fathers.

The Denver Broncos, who show up at the Drunken Barn Dance. They can also be seen in "Cartman's Mom Is Still a Dirty Slut" (page 40).

OBSCENITY REPORT

Cartman uses the F word for the first time in this episode.

POINTLESS OBSERVATIONS

A fake commercial for a Terrence and Phillip movie, *Not Without My Anus*, is shown. This was actually the next episode shown (page 38). It premiered on April 1, 1998, and was offered as an April Fool's joke to fans waiting to find out who Cartman's dad was.

At Cartman's tea party, we meet Polly Prissypants, Rumper Tumpskin, Peter Panda, and Clyde Frog (Cartman later calls Clyde Frog "the best stuffed animal he ever had" in "Die Hippie, Die"). These stuffed animals will all make appearances in future episodes. Peter Panda looks an awful lot like Peetie the Sexual Harassment Panda mascot, who we meet in "Sexual Harassment Panda" (page 86).

When Cartman is all thugged out, he has a knuckle ring that reads "PIE." He's also wearing a clock around his neck, much like rapper Flavor Flav of Public Enemy.

POP CULTURE REFERENCES

America's Stupidest Home Videos is a takeoff of *America's Funniest Home Videos*.

On this episode, Jay Leno guest stars as "Kitty." He has three lines, all of which are cat noises.

The lustful song "Like a Throbbing Star. . ." plays every time Cartman's mom "falls in love." This is a rip on the song "My Heart Will Go On" from *Titanic*.

WHAT STAN LEARNED

"Wow, I always knew Cartman's mom was a slut, but God damn!"

SEASON

2

TERRANCE AND PHILLIP IN NOT WITHOUT MY ANUS

Original Air Date: April 1, 1998
Episode No. 201

THE STORY: This "special," very fart-intensive episode is a full-length Terrance and Phillip story, in which the two friends defeat an attempt by Saddam Hussein to conquer Canada. The story opens with Terrance's acquittal during a murder trial, in spite of overwhelming evidence of his guilt. Afterward the prosecutor, nicknamed "Scott the Dick," swears to get the two no matter what.

He soon has his chance. Scott the Dick allies himself with Saddam Hussein, who promises to eliminate Terrance and Phillip in exchange for Scott's help in a not-yet-explained scheme.

Word soon comes that Terrance's daughter, Sally (whose mother is Celine Dion), has been kidnapped in Iran. Terrance and Phillip fly off to Tehran, find the girl within minutes of landing and immediately go home.

They find Canada occupied by the vanguard of Hussein's army, which was smuggled into the country on Terrance and Phillip's return flight. Scott the Dick, realizing his folly, tells the two that this is the beginning of an invasion. The friends decide to strike back during an Ottawa Rough Riders/Vancouver Rough Riders Canadian Football League game, where Hussein plans to reveal his power grab and force Celine Dion to sing the Iraqi national anthem.

The coup is foiled when the crowd at the game farts in unison, unleashing a gas cloud that kills Hussein and his henchmen. Celine Dion then leads everyone in the singing of the Canadian national anthem.

MEMORABLE LINES

"Hey, relax guy."
—*Saddam Hussein*

"I'm going to have a freak baby!"
—*Celine Dion*

"I'm trying to give you cancer with my mind."
—*Scott the Dick*

"Oh Phillip, you saved me from the gas chamber!"
—*Terrance*

"Well, you know what they say: 'A friend in need is a friend with Kroff dinner.'"
—*Phillip*

"Let's look for treasure!"
—*Terrance*

BODY COUNT

Saddam Hussein and his henchmen, all overcome by poisonous anal emissions. Kenny doesn't die, because Kenny (nor any of the other regular cast members except, briefly, for Cartman) doesn't appear.

CHARACTER DEBUTS

While we've seen Terrance and Phillip on TV many times prior to this, it's the first time we meet them in person. Also, we meet their dog and cat, Barkie and Purry, as well as Terrance's "bastard daughter" Sally. And Celine Dion, of course.

Saddam Hussein, portrayed using real-life photos of the actual Iraqi dictator.

Also Ugly Bob and Scott the Dick, who will make another appearance in "Christmas in Canada."

WHERE DID THE IDEA COME FROM?

It was an April Fool's joke at the expense of eager viewers waiting for resolution of Season One's cliffhanger, "Cartman's Mom Is A Dirty Slut" (page 34). South Park thought their fans would appreciate the joke, but quite a few devoted fans were deeply upset about this.

POP CULTURE REFERENCES

The episode's title is an homage to the 1991 Sally Field film *Not Without My Daughter*, in which she rescues her child from Iran. Terrance's daughter is, not surprisingly, named Sally. Also, when Scott questions Saddam about his plans for Canada, he replies by saying, "I changed my mind. Pray that I do not change it any more," to which Scott replies, "This deal's getting worse all the time." The lines were originally spoken by Darth Vader and Lando Calrissian in *The Empire Strikes Back*.

Terrance and Phillip eagerly flip on American TV, first watching what appears to be *Jerry Springer* (on which several townspeople from South Park get into a brawl), and then *South Park* itself (the episode "Cartman's Mom is a Dirty Slut" plays). Phillip laughs, "God damn, their TV shows are lame!"

POINTLESS OBSERVATIONS

Terrance and Phillip (and indeed, all Canadians) seem fascinated by the cheesy stovetop dish Kraft Dinner—here called "Kroff Dinner," in deference to the Canadian accent. Also, the football game between two teams called the Rough Riders is a jab at the Canadian Football League, which until 1996 really did have two teams with that same name.

Saddam is killed by fart poison, then decapitated, but comes back as a villain in *many* future episodes.

CELEBRITIES IMPUGNED

Celine Dion, who not only bore Terrance's love child, but also became pregnant by Ugly Bob, a character so grotesque that he wears a bag over his head. Interestingly, when he takes off the bag he looks exactly like everyone else.

WHAT SCOTT THE DICK LEARNED

"I hate you Terrance and Phillip!"

CARTMAN'S MOM IS STILL A DIRTY SLUT

Original Air Date: April 22, 1998
Episode No. 202

THE STORY: The second half of the first-season cliffhanger finds most of South Park's male population still nervously awaiting Dr. Mephesto's DNA test results. But just as they're about to be revealed, the lights go out and Mephesto is shot twice. Chef rushes him to the hospital.

A crew from *America's Most Wanted* promptly shows up and prepares to do a segment on the crime. At the hospital Dr. Doctor and his nurse, the armless Nurse Goodley, manage to stabilize the still-unconscious Mephesto. Meanwhile, a powerful snowstorm traps the *America's Most Wanted* crew in a TV studio, along with a large group of locals reenacting the shooting. Almost immediately (and in spite of the fact that they've only been without food for a few hours) they resort to cannibalism. Soon much of the *Most Wanted* crew and studio audience is consumed, along with the townies who aren't recurring characters.

Power goes out at the hospital, and Kenny is sent on a dangerous solo mission to restore it. Not surprisingly, he's electrocuted. The power returns and Mephesto regains consciousness. He says the shooter was probably his brother, who tries to kill him once a month. The potential dads gather at the hospital to find out who fathered Cartman.

It turns out none of them did. Eric's mom is a hermaphrodite with both male and female genitals. She impregnated another woman, raising the question of who Cartman's *mother* might be. Cartman, disgusted, drops the matter.

MEMORABLE LINES

"I'm bringing home some Eric Roberts in a doggy bag. Does anyone else want some?"
—*Mr. Garrison*

"Officer Barbrady, let's pretend for one second that we had a competent law enforcer in this town. What would he do?"
—*Mayor McDaniels*

"Oh my God! They killed Mephesto!"
—*Kenny*

"Ummm, Mrs. Cartman, 8 years old is a little late to be considering abortion."
—*Nurse at Unplanned Parenthood*

"The father is . . . Mrs. Cartman!"
—*Dr. Mephesto*

BODY COUNT

Kenny (aka 'Team B'), who's electrocuted while restoring power to the hospital.

Eric Roberts, as well as Sid Greenfield and most of the *America's Most Wanted* crew, are cannibalized by the Mayor, Jimbo, Garrison, Ned, and Barbrady.

POP CULTURE REFERENCES

Kenny's quest to restore the hospital's power mirrors a similar scene in *Jurassic Park*. Also Cartman offers a stirring rendition of "Come Sail Away" by Styx (he admits that if he hears the first part of that song, he has to finish it).

When the power gets cut out during the feed of *America's Most Wanted*, they switch over to their feature movie *Who Framed Roger Rabbit?*

Dr. Doctor enlists Chef's help in the operating room after Chef admits he "used to watch *Quincy*." This is a reference to "*Quincy M.E.*," a medical drama from the late 70s.

John Walsh, the host of *America's Most Wanted*, also makes a cameo.

CELEBRITIES IMPUGNED

It's revealed that Chef owns a "Meredith Baxter-Birney memorial towel." Apparently Chef had sex with the former star of TV's *Family Ties*, then the two of them used the towel to . . . freshen up.

Eric Roberts, star of the TV show *Less Than Perfect*, plays the part of Dr. Mephesto's "little monkey guy" (aka Kevin) in the *America's Most Wanted* reenactment. He is also the first person to be cannibalized; as the Mayor puts it: "Nobody gives a shit about Eric Roberts."

CHARACTER DEBUTS

Dr. Doctor and Nurse Goodley, the no-armed hospital aide.

Sid Greenfield, the director of *America's Most Wanted*, although he's eaten at the end of the episode.

Bill Clinton (the sitting President when this aired) makes his debut in bed with Cartman's mom. He can also be seen in "The Red Badge of Gayness" (page 102) and "Chinpoko Mon" (page 96).

CANNIBALISM NOTES

The scene in which the South Park residents draw straws to determine who gets eaten is from a deleted moment in *Cannibal! The Musical*. Also, when the survivors emerge from the TV studio, they're accompanied by Aaron Neville's version of "Ave Maria," which played in the great cannibal movie *Alive*.

POINTLESS OBSERVATION:

Mephesto's first name is Alphonse. Kenny was killed in Part I of this double-episode after being run over by a train, but in the beginning of this show, he angelically materializes out of thin air. He dies again a few minutes later.

During the final scene, where all of Cartman's potential fathers are gathered, there's an alien present.

WHAT STAN LEARNED

"Dude! You're a big fatass and your mom's a hermaphlite!"

CHICKENLOVER

Original Air Date: May 20, 1998
Episode No. 203

THE STORY: The boys are intrigued by the local bookmobile (called the Booktastic Bus), until they get a look at its bizarre-looking operator. Meanwhile, the town is up in arms because someone is having sex with all the local chickens. Officer Barbrady, charged with finding the culprit, must first confront the fact that he can't read. He resigns his post and enrolls in the boys' class at school, where he deputizes Stan, Kyle, Cartman and Kenny. Cartman in particular enjoys this new honor, patrolling town on his Big Wheel, dealing out violent justice and admonishing anyone who will listen to "Respect my authoritah!"

The chicken "person" is apprehended at the local petting zoo while wearing a Richard Nixon mask. It turns out to be the Booktastic Bus driver, who says his chicken molesting rampage was all part of a scheme to help Barbrady learn to read. He then gives him a copy of Ayn Rand's *Atlas Shrugged.*

Cartman promptly begins clubbing the bookmobile guy in the shins. Officer Barbrady helps, beating the man's head until he dies. Barbrady then takes a crack at *Atlas Shrugged*, but the experience convinces him that reading "totally sucks ass." He vows never to do it again.

MEMORABLE LINES

"Keep your eyes peeled, boys. Someone's going to make love to this chicken any second now."
—*Officer Barbrady*

"I need to go poopies."
—*Officer Barbrady*

"Respect my authoritah!"
—*Cartman*

"This ain't no podunk little town!"
—*Officer Barbrady*

"Reading sucks ass."
—*Cartman*

"Poor people tend to live in clusters."
—*Cartman*

"Bzzzzd. WRONG! Try again, dumbass!!"
—*Mr. Garrison*

POINTLESS OBSERVATIONS

There's a poster at the back of the classroom for Trey Parker's short animated film, *American History*. It also appears in several other episodes.

This is the second time that "Halfie" (a hippie-looking man with no legs) has vouched for sexual activity that he's not responsible for, the first being in "Cartman's Mom is a Dirty Slut" (page 34). Both times he's been scolded for not having legs, to which he responds "Oh yeah."

This episode features a pretty infamous scene in which Cartman dresses up like a hooker. It will happen again (for different reasons) when he dresses up as Ming Lee, a Vietnamese prostitute, in "Cow Days" (page 62), as well as "Freak Strike."

Robert T. Pooner is credited at the fake ending as the Executive Producer. This fake alias will be used in future episodes.

BODY COUNT

The bookmobile guy and, of course, Kenny. He takes an extraordinarily long time to die, cheating the Reaper on several occasions before finally being crushed by a tree. During each near-death experience Stan starts uttering the famous "Oh my God, they killed Kenny!" line before realizing his friend survived. Ironically, when Kenny finally dies Stan doesn't say a word.

POP CULTURE REFERENCES

During a set of fake closing credits, a picture of *Dukes of Hazard* star Tom Wopat appears. And speaking of closing credits, when Officer Barbrady freezes while the credits flash over him, he's offering an homage to countless '60s and '70s cop shows that used this lame technique each week. The fact that he's the only person who freezes, while other cast members continue moving, is a nod to the short-lived yet hilarious cop show satire *Police Squad*.

COPS, the popular reality TV show, follows Officer Barbrady around. Later, they follow Deputy Cartman, and the show is called *Cartman*.

While trying to teach Officer Barbrady to read, Mr. Garrison writes "Oprah Winfrey has huge knockers" on the chalkboard.

For Cartman's book report on *The Lion, The Witch, and the Wardrobe* he recaps that "a bunch of, uh, hippies walk around and paint stuff. They eat lunch, and then they find a magical . . . camel, which they have to eat to stay alive." He gets an F on the report. Officer Barbrady reads *Go Dog Go*, an easy-reading book, and gets an A.

OBSCENITY WATCH

Matt and Trey originally wanted to call the episode "Chickenfucker."

CELEBRITIES IMPUGNED

Author and philosopher Ayn Rand, whose immense novel *Atlas Shrugged* single-handedly turns Officer Barbrady off of reading forever.

WHAT KYLE LEARNED
"Wow, I guess reading really does suck ass!"

IKE'S WEE WEE

Original Air Date: May 27, 1998
Episode No. 204

THE STORY: Mr. Mackey is fired when, during a lecture on the evils of drugs and alcohol, a marijuana sample that he passes around the class mysteriously vanishes (stolen, it turns out, by Mr. Garrison). In short order Mr. Mackey is kicked out of his house and winds up on drugs—which turn out to be kind of enjoyable. He hooks up with a hippie chick and they decide to get married and honeymoon in India.

Meanwhile, Kyle is horrified to learn that his little brother Ike is about to have a bris—something he misconstrues as a party at which his penis will be cut off. He puts his brother on a train to Nebraska and replaces him with a life-sized doll. But a dog runs off with it, then is struck by a truck,

which explodes. At Ike's "funeral" it's revealed that the baby was adopted from Canada. Since Ike isn't his "real" brother," Kyle no longer cares about him and tells his parents where he can be found.

Mr. Mackey, while honeymooning in India, is captured by the A-Team and tossed into the Betty Ford Clinic where he's "cured" of his addiction. Kyle has second thoughts about his relationship to Ike on the day of the bris, when his little brother flees to his room in terror. Kyle defends him fiercely against the besieging adults, until they explain that they won't cut off his *entire* penis. Just a little bit at the end "to make it look bigger." Stan and Cartman promptly demand to be circumcised too.

MEMORABLE LINES

"**This is all I'm going to say about drugs. Stay away from them. There's a time and a place for everything, and it's called college.**"
—*Chef*

"Dude! That is not cool! Choppin' off wee-wees is not cool!!"
—*Cartman*

"Don't you understand that us males are defined by our firemen?"
—*Kyle*

"The fireman is very magical. Rub his helmet and he spits in your eyes."
—*Cartman*

"I'm sorry, but we can't just throw Caucasian babies on an outgoing train."
—*Train Operator*

"Drugs are bad, because if you do drugs you're a hippie, and hippies suck!"
—*Cartman*

"Oh kick ass! I wanna have a bris!"
—*Cartman*

"I don't wanna be in your penis choppin' family anyway!"
—*Cartman*

"Drugs are bad, mkay."
—*Mr. Mackey*

BODY COUNT

Just Kenny, who falls into an empty grave during Ike's "funeral" and gets brained by a headstone. Also the person driving the exploding truck that "kills" Ike, and Sylvester the dog.

POINTLESS OBSERVATIONS

The alphabet above the classroom's chalkboard reads DiOsMiO-hAnMaTaDoHaKeNnYbAsTaRdOs. That spells *"Dios Mio han matado ha Kenny, bastardos,"* which is loosely Spanish for "Oh my God they killed Kenny, you bastards."

This is the second time Kyle uses "kick the baby" with Ike, the first being in "Cartman Gets an Anal Probe" (page 10).

This is the only episode where you can see Mr. Mackey with a normal sized head. We learn here that his necktie is responsible for making his head balloon up so large.

POP CULTURE REFERENCES

While staggering home from a bar, Mr. Mackey sings Pat Benatar's "Love is a Battlefield." Dr. Schwartz tries to explain the bris by telling Kyle that "a circumcision is a very common thing for Ike to have. His father had it, his grandfather had it, and . . . his brother . . . had it." The lines echo an encounter in *Return of the Jedi* between Luke Skywalker and Princess Leia, when Luke breaks the news that they are brother and sister. Finally, after Mr. Garrison smokes the stolen marijuana he sits around watching *Teletubbies*.

Mr. Mackey says that LSD is a drug made famous by John Lennon and Paul McCartney.

Mr. T and the A-Team kidnap Mr. Mackey and take him to the Betty Ford Clinic, a well-known rehab clinic outside of Los Angeles famous for its celebrity guests. Mr. T can also be seen in "Cartoon Wars: Part I."

CHARACTER DEBUTS

Dr. Schwartz, the Jewish doctor brought in to perform Ike's bris. Mr. Mackey also runs into Two Hippie Dudes, who give him a dose of LSD and cause his head to float away. These two can also be seen jamming out to some Laser Loggins in "Roger Ebert Should Lay Off the Fatty Foods" (page 58).

CHARACTER DEPARTURE

The canine that steals the Ike doll and then gets run over is Sylvester, the toughest dog in town, first seen in "Big Gay Al's Big Gay Boat Ride" (page 16).

CARTOON REFERENCE

Someone in a car harasses Mr. Mackey by shouting, "Now we see what you and Homer Simpson have in common—dope!"

WHAT KYLE LEARNED

"Family isn't about whose blood you have, it's about who you care about. That's why I feel you guys are more than just my friends. You're my family. Except for Cartman."

45

CONJOINED FETUS LADY

Original Air Date: June 3, 1998
Episode No. 205

THE STORY: Pip, for once showing some backbone, pops Kyle in the face during a dodgeball game, giving him a bloody nose. Kyle is sent to see Nurse Gollum, who (he is horrified to discover) has a dead conjoined fetus on the side of her head. Apparently she suffers from something called Conjoined Twin Myslexia.

The boys naturally make fun of her hideous condition. Kyle's mom overhears and tries to raise their consciousness, telling them that sometimes a dead twin can be inside a live one, and that any one of them might also have a dead, conjoined sibling somewhere in their bodies. Stan flips out, goes home and tries to hack open his head with an ice pick.

Kyle's mom then decides to raise awareness of the problem and champions a "Conjoined Twin Myslexia Week," for the community's sole sufferer, who would greatly prefer to remain in relative anonymity.

At the same time the school's dodgeball team wins the state championship—primarily on the strength of Pip's performance. He becomes a rage-filled, superhuman dodgeball machine whenever anyone mistakes him for being French. Which seems to happen quite a bit. The team goes on to win the national championship, then takes on international powerhouse China.

Pip single-handedly wipes out the entire Chinese squad when they (at the prompting of the South Park players) call him French. The kids become world champions, but no one cares because dodgeball sucks.

Back in South Park the town stages a parade for Nurse Gollum. The locals don hats that make them look like they have fetuses on their heads. Nurse Gollum, her patience at an end, states that she just wants to be harassed and abused like everyone else. For this she's called "ungrateful."

MEMORABLE LINES

"My mom says there's a lot of black people in China."
—*Cartman*

"Oh. I see you've noticed my disorder. I have a stillborn fetus growth attached to my head."
—*Nurse Gollum*

"This may sound odd coming from a woman with a fetus sticking out of her head, but . . . you're all a bunch of freaks!"
—*Nurse Gollum*

"You see, it's NOT okay to make fun of an American because they're black or brown or whatever, but it IS okay to make fun of foreigners because they're from another country."
—*Chef*

"Oh, what jolly good fun!"
—*Pip*

"You shouldn't make fun of foreigners. And besides, I hate French people."
—*Pip*

BODY COUNT

Kenny, killed by a dodgeball thrown with too much mustard during the match against China.

Several other competing children fall under the gun of an angry, dodgeball-hurling Pip.

Also a Washington, D.C. tourist run over by Ms. Crabtree's bus.

POINTLESS OBSERVATION

The boys travel to their various dodgeball matches via Mrs. Crabtree's bus—even to the one in China.

The Nurse's name "Gollum" is actually the name of the creepy, monster-like character from J.R.R. Tolkien's *Lord of the Rings*. Also, "golem" is a Yiddish term referring to "an animate being created out of inanimate matter."

The newspaper Kyle's Dad is reading at breakfast has a section on it called "Priests & Kids."

POP CULTURE REFERENCES

Cartman's taunt, "So, Captain Ahab has to get his whale, huh?" is a *Moby Dick* reference skimmed from *Star Trek: First Contact*.

ORIGINAL SONGS

There's two little snippets of songs: Chef's "Whooped Yo Ass," which he sings after beating the Denver team, as well as the Neil Diamond-esque piano ballad "Dead Fetus on Your Head" which plays over the Nurse Gollum tribute video.

CHARACTER DEBUTS

Nurse Gollum. Also Butters is seen (but not heard) in this episode, where he is referred to as "Swanson." He won't get to talk until "Two Guys Naked In A Hot Tub" (page 90). The black-haired kid Kevin (he's referred to as "Casey" in "An Elephant Makes Love to a Pig" (page 18)) has his speaking debut.

CELEBRITIES IMPUGNED

When Kyle's mom shows the boys a picture of conjoined twins from a book called *Freaks A-Z*, it's really a picture of Mickey Dolenz and Michael Nesmith from The Monkees.

WHAT CHEF LEARNED

"I have been obsessed, and obsession isn't good. If we had won the world championship, what then? It would only be a bigger letdown the next year if we didn't win! Our lives would have to revolve around dodgeball. Our lives were fine before!"

THE MEXICAN STARING FROG OF SOUTHERN SRI LANKA

Original Air Date: June 10, 1998
Episode No. 206

THE STORY: The Boys interview Jimbo and Ned about their Vietnam experiences for a class project. Unfortunately the men are less than truthful, stating, among a great many other things, that American military camps were equipped with amusement park rides and that they single-handedly defeated the Viet Cong. The boys get an F from Mr. Garrison, who assumes they made it all up.

To get revenge, the boys fake videos of the legendary Mexican Staring Frog of Southern Sri Lanka, which can kill at a glance. Jimbo and Ned air them on their cable access show, *Huntin' and Killin' With Jimbo and Ned*. They're a big hit with the program's incredulous viewers, who abandon its competitor, *Jesus and Pals*, in droves. Or maybe not exactly in droves, because the view-

ership for both shows is in the low tens. Jesus' producer fights back by changing his program's format into something a bit more *Springer*-esque.

Disaster ensues when Jimbo and Ned decide to pursue the Staring Frog. When Ned sees a fake one set up by the boys he becomes comatose with fright. At the hospital the kids own up to their fakery.

Jimbo, Ned and the boys appear on *Jesus and Pals* to iron out their differences. Thanks to the show's producer, who encourages them to lie, it doesn't work out that way. Jimbo claims Stan is a drug-addicted Satan worshipper, while Stan says Jimbo molested him. Chaos ensues, which Jesus ends with a very un-Savior-like "Shut the fuck up!" He sends his producer to Hell for her transgressions.

MEMORABLE LINES

"Comin' up next, we're gonna drop some napalm on an unsuspecting family of beavers."
—*Jimbo*

"We did it Ned! We killed the entire Viet Cong army!"
—*Jimbo*

"No, I wasn't in Vietnam. But sometimes I like to pretend I was."
—*Mr. Garrison*

"Revenge is so very, very sweet."
—*Cartman*

"Oh J, you are so omnipotent and yet so naïve."
—*Show Producer*

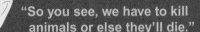

"So you see, we have to kill animals or else they'll die."
—*Jimbo*

"Put your hands together and welcome the only man in town who always has a fully-stocked wine cellar, Jeeeeeeeeeeeeeeeeeeeeeeeesus Christ!"
—*Jesus and Pals announcer*

BODY COUNT

Kenny is ripped in half by rowdy, brawling audience members on *Jesus and Pals*. Ned and Jimbo kill a bunch of woodland animals on their show *Huntin' and Killin'*, and according to their flashbacks, the entire Viet Cong army. Also, the producer of *Jesus and Pals* is cast into hell by Jesus himself.

CELEBRITIES IMPUGNED

One of Jesus' audience members mistakenly refers to him as "Montel," as in Montel Williams. He then launches into a largely irrelevant defense of Michael Jackson, who at the time had once again been accused of child molestation.

Bob Denver, best known as Gilligan from the TV show *Gilligan's Island*, makes an awkward appearance on Jesus' show.

OBSCENITY WATCH

Jesus drops an F-bomb. The exact quote is, "Shut the fuck up! Jesus, what is wrong with you people?!"

WHERE DID THE IDEA COME FROM?

The title of the episode is a play on *The Giant Beaver of Southern Sri Lanka*, a student film that Matt and Trey met while working on. It was in turn a satire of Mark Twain's *The Celebrated Jumping Frog of Calaveras County*.

POINTLESS OBSERVATIONS

When Jesus' producer goes to Hell, she meets Satan and Saddam Hussein. It's the first time they're portrayed as lovers. Also, during Jimbo's Vietnam flashback we learn that Ned formerly possessed a beautiful, melodious man voice.

This is the first and last time we'll see Ned and Jimbo's public access show *Huntin' and Killin'*. We also learn that their go-to phrase "It's coming right for us!" no longer works. Instead, they yell "Thin out their numbers!"

During the flashbacks, animators spliced in real video footage of the Vietnam War.

In this episode, we actually see how Ned lost his arm: a grenade went off in his hands while ambushing the Viet Congs.

POP CULTURE REFERENCES

While in the hospital Jimbo reads S. E. Hinton's *The Outsiders* to Ned. Also, when Cartman asks Mr. Garrison what Vietnam is, he says, "What's Vietnam? A question a child might ask, but not a childish question." The line is from a TV commercial for a Time-Life book series about the war.

On *Huntin' and Killin'*, there's a part of the show called "Jimbo's Mysteries of the Unexplained." This is a nod to the popular show *Unexplained Mysteries*.

The spacey, late-60s song "Time of the Season" by The Zombies is used during Jimbo's Vietnam flashback. Also, the song "Nothing From Nothing" by Billy Preston is covered by Jesus' studio band The Disciples.

Jesus and Pals is reformatted to be very similar to *Jerry Springer*. Furthermore, Jesus releases "Too Hot For TV" featuring raunchy and vulgar outtakes from his show. This is spoof on Springer's tape series of the same name.

WHAT CARTMAN LEARNED

"Lying kicks ass!"

CITY ON THE EDGE OF FOREVER

Original Air Date: June 17, 1998
Episode No. 207

THE STORY: When Ms. Crabtree's school bus slides on some ice and winds up teetering on the edge of a cliff, she goes for help while telling the children that if they try to leave, a monster will eat them. To fight the boredom, they start having flashbacks to previous episodes.

Except that these flashbacks are all wrong. They mess with the reality of the episode they reference. Stan succeeds in kissing Wendy instead of vomiting on her ("Cartman Gets An Anal Probe," page 10); Mr. Garrison succeeds in shooting Kathie Lee Gifford ("Weight Gain 4000," page 12), who turns out to be an alien; and Kenny kills Death instead of the other way around ("Death," page 20). There's even a flashback to an old *Happy Days* episode in which Fonzie jumps his motorcycle over a line of busses.

Each vignette somehow involves ice cream and ends with the child who recalls it saying, "Now that's what I call a sticky situation!"

Finally one kid, dressed tellingly in a red Starfleet uniform, ventures off the bus. He's promptly eaten by an enormous black monster voiced by Henry Winkler.

Meanwhile Ms. Crabtree meets a trucker named Marcus, who's hauling a load of the date rape drug "rufies." She then stumbles into a theatrical agent who launches her on a career as a successful comedian. Then Cartman and Kyle get in an altercation on the bus, causing it to fall down the cliff. But disaster is averted when it lands in a pile of ice cream. Which makes no sense. Realizing this, Cartman suddenly wakes up in his own bed. His mother brings him a bowl of beetles to eat.

This causes Kyle, who's *actually* having the dream, to wake up. The show closes with Ms. Crabtree and Marcus (who's also referred to as Mitch) watching a sunset. Even though their union is just the product of a child's dream, they don't care because they're happy.

MEMORABLE LINES

"Please, call me muffin."
—*Ms. Crabtree*

"Y'all be quiet or the cute little bunny dies!"
—*Ms. Crabtree*

"KIDS! Do not get off this bus! If you do, a big, scary monster will EAT YOU!"—*Ms. Crabtree*

"I don't wanna die on this bus with you assholes! You guys suck!"
—*Cartman*

"Dude, that's a pretty fucked up dream."
—*Kyle*

"My father is John Elway! My father is John Elway!!"
—*Cartman*

"Now that's what I call a sticky situation!"
—*Stan, Kyle, Cartman, and Kenny*

"Oh my God! Kenny . . . killed . . . Death."
—*Stan*

BODY COUNT

Technically, nobody died because it was a dream. But there were some dreamt casualties: the 3rd grade kid in the *Star Trek* shirt, and Kenny—twice (once by the monster and once by Fonzie's motorcycle).

CELEBRITIES IMPUGNED

In a flashback sportscaster Brent Musburger (who plays himself) serves as Scuzzlebutt's leg, rather than Patrick Duffy as in "Volcano" (page 14). In the closing credits his name is misspelled as Musberger.

The comedy club Mrs. Crabtree stumbles into is called "Pauly Shore's Funny Pit!!" and the comedian on stage is Carrot Top (the name on the marquee is "Carrot Ass"). Mrs. Crabtree humiliates him with her "Sit down and shut up" routine, and Carrot Top pees his pants on stage.

Jay Leno, who's shown with a chin the size of his entire body.

POINTLESS OBSERVATION

The red-shirted kid who's killed by the monster is a reference to the original *Star Trek* series, where extras in red shirts were always the first (and usually only) cast members to die.

This is the only episode in which Stan actually kisses Wendy. He smooches her twice.

The Talent Agency that reps Ms. Crabtree also has pictures of Kathie Lee Gifford, Leonard Maltin, and Carrot Top on their wall.

When the parents are posting up pictures of their missing kids, there's a picture of Macaulay Culkin (famous child actor and star of *Home Alone*) on one of the posters reading: "Find Me."

ORIGINAL SONGS

The parents all join together in a "Band Aid"-type collaboration to sing "Please Come Home," with hopes that their "runaway children" would hear it and return home.

POP CULTURE REFERENCES

The title was taken from a *Star Trek* episode of the same name. Also, Ms. Crabtree's comedy "stylings" are featured on *The Tonight Show* with Jay Leno.

Marcus, the truck driver, is humming the tune "Lookin' For Love" when he picks up Ms. Crabtree. It's a country tune made popular by Johnny Lee.

Cartman complains that he's missing the new *Fantasy Island* on the bus, then later complains about missing *Barnaby Jones*. Both shows were on TV before Cartman was ever born.

John Elway is shown as Cartman's father, even though this clearly isn't true.

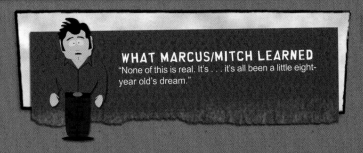

WHAT MARCUS/MITCH LEARNED

"None of this is real. It's . . . it's all been a little eight-year old's dream."

SUMMER SUCKS

Original Air Date: June 24, 1998
Episode No. 208

THE STORY: South Park's hot, boring summer is made even worse by a new, state-wide fireworks ban. The only thing still legal are snakes—little black tablets that create a long, twisting tail of ash when lit. The mayor has the largest one in the world created for the town's Fourth of July celebration. But after lighting it, the manufacturer points out that it won't burn out until November of the next year. In the meantime it makes a huge trail of ash that destroys everything it touches.

Mr. Garrison undergoes a personal crisis when Mr. Hat suddenly vanishes (the puppet is briefly seen in a sauna). He visits a New York City psychiatrist, who tells him Mr. Hat represents his own gay side. Before they can make much progress,

the snake (which now spans the country) breaks through a window and incinerates the psychiatrist.

But help is on the way. Jimbo and Ned return to town with a huge cache of illegal Mexican fireworks, which the boys use to destroy the giant snake. Ash from the pulverized monstrosity rains down on the town (which is, for the first time in the show's history, shown completely free of snow). The residents use the sooty fallout for sledding and other winter activities.

Mr. Garrison returns to town with a new puppet, Mr. Twig (literally a twig). Chef, returning from a vacation in Aruba, mistakenly thinks South Park's soot-covered residents are wearing blackface.

MEMORABLE LINES

"Hey! If you so much as touch Kitty's ass, I'll put firecrackers in your nutsack and blow your balls all over your pants!"
—*Cartman*

"Okay, everybody get in a line so I can whoop all your asses!"
—*Chef*

"Hell, everything's legal in Mexico. It's the American way."
—*Jimbo*

"Look how much happiness a little firepower can bring to a child."
—*Jimbo*

"Summer sucks ass, Mr. Garrison."
—*Stan*

"I only know how to do it doggy style."
—*Cartman*

"Serves you right, you gay-bashing homo!"
—*Mr. Garrison*

"Well I can tell you that I'm 100 percent NOT GAY!"
—*Mr. Garrison*

BODY COUNT

Kenny (killed when some bleachers collapse on him as he dodges the giant snake). Also Mr. Garrison's psychiatrist and various other citizens across the country that get in the snake's way. Technically Kenny gets it twice, because during a flashback he's seen blowing himself up with a firecracker in kindergarten. In response baby Stan says something to the effect of, "Oooh das kill Kenny!" and Kyle says, "Oooh bastards!"

POINTLESS OBSERVATIONS

Pip states that his biological parents are dead.

This is the first time we see Cartman (or any of the boys) without their shirt on.

Mr. Mackey prank-calls Mr. Garrison in this episode, asking "if Mr. Hat is there." Mr. Garrison has no idea who it is.

This is the first of many episodes in which Mormons are featured (here, performing a baptism before being killed by the snake). Matt and Trey grew up in an area with a lot of Mormons, hence their interest in the topic.

POP CULTURE REFERENCES

The psychiatrist Mr. Garrison visits in New York City is Dr. Jonathan Katz, the lead character in another Comedy Central animated program that was popular at the time.

For the conclusion of Charlie's "Giant Snake" presentation, he flips to a photo of Abe Vigoda tipping his hat.

With the snake on the verge of destroying the town, the boys pick up musical instruments and start playing sad music, just as the band in *Titanic* does while the ship is sinking.

CHARACTER DEBUTS

Mr. Twig, a little wooden twig with a pink-triangle t-shirt, makes his hand-held debut. Mr. Twig is Mr. Garrison's replacement for Mr. Hat who has gone missing.

A kid named Kevin who's been missing for months. When a particularly large mound of snow melts he's found beneath it, still alive and none the worse for wear.

Stu, of Stu's Firework Shack, and Charlie, the DYNO-MIGHT firework company owner. Charlie's responsible for creating the giant snake that destroys the town. We also meet Mr. Romero, the school's skinny music teacher.

CELEBRITIES IMPUGNED

Mr. Garrison, distraught over losing Mr. Hat, fantasizes about murdering PBS fixtures Shari and Lamb Chop with an ax.

Mr. Garrison confesses, "Sometimes Mr. Hat liked to pretend he was in a sauna with Brett Favre and a bottle of 1000 Island dressing." We later see a scene where this actually happens (minus the 1000 Island dressing).

WHAT-THE-FUCK MOMENT

While Mayor McDaniels fields phone calls in her office, Officer Barbrady's head suddenly pops up from underneath her desk, complaining that he "couldn't find the little man in the boat." The mayor tells him to keep looking and pushes his head back down.

ORIGINAL SONGS

While vacationing in Aruba, Chef sings "Simultaneous Love" surrounded by a bunch of bikini-clad ladies.

WHAT JIMBO LEARNED

"Look how much happiness a little fire-power can bring to a child."

CHEF'S CHOCOLATE SALTY BALLS

Original Air Date: August 19, 1998
Episode No. 209

THE STORY: Robert Redford decides to move the Sundance Film Festival from Park City, Utah, to South Park. The town is immediately overwhelmed by tourists and celebrities. Mr. Garrison tells his class to see and write a report about one independent film, while Chef makes money by selling a special confection called Chocolate Salty Balls.

That evening Kyle thinks he hears Mr. Hankey, the Christmas Poo, calling from inside the toilet. Stan, Cartman and Kenny join him on a trip into the sewers, where they find a very ill Mr. Hankey. It seems that the influx of out-of-towners with strange, healthful diets has dangerously disrupted the sewer's "ecosystem."

The boys try to tell the town's guests about the problem, but everyone thinks they're trying to pitch a script. An agent even convinces Cartman to sell the rights to Kyle's story. Within hours a Mr. Hankey movie appears, with Tom Hanks as Kyle and a monkey as Mr. Hankey.

Meanwhile, the real Mr. Hankey has turned ghostly white and lingers near death. But the timely consumption of one of Chef's Chocolate Salty Balls revives him. After giving Robert Redford one last chance to take his festival elsewhere, Mr. Hankey causes sewage to inundate the town, killing Redford and his wife and sending the festival's attendees fleeing for their lives. South Park's residents are happy to have their town to themselves—even though it's now covered in human feces.

MEMORABLE LINES

"Don't forget to change your sheets once a week."
—*Mr. Hankey*

"You've got the best balls in the whole world, Chef."
—*Stan*

"Does poo go to heaven?"
—*Kyle*

"One time, when you were sleeping, I put myself in your mouth and had my friend take a picture."
—*Mr. Hankey*

"You show me one independent film that isn't about gay cowboys eating pudding!"
—*Cartman*

"If you work in the entertainment business and you make money, you're a sellout."
—*Stan*

"I'll always love you, Mr. Hankey."
—*Tom Hanks*

BODY COUNT

Kenny is trampled by an audience leaving a movie screening. Because Stan and Kyle aren't around, a passerby says, "Oh my God, I found a penny!" To which his companion replies, "You bastard!" Also Robert Redford and his wife are drowned by raw sewage.

POINTLESS OBSERVATION

Chef develops several other suggestively named products besides *Chocolate Salty Balls,* including Fudge Ems, Fudge This, Go Fudge Yourself, I Don't Really Give A Flying Fudge, and I Just Went and Fudged Your Mama.

The boys run into Mr. Garrison in the sewers, covered in poo and in full snorkel gear, saying he was "just hanging out."

Stan holds hands with Wendy for the first time in this episode . . . and pukes all over the movie patron in front of him.

POP CULTURE REFERENCE THAT NOW SEEMS STRANGELY PROPHETIC

One of the films screened at the festival was called *A Bunch of Gay Cowboys Eating Pudding.* This was long before 2005's *Brokeback Mountain,* which made gay cowboys (though not pudding) a big deal.

WHERE DID THE IDEA COME FROM?

A couple of years earlier the Sundance Festival rejected Trey and Matt's film *Cannibal! The Musical.* Actually "rejected" doesn't quite cover it. The Sundance people never even bothered to respond to their submission.

POP CULTURE REFERENCES

The movies *Godzilla* (the American remake) and *Independence Day* are singled out for scorn. Also, when Mr. Hankey seems about to die, he motions Kyle toward him and says, "There is another Skywalker." Yoda says this to Luke Skywalker in *Return of the Jedi.* Finally, Mr. Hankey's climactic sewage assault is an homage to the *Sorcerer's Apprentice* segment in *Fantasia.* Mr. Hankey even wears a wizard's robe and hat.

In the exploratory, independent lesbian film *Witness to Denial,* one of the women is wearing a "Lillith Fare" t-shirt. This is a reference to the "Lilith Fair" concert tour, which only featured bands with female vocalists.

Robert Redford "honors" South Park by demolishing the town library to make way for a Hollywood Planet restaurant. This is a take-off on the popular tinsel-town themed chain Planet Hollywood.

After Mr. Hankey dries out and "dies," a man in a HAZMAT suit comes by and scoops him up. This, as well as the following scene in the white containment room, is a take-off on the film *E.T.: The Extra Terrestrial,* where the sick alien is taken away from his friend Elliot and put into a containment facility.

CELEBRITIES IMPUGNED

Robert Redford, who gets a steaming plate of payback with a side order of cous cous for blowing off *Cannibal! The Musical.* Also Tom Hanks, whom Cartman asserts ". . . can't act his way out of a nutsack." The movie he stars in, *Mr. Hankey and Me,* is a parody of *Philadelphia.* Finally Fred Savage, diminutive star of TV's *The Wonder Years,* is singled out for mockery. When he exits a limo, the nearby crowd groans in disappointment.

PUBLIC REACTION

The song *Chocolate Salty Balls (P.S. I Love You),* performed by Isaac Hayes, hit No. 1 in Great Britain and Ireland.

WHAT WENDY LEARNED

"Sometimes I forget that even though a few independent films are great, most of them suck ass."

WHAT CARTMAN LEARNED

"Being a sellout is sweet, because you make a lot of money, and when you have money you don't have to hang out with any poor-ass losers like you guys."

CHICKENPOX

Original Air Date: August 26, 1998
Episode No. 210

THE STORY: A chickenpox epidemic sweeps through South Park, infecting Kenny and Stan's sister, Shelly. Stan, Kyle and Cartman haven't caught it yet, so their mothers, to get it out of the way, arrange for them to stay overnight at Kenny's house so they can be exposed. Cartman and Stan both get sick. Stan gets so bad that he's hospitalized with Shelly. Kyle, so far uninfected, discovers his mom's plan to "expose" them.

Kyle's mom has her hands full just now, because she's also trying to patch up a former friendship between her husband and Kenny's dad. The two men go away together on a fishing trip, but a fistfight soon erupts. Kenny's dad is jealous of Kyle's dad's success. Kyle's dad then makes a speech to Kyle about how, in a capitalist society, there has to be a hierarchy of "gods and clods."

Kyle writes a school paper called "My Final Solution," in which he outlines a plan to eliminate all the clods. Not surprisingly, his father sees the error of his views.

The boys are outraged when they discover their moms planned to get them all sick. Stan (unaware that he's deathly ill) escapes the hospital, rallies the boys and convinces them to take revenge on the adults. They hire a herpes-infected prostitute named Frida to visit their families' homes and lick and touch things. The parents find the kids and return them to the hospital. Suddenly Kyle becomes ill and passes out.

All four wind up in hospital beds, and all the parents get herpes. Everyone has a hearty laugh about it. Then Kenny flatlines. Then everyone laughs some more.

MEMORABLE LINES

"I can't believe you boys gave us herpes . . . you little rascals!"
—*Kyle's dad*

"Lord, we thank you for this staggering payload of frozen waffles you have bestowed upon us."
—*Kenny's dad*

"We humans work as a society. And in order for a society to thrive, we need Gods and Clods."
—*Kyle's dad*

"Dude, seriously, you better stop being so poor or else I'm gonna start huckin' rocks at you."
—*Cartman*

"I'm gonna go downstairs and kick her square in the nuts!"
—*Cartman*

"When you're unemployed, weekends are meaningless."
—*Kenny's dad*

BODY COUNT
Just Kenny.

POINTLESS OBSERVATIONS

Kenny's brother's name is revealed to be Kevin. The bumper sticker on Kenny's dad's truck says "Know Fear."

Shelly likes the TV show *Passion Cramps*.

Kyle's Mom introduces a game called Ookie Mouth, the point of which is to have someone spit in your mouth, and try to swallow the spit while saying "ookie mouth" at the same time. Kyle can't do it.

CHARACTER DEBUTS
Frida the prostitute.

POP CULTURE REFERENCES

The Monkees song "I'm A Believer" plays during a montage shot of Frida spreading herpes across town. Also Cartman sings Elvis Presley's "In The Ghetto" for the first (but not last) time while visiting Kenny's house. Finally, Cartman takes his Steve Urkel sleeping bag along for the sleepover.

The "entertainment system" at Kenny's house is a black-and-white TV and ColecoVision (an old, not-popular gaming console from the early 80s). After hearing the news, Kyle says, "Oh my god, this is like a third world country."

For his paper on "How I would make America better," Stan closes his argument with ". . . and so that's why *Knight Rider* was the best show in America." Cartman takes a similar approach, finishing with this *Star Wars* reference ". . . I hope that one day America could be more like Endor, where the Ewoks live. Endor is very cool." Cartman will again display his love for Ewoks in "Clubhouses" (page 60).

CELEBRITIES IMPUGNED

Dr. Doctor informs Stan's parents that he's suffering from a dangerous case of chickenpox that could "move through his inner ear to his brain, making him think he's David Duchovny."

WHAT KYLE'S DAD LEARNED
"I've realized I shouldn't be so cold towards people that are less fortunate than me."

ROGER EBERT SHOULD LAY OFF THE FATTY FOODS

Original Air Date: September 2, 1998
Episode No. 211

THE STORY: Cartman slips away from a field trip to the local planetarium to audition for a chance to sing the Cheesy Poofs jingle on the company's next commercial. The rest of the class is brainwashed by the planetarium's director, Dr. Adams, when he uses a powerful machine to scramble the stars, thereby hypnotizing the audience during the light show. After they watch the show the kids develop an overwhelming desire not just to revisit the planetarium, but to volunteer there as well.

Meanwhile Cartman cheats his way into singing the Cheesy Poofs song. But his singing is so terrible that only one word of his makes it into the ad. He's thrilled however, because he's been on TV.

Mr. Mackey, concerned over the children's be-havior, mind melds (an ancient technique passed down from school counselor to school counselor) with a kid who escaped from the planetarium and learns of the brainwashing. He, Nurse Gollum, Stan and Kyle then confront Dr. Adams and Officer Barbrady, who's been made to believe he's Elvis. They are quickly overwhelmed by the drones who are working for the planetarium, tied up and about to have their minds wiped. But in the middle of the process Cartman bursts in, furious that the other boys missed his TV commercial. Angrily kicking over the star projector, he sends a full blast of mind control beams into Dr. Adams' brain, turning him into a drooling vegetable. Everyone is saved. Cartman is a hero.

MEMORABLE LINES

"You guys can all kiss my ass, because I was on television!!"
—*Cartman*

"A haiku is just like a normal American poem except it doesn't rhyme and it's totally stupid."—*Mr. Garrison*

"Okay children, now I'm going to remind you that this is a planetarium, not a Bangkok brothel, so let's behave ourselves."
—*Mr. Garrison*

"Can't we just be like normal third graders for a little while?"
—*Stan*

"Stars are actually made of hot gas, which is exactly what comes out of Roger Ebert's mouth."
—*Dr. Adams*

"Please, nurse, for a woman with a dead fetus on her head, you're not being very open-minded!"
—*Mr. Mackey*

BODY COUNT

Kenny, whose head explodes when Stan and Kyle accidentally overdose him with the brainwashing ray.

WHERE DID THE IDEA COME FROM?

The story is an homage to "Dagger of the Mind," an episode from the original *Star Trek*. Interestingly, the entire thing is named in "honor" of film critic Roger Ebert, even though he's only mentioned in a single sight gag and in a half-heard remark by Dr. Adams.

WHAT-THE-FUCK MOMENT

Dr. Adams, the Planetarium Director, pronounces the word, "plane arium," because a bone disorder makes it impossible for him to pronounce the "T".

POINTLESS OBSERVATIONS

The planetarium sports the Latin phrase "Me transmitte sursum, Caledoini!" It loosely translates to "Beam me up, Scotty," or (more accurately) "Bring me up, Scotsman." Also, a sign at the South Park police station reads, "South Park Police: To Serve and Neglect."

Chef is one of many people that gets brainwashed at the Planetarium. But this isn't the last time he'll have his mind erased; it happens again in "The Return of Chef."

Although she hasn't been officially introduced yet, Red is one of the children featured in Cartman's Cheesy Poof commercials. She can be seen in the vat of Cheesy Poofs, eating her heart out.

POP CULTURE REFERENCES

When trying to explain just how lame the planetarium is, Cartman says it's "*Night Court* in its fifth season lame." Also Cartman auditions for the Cheesy Poofs commercial by singing Donna Summer's "She Works Hard for the Money."

At the beginning of this episode, we learn that Garrison has been teaching the class via *Barnaby Jones* reruns. Cartman also mentions this TV show in "City on the Edge of Forever" (page 50). Actress and model Daisy Fuentes is mentioned by a mind-warped Vangelder, blurting out "Why?! Why *America's Funniest Home Videos*?? Why?!?" Apparently, her choice to host the home video show was emotionally scarring.

Principal Victoria goes to see *Laser Loggins* at the Planetarium, a laser rock show featuring music by Kenny Loggins. His hit "Footloose" blasts on screen.

CHARACTER DEBUTS

Dr. Adams, the brainwashing leader of the Planetarium.

Vangelder, a little brainwashed kid from the Planetarium that escaped with Mr. Garrison's class.

Cartman's Grandmother is also briefly introduced. You will see her later in "Merry Christmas Charlie Manson!" (page 68).

CELEBRITIES IMPUGNED

William Shatner, sort of. At the end of the episode, as Kyle contemplates the now-mindless Dr. Adams, he breaks into his best Captain Kirk-speak, saying, "Can you . . . imagine it, Stan? A mind . . . emptied . . . by that thing." And of course there's Roger Ebert.

The reporter for Channel 4 news is introduced as "a 34 year old Asian man who looks strikingly similar to Ricardo Montalbán."

Dr. Adams brainwashes Officer Barbrady to think he's Elvis Presley, leading him to speak in broken Elvis talk. Mr. Mackey mistakenly thinks he's impersonating Charlton Heston.

BIOGRAPHICAL TRIVIA

Cartman's middle name is revealed to be Theodore.

CLUBHOUSES

Original Air Date: September 23, 1998
Episode No. 212

THE STORY: Stan and Kyle build a tree house so they can play Truth or Dare with Wendy and Bebe (who has a crush on Kyle). Kyle doesn't reciprocate, but goes along with the plan when Stan says they can make the girls "eat bugs."

When Cartman and Kenny hear of the scheme, they construct their own insanely elaborate pre-fab structure called the Ewok Village 2000 Deluxe Club House Kit. Not surprisingly, Kenny does all the work.

As the two structures go up, the marriage of Stan's parents, Randy and Sharon, falls apart. They divorce and Sharon takes up with a guy named Roy who moves into the family home. Stan and Roy's relationship quickly goes south.

Cartman and Kenny finish their clubhouse first

and use it to attract two older female runaways. They host a huge party, during which Kenny dies in a mosh pit mishap. Stan and Kyle finally get their own clubhouse online (in spite of not being allowed to use nails) and invite Bebe and Wendy over. Wendy dares Kyle to kiss Bebe on the lips. He does it, then freaks out and flees.

Bebe breaks up with Kyle and takes up with Clyde. They play Truth or Dare again with Stan and Wendy. Stan picks dare, but instead of being asked to kiss Wendy, she tells him to "Take this twig and jam it up your pee hole."

Randy and Sharon reconcile, and wind up making sweet love in Stan's tree house. Roy spends the interlude hanging from a tree in a bear trap.

MEMORABLE LINES

"Now Stanley, you have to understand how divorce works. When I say, 'You're the most important thing to me,' what I mean is, you're the most important thing after me and my happiness and my new romances."
—Stan's mom

"That's fine! I LIKE playing with myself!! I'll play with myself all day long!!"
—Cartman

"I'd like to live with you and wear your ass as a hat for all eternity."
—Note read by Stan

"Don't lie, Stan. Lying makes you sterile."
—Mr. Garrison

"Wow, cartoons are getting really dirty."
—Kyle

BODY COUNT
Just Kenny.

CHARACTER DEBUTS
Roy, Sharon's new bearded boyfriend.

POINTLESS OBSERVATIONS
This is the first episode in which Stan doesn't throw up in Wendy's presence. Also, one of the runaways staying in Cartman's clubhouse wears a D.V.D.A. t-shirt. It is the name of Matt and Trey's band, and their songs have been featured in several *South Park* episodes.

Despite the fact that Randy and Sharon get "divorced" briefly, this is the only time that there are hints of their marriage being broken.

The leader of the Sixth Graders can be seen partying at Cartman's clubhouse (notably wearing a green t-shirt with a picture of himself on it). Though he's just a background character here, he will eventually become a main antagonist, featured in episodes such as "Korn's Groovy Pirate Ghost Mystery" (page 94), "The Return of the Fellowship of the Ring to the Two Towers," and "Pre-School."

CELEBRITIES IMPUGNED
Bill Cosby, portrayed during the cartoon *Fat Abbot* as a doddering pudding salesman.

POP CULTURE REFERENCES
Banned from watching *Terrance and Phillip*, Stan instead tunes to *Fat Abbot*, a foul-mouthed takeoff on *Fat Albert and the Cosby Kids*. During one episode, Fat Abbot says "You punk ass blasphemous dope fiend bitch!" The line is from the 1991 film *New Jack City*.

Mr. Garrison calls out Stan for not paying attention, but Stan is able to guess what he said anyway: "Even though Charo appeared twelve times on *The Love Boat*, the episode with Captain and Tennille got higher ratings."

After he sends Kenny off to score chicks, Cartman pleads with his mom to watch *American Gladiators*.

WHAT STAN LEARNED
"Wow. Clubhouses are magical."

COW DAYS

Original Air Date: September 30, 1998
Episode No. 213

THE STORY: Two game show participants named Tom and Mary win a trip to South Park for its notoriously lame Cow Days festival. The celebration includes a third-rate carnival, where Stan, Kyle, Cartman and Kenny discover a ball-throwing game that offers Terrance and Phillip dolls as a prize. The object is to toss balls at Jennifer Love Hewitt's mouth. But the balls are too big to fit in the appropriate space. Undaunted, the boys enter Cartman in a bull-riding contest, figuring the top prize of $5,000 will buy them enough chances at the game to win.

Meanwhile, the town's cows steal a giant cow-shaped clock and carry it off to worship as a god. Tom and Mary (the game show winners) are accused of carrying off both the clock and the cows, and are tossed in jail. The fugitive cows are found and confronted, but rather than surrender the stat-

ue and return to their former lives, they commit mass suicide by walking off a cliff.

Cartman is thrown from a bull during practice, hits his head and assumes the personality of a Vietnamese prostitute named Ming Li. He nevertheless wins the bull riding contest. Then he spends the night with Leonardo DiCaprio. Then (and only then) his memory returns.

The carny in charge of the Jennifer Love Hewitt game gives the boys the dolls in exchange for their $5,000. But they turn out to be cheap knockoffs. The townspeople get wind of the swindle, decide the entire carnival sucks and attack the carnies.

Amidst all the distractions, Tom and Mary quietly starve to death in their cell. The mayor tells Officer Barbrady to say that the couple never arrived in town in the first place.

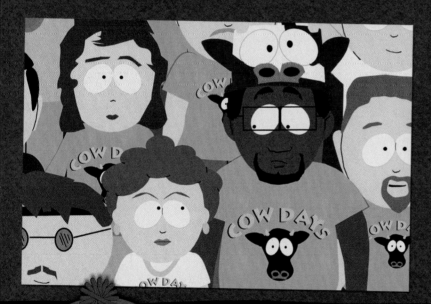

MEMORABLE LINES

"I'm starting to think that maybe it's wrong to put someone who thinks they're a Vietnamese prostitute onto a bull."
—Stan

"Young man, you can't just go around declaring shenanigans on innocent people. That's how wars get started."
—Officer Barbrady

"Screw you guys . . . I hate you guys."
—Cartman

"Shenanigans!!"
—Kyle

"Everybody grab a broom! It's shenanigans!"
—Officer Barbrady

"Me so horny! Me love you long time!"
—Cartman/Ming Lee

"Sucky sucky? Five dorra!"
—Cartman/Ming Li

"Oh my god! They killed Cartman!"
—Kenny

POINTLESS OBSERVATIONS

The lame carnival rides include the Chamber of Farts, which is shaped like a giant purple butt.

The Announcer for the game show W.T.H.I.T.? is voiced by Dian Bachar, an actor that has appeared in several other projects by Stone and Parker. He also lends a voice in "Merry Christmas Charlie Manson!" (page 68), "Do the Handicapped Go To Hell?" (page 128), and "Probably" (page 130).

According to carny math, roughly 7 Bon Jovi toothpicks is equal to one cheaply-made Terrance and Phillip doll.

The end of this episode is a nod to the first *South Park* episode, "Cartman Gets An Anal Probe" (page 10).

POP CULTURE REFERENCES

Much of Cartman's prostitute-speak is lifted from the movie *Full Metal Jacket*.

The "Running of the Cows" is a parody of the famous "Running of the Bulls" which takes place every year in Pamplona, Spain.

BODY COUNT

Kenny (killed by a bull), Tom and Mary, a bull rider impaled on a bull's horns, and one participant in the annual "running of the cows" extravaganza.

Oh yeah, and every cow in South Park. They all decide to commit mass cow suicide instead of being rounded back up.

CELEBRITIES IMPUGNED

Leonardo DiCaprio, who (according to the episode) likes to spank Vietnamese prostitutes.

Jennifer Love Hewitt, who's balls-in-mouth game is the subject of the boys' quest.

WHAT MAYOR McDANIELS LEARNED

"Perhaps one day cows will learn that cults are never a good thing."

CHEF AID

Original Air Date: October 7, 1998
Episode No. 214

THE STORY: When Chef discovers that Alanis Morissette has turned "Stinky Britches," a song he wrote years ago, into a hit, he approaches the record company about having his name listed as the composer. Instead the label hires celebrity lawyer Johnnie Cochran to sue Chef for harassment. Cochran wins damages of $2 million. If Chef doesn't pay within 24 hours he gets four years in jail.

Chef decides to become a male prostitute, sleeping with all the women in town until he raises $2 million—not to pay off the fine, but to hire Cochran to sue the record company on his behalf.

On a different front, someone is making attempts on the "life" of Mr. Garrison's puppet, Mr. Twig. All evidence points to Mr. Hat. After sever-

al misadventures, Mr. Hat and Mr. Garrison reconcile and get back together.

The boys also try to raise cash to help Chef. They begin by selling candy to all of Chef's old rock star friends. Then they organize a benefit concert which consists of Cartman in lederhosen performing something called "The German Dance." Then Elton John and other performers show up and agree to put on a show for Chef.

The show is sabotaged by a record company executive, but the event touches Johnnie Cochran, who agrees to represent Chef for free. Using exactly the same tactics he employed the first time around, he gets the new jury to reach a completely different verdict. Chef gets his name on the album.

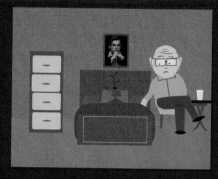

MEMORABLE LINES

**"Well I'll be sodom-
ized on Christmas!"**
—*Chef*

**"My only hope . . . is to whore myself
to every woman in town."**
—*Chef*

"You still aren't entertaining any ideas of raping me here in this prison cell, are you Chef?"
—*Garrison*

"I'm afraid it's the big house for you, fruitcake."
—*Officer Barbrady*

"If Chewbacca lives on Endor,
you must acquit!"
—*Johnnie Cochran*

POINTLESS OBSERVATIONS

Mr. Twig is first found in a pot of boiling water (a reference to the boiled bunny in *Fatal Attraction*), then broken in half while in bed (an homage to the horse-head-in-the-bed scene in *The Godfather*.

In Chef's memory book, we see that he played with The Beatles, Janis Joplin, Elton John, the Sex Pistols, and also a German goat.

There's a picture of Leonardo DiCaprio above Mr. Twig's bed. The actor is apparently quite popular around South Park, having spent some quality time with Ming Lee in the previous episode "Cow Days" (page 62).

This is a big episode for Mr. Hat. Up to this point, everyone assumed he was just a puppet (a very gay one), but here, he drives a car and busts Garrison and Chef out of jail. How he reached the pedals is still a mystery. . . .

BODY COUNT

Ozzy Osbourne bites off Kenny's head. Also a juror's head explodes.

CHARACTER DEBUTS

Judge Moses, the wild-haired judge that resides over Chef's court case, and the Record Producer, who's constantly applying spooge to his comb-over.

Also, the Band Announcer during Chef Aid will also make another cameo in "Timmy 2000" (page 116).

BIOGRAPHICAL TRIVIA

Chef's real name is revealed to be Jerome McElroy.

POP CULTURE REFERENCES

Mr. Garrison drives Chef to the benefit concert in a white Bronco, a la O.J. Simpson. Also the episode's narrator says that when Johnnie Cochran witnessed the show his ". . . small heart grew three sizes that day." It's an obvious parody of *How the Grinch Stole Christmas*.

Alanis Morissette's crappy music video for "Stinky Britches" plays briefly in the beginning of the episode. It resembles the video for her hit song "Ironic."

LEGAL BRIEFS

To win his South Park cases Cochran employed the Chewbacca defense—basically baffling a jury with so much extraneous information that their minds shut down. When he represents Chef, he takes this tactic to its extreme, producing a puppet during closing arguments and shouting "Here, look at the monkey. Look at the silly monkey!" His antics cause one juror's head to explode. The creepy thing is that the term "Chewbacca defense" is actually now used in the legal community.

MUSICAL CAMEOS

Episode guest stars included Rick James, DMX, Elton John, Meat Loaf, Primus, Rancid, Ol' Dirty Bastard, Joe Strummer, The Crystal Method, Ween and Ozzy Osbourne. The album released in conjunction with the episode, *Chef Aid: The South Park Album,* included 21 songs.

WHAT MR. TWIG LEARNED

"Love isn't a decision, it's a feeling. If we could decide who we love, it would be much simpler, but much less magical."

SPOOKYFISH

Original Air Date: October 28, 1998
Episode No. 215

THE STORY: It's Halloween and Cartman is acting weird. Sometimes he's his regular, obnoxious self, endlessly saying the word "hella." Other times he shows such un-Cartman-like traits as compassion and consideration for others.

Speaking of weirdness, Stan's mother Sharon tells Stan that her Aunt Flo, who visits each month, has given him a fish as a present. A fish that murders people at night. Sharon, convinced Stan is the killer, dutifully buries the bodies to cover her son's tracks. She even kidnaps Officer Barbrady when he comes snooping around and keeps him pants-less in the basement. The fish also kills Aunt Flo, and of course, Kenny.

The boys discover that Cartman is actually two separate people. The "good" one is from an evil parallel universe—as is the pet fish. They promptly return the fish to the Ancient Indian Burial Ground Pet Store (where the portal between worlds resides). They learn that nine other "evil" pets, complete with glowing red eyes, have already been returned.

After they leave, versions of Stan and Kyle cross over from the parallel universe. They release the evil pets, which go on a killing spree. They also ally themselves with the "real" Cartman from this world and go gunning for Stan, Kyle and parallel-universe Cartman.

After a vicious struggle the evil Stan and Kyle are vanquished back to their own world using a "gingerfication gun." But the good Stan and Kyle—who want to send *their* Cartman back to the evil parallel universe and keep the alternate Cartman—lose track of which is which and don't know who to blast. One of the Cartmans says they should shoot them both, just to be sure. Figuring only alternate-universe Cartman would be capable of such altruism, they zap the other one instead.

Mistake. They're stuck with the "real" Cartman, who figured the two would fall for such a lame ruse.

MEMORABLE LINES

"Hush little baby, don't say a word, momma's gonna buy you a mockingbird. If that mockingbird don't sing, momma's gonna bury it in the backyard. . . ."
—*Stan's mom*

"I've got such a good boy, such a handsome boy. . . ."
—*Stan's mom*

"You guys can kiss my black ass."
—*Cartman*

"Let's see . . . I hate you guys. . . . You're hella-stupid."
—*Cartman*

"Man, you guys are hella stupid."
—*Cartman*

"You kick ass Evil Cartman!"
—*Kyle*

"You guys are my best friends! Through thick and thin, we've always been to-gether! We're four of a kind! Havin' fun all day! Pallin' around and laughin' away!"
—*Evil Cartman*

BODY COUNT

Close to a dozen people (including Kenny and Aunt Flo) finished off by the Spookyfish. The other evil pets also claimed an unde-termined number of South Park residents.

POINTLESS OBSERVATIONS

When Officer Barbrady shows Stan's mom photos of people who have gone missing, the lineup includes a shot of William Shatner.

When Cartman and Evil Cartman appear in the same scenes together, there is a clear seam in the animation to give the effect that the image was crudely mirrored. This was done on purpose, as a tribute to shows and films that actually used this old-school effect.

The boys can't stand Cartman's constant use of the term "hella" in this episode. However, when Bebe sprouts boobs in "Bebe's Boobs Destroy Society," she uses the term "hella" and everyone loves it.

POP CULTURE REFERENCES

Evil Stan, Kyle and Cartman all have goatees—a reference to the *Star Trek* episode *Mirror, Mirror*, in which an evil, alternate-uni-verse Spock sports similar facial adornment. Also, when Kyle re-marks about a puny squash Kenny wanted to use for a pump-kin-carving contest, he says, "I never thought it was such a bad little squash. It just needed some tender loving care." It's a direct reference to a similar line in *A Charlie Brown Christmas*.

The notion of murderous pets coming out of an Indian bur-ial ground borrows from Stephen King's horror story *Pet Sematary*. Furthermore, the closet doorway that holds an entrance to the parallel universe is a reference to the cult classic film *Poltergeist*.

CELEBRITIES IMPUGNED

Barbara Streisand, again. After being savaged in "Mecha-Streisand" (page 32), her image is emblazoned on all four corners of the screen, along with the words "spooky vision," during the entire episode. Her "spooky" picture changes 4 times throughout the show; a dif-ferent picture is shown in each act.

MERRY CHRISTMAS CHARLIE MANSON!

Original Air Date: December 9, 1998
Episode No. 216

THE STORY: Kyle, Kenny and Stan (against his parents' wishes) accompany Cartman to Nebraska to visit his grandmother for the holidays. It turns into the road trip from hell. All of Cartman's relatives are in attendance, and they're just as fat and obnoxious as him. The guest list includes Uncle Howard, who gets in touch via a satellite link from state prison. That evening he pays an in-person visit, having broken out with another inmate, his friend, criminal mastermind and noted lunatic Charles Manson.

Manson volunteers to drive the boys to the nearby Mall of Nebraska, where Mr. Hankey is allegedly appearing. Once there, the infamous killer parks himself in front of a department store television display and becomes engrossed in watching Christmas specials.

Meanwhile Kyle and Stan visit the supposed Mr. Hankey, who turns out to be a guy in a costume. Disappointed, they "out" the imposter to the mob of kids waiting to see him. A bloody riot erupts and police are called in. They recognize Manson and a televised, high-speed car chase ensues.

Manson and Uncle Howard make it back to the Cartman residence and hold everyone hostage—a development the Cartmans, busy watching *Terrance and Phillip* on TV, barely notice. When Stan's furious parents arrive to take him home, he asks the two criminals if he can go on the lam with them. Instead Manson, who's suffered some sort of holiday-TV-special-induced epiphany, lectures him about the importance of family.

Stan changes his mind about leaving. Kenny is gunned down by the cops. Manson and Uncle Howard surrender and go back to prison. The Cartmans, plus Stan and Kyle, surprise him in his cell by shouting, "Merry Christmas Charlie Manson!" and singing "Hark the Herald Angels Sing."

MEMORABLE LINES

"Mister Hankey kicks ass!"
—*Cousin Elvin*

"Oh my God! They killed the little orange coat kid!"
—*Charlie Manson*

"No, Jimmy! That's grandpa's pot pie!!"
—*Grandma Cartman*

"Folks need to understand that I am terror. I am fear! I AM—Oh look, another holiday special. . ."
—*Charlie Manson*

"The holidays are bullcrap!!"
—*Cartman*

"I'm glad I'm not you right now kid."
—*Charlie Manson*

"Stan, don't be such a dumbass. You have to trust people."
—*Cartman*

POINTLESS OBSERVATIONS

The Mall of Nebraska crowd unaccountably includes Craig, Red and Butters. Cartman sleeps in his Weight Gain 4000 t-shirt from the episode of the same name (page 12). We also get to see his hair for the first time.

To get his cousin Elvin to stop crying, Cartman takes a stick and whacks him over the head. He will do the same thing to an Underpants Gnome in "Gnomes" (page 70), and an endangered monkey in "Rainforest Shmainforest" (page 76).

The reporter covering the Manson chase is named Robert Pooner. This alias was also used as the name of the "Executive Producer" for Barbrady's cop show in "Chickenlover" (page 42). Pooner signs off with "God bless us, every one," a classic line from *A Christmas Carol*.

Kyle complains that "ever since Mr. Hankey was in that movie, he got all famous." He's talking about the Tom Hanks independent film *Mr. Hankey and Me* from "Chef's Chocolate Salty Balls" (page 54).

BODY COUNT

Kenny for sure; he's been shot, beaten with a baton, and then handcuffed by policemen. There's also a massive pileup during the police chase that leaves a lot of cops in bad shape.

CHARACTER DEBUTS

Although we briefly saw Cartman's grandmother in "Roger Ebert Should Lay Off The Fatty Foods" (page 58), the rest of his extended family is introduced: Uncle Stinky, Grandpa Cartman, Cousin Fred, Cousin Alexandra, Fat Bob, Jimmy (the bulldog), little Cousin Elvin, Uncle Howard, and great grandma Florence. And, of course, Charlie Manson.

POP CULTURE REFERENCES

The prison sing-along at the end of the episode is lifted from a similar scene in *A Charlie Brown Christmas*. Manson is also mesmerized by a Christmas special called *Grinchy Poo*—a reference to *How The Grinch Stole Christmas*. Finally Manson, once back in jail, pens a series of introspective books, including *Are You There God? It's Me, Manson*. This is a rip on the novel by Judy Bloom, *Are You There God? It's Me, Margaret*.

In the *Terrance and Phillip Christmas Special*, Terrance and Phillip take turns farting on a reindeer whose nose glows red with every fart—an obvious homage to *Rudolph the Red-Nosed Reindeer*.

CELEBRITIES IMPUGNED

Jimmy Stewart. In a scene allegedly from *It's A Wonderful Life* he tells Mr. Potter, "You know what you are? You're a little bitch. That's right, you're a bitch and I'll bet you'd like to suck it, wouldn't you?" Also the entire state of Nebraska, which is portrayed as pool table-flat and covered with wheat. A sign at the state line reads "You are now in Nebraska . . . sorry."

WHAT CHARLES MANSON LEARNED

"I'm sorry for what I did, but that doesn't make up for it. I deserve to be in jail. All I hope is that I don't make mankind lose faith in itself. Yes there's murderers in the world, there's rapists and thieves, but those are the vast minority. The majority of mankind is made up of caring people who try every day to do what they think is right. And that's the spirit of the season."

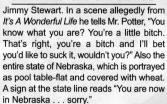

ORIGINAL SONGS

Manson breaks out into song after his Christmas epiphany, singing the jolly yule tune "Happy, Happy Holiday."

GNOMES

Original Air Date: December 16, 1998
Episode No. 217

THE STORY: Mr. Garrison's job is on thin ice. To prove he's a good teacher he tells his kids to prepare oral presentations on current events for delivery to the South Park Town Committee. The boys are paired up with Tweek, an extremely twitchy kid obsessed with Underpants Gnomes—tiny men who visit his room every night at 3:30 a.m. to steal his undergarments.

Tweek's nervousness is explained when he invites Stan, Kyle, Cartman and Kenny to his home for a sleepover. His parents run a coffee shop and aren't shy about giving their son (and the other boys) enough java to send them into a caffeine-fueled frenzy. That night the gnomes file in at 3:30 a.m., as usual, to steal several pairs of Tweek's underwear. But the kids are so burnt out from their coffee buzz that none of them (except, of course, Tweek) notice.

Aware that the boys are having trouble coming up with a topic for their paper, Tweek's dad volunteers to write one for them. It's about his store's struggle against a huge coffee shop chain called Harbucks. The kids read the paper aloud to the South Park Town Committee, which promptly creates a special proposition, called Prop 10, to kick the chain out of town. Mr. Garrison suspects the boys cheated, but tells them they must stick to their story since his job is at stake.

The kids panic when they learn they have to talk about corporate greed at a Prop 10 rally. While gathered at Tweek's house to figure out what to do, they finally encounter the Underpants Gnomes. The magical creatures take the boys to their underground lair and explain their not-very-well-thought-out plan for making money with underpants.

Also, in exchange for the boys' underwear, the Gnomes agree to tell them about the nature of corporations. At the rally before the no-Harbucks proposition is to be voted on, the kids state that corporations have done a lot of good—and that they didn't write their previous presentation. Mrs. Tweek, upset that her husband used the boys as pawns, encourages everyone to try Harbucks Coffee. Which turns out to be pretty good. "It doesn't have that bland, raw sewage taste that Tweek's coffee has," someone remarks.

MEMORABLE LINES

"Time to go to work, work all night, search for underpants yay, we won't stop till we have underpants, yum tum yummy tum yay!"
—*Underpants Gnomes*

"They really have my balls in a salad shooter."
—*Mr. Tweek*

"Well, I must say Garrison, perhaps you're not as stupid and crazy as I always tell people you are."
—*Mayor*

"Stealing underpants is big business."
—*Underpants Gnome*

"Holy shit! We killed your friend!"
—*Underpants Gnome*

"Agh! Maybe it was all in my head! Maybe I'm going insane!! OH NO! I'M GOING INSANE!"
—*Tweek*

"They're taking my underpants!!"
—*Tweek*

BODY COUNT

Kenny gets crushed by one of the Underpants Gnomes' underpants-filled trolley carts.

POINTLESS OBSERVATIONS

The band Toto performs at a Prop 10 rally. A costumed character named Camel Joe, used by Harbucks to drum up business with kids, is a thinly veiled reference to Joe Camel.

This is the first time that Token is actually referred to as "Token." Up to this point, he has just been a background character.

The logline for Tweek Bros. Coffee is "30 Years of Tweekers."

CHARACTER DEBUTS

The overly caffeinated Tweek and his parents.

The Underpants Gnomes also make their hard-working debut here.

POP CULTURE REFERENCES

The Harbucks representative, Mr. Postum, is named after an instant coffee alternative beverage made from wheat and molasses.

When Stan mentions his reluctance to work with Tweek, Mr. Garrison launches into a monologue about the popular 70s hospital drama *Medical Center*: "That's what Chad Everett thought when the new female intern joined the cast of *Medical Center*. He thought, 'Who is this woman with her gazungas and high heels. What does she know of medicine?' Well, that intern soon saved Chad Everett's brother with a kidney transplant."

Cartman suggests they do their presentation on "that Raymond guy on TV . . . you know, *Everybody Loves Raymond*." Kyle counters, "No Cartman! We can't do it on Raymond AGAIN!"

CELEBRITIES IMPUGNED

When Mrs. Tweek admits to using the children to gain sympathy for their business, she says, "We're as low and despicable as Rob Reiner." Reiner will later get proper *South Park* honors with his very own episode, "Butt Out."

PREHISTORIC ICE MAN

Original Air Date: January 20, 1999
Episode No. 218

THE STORY: After watching a TV show about a wild Australian tracker who sticks his thumb up wild animals' buttholes, the boys decide to hunt for crocodiles. Kyle falls down a very deep hole, and when Stan attempts to rescue him, they discover a man frozen in ice. The body is brought to Dr. Mephesto.

Stan and Kyle have a serious argument over what to name the Ice Man, the former favoring Gorak and the latter favoring Steve.

Mephesto discovers that the "Ice Man" is still alive, and thaws him out. He's from the year 1996—about 32 months earlier. Mephesto treats him like a discovery from another era and the Ice Man is displayed in a special habitat that's fitted out to look like 1996. A conveyor belt trundles visitors past. It also drags Kenny to his death.

The Ice Man hates the way he's being treated, as do Stan and Kyle. They put aside their disagreement until later while they help him escape.

Meanwhile the Ice Man, whose real name is Larry, learns his wife has remarried and has two children—ages 8 and 13. Realizing he can't survive in this new reality, he accepts the boys' suggestion to take a train to Des Moines, which is supposedly three years behind the rest of the world.

The boys free Larry and get him to the train station where chaos ensues. Kyle and Stan resume their argument and get into a fistfight. The FBI (with the aid of the Australian Outback Guy) attempt to capture Larry. The Australian Outback Guy actually does catch him and sticks his thumb in his butthole. Finally, Larry escapes by helicopter and the Outback Guy is hacked to pieces by its blades.

Stan and Kyle finally bury the hatchet. Cartman tries to put his thumb in a cow's butthole, but the animal sits on him.

MEMORABLE LINES

"Little boy, sometimes what's right isn't as important as what's profitable."
—*Man in Suit*

"Good job, Cartman. You killed Kyle!"
—*Stan*

"First one to die loses."
—*Stan*

"YOU'RE a dick, and I have had it with your dickdetry!"
—*Stan*

"You suck as a best friend, Cartman."
—*Kyle*

"Oh my God, they revived Gorak!"
—*Stan*

"I'm gonna jam my thumb in its butthole now. This should REALLY piss it off!"
—*Australian Outback Guy*

POINTLESS OBSERVATIONS

Mephesto has an ass-shaped door buzzer. Also Marilyn Manson performs a snippet from *Stinky Britches* about halfway through the episode and during the closing credits. The Ice Man's enclosure is a couple of doors down from Mephesto's five-assed monkey, first seen in "An Elephant Makes Love To A Pig" (page 18).

Kyle doesn't add his signature "You bastards!" after Kenny is killed, due to the fact that he's not talking to Stan.

There are movie posters for *Fargo* and *ID4* (*Independence Day*), as well as a *Hunchback of Notre Dame* blanket in the Ice Man's "habitat." There's also a "Re-Elect Clinton" poster.

POP CULTURE REFERENCES

The Outback Guy is of course Steve Irwin, who was just beginning to catch on in the U.S. as *The Crocodile Hunter*. Also Stan wants to call the ice man Steve because he thinks he looks like Steve Austin from *The Six Million Dollar Man*.

When the boys find the frozen ice man, Cartman says "this is just like that one movie where John Travolta and that . . . French chick were doing it all summer long, and then they went back to school and sang songs about Grease Lighting. . ." He's referring to the movie *Grease*, which has absolutely nothing to do with an ice man.

Dr. Mephesto determines that the Ice Man's clothes are from Eddie Baur, which he hasn't seen anyone wear since . . . 1996.

When trying to buy a train ticket, Kyle says, "We have to get him to Des Moines or else he's gonna melt away." Stan yells back: "That's Frosty, you stupid butthole!"

BODY COUNT

Kenny and the Australian Outback Guy.

CELEBRITIES IMPUGNED

Music from the band Ace of Base is pumped into the Ice Man's habitat because, Mephesto states, ". . . their primitive drumming soothed his people's tempers."

WHAT GORAK/ STEVE/LARRY LEARNED

"You boys have really shown me the true meaning of friendship. You didn't care about anything but my happiness. You put me in front of yourselves, and that's what true friendship is all about."

SEASON

3

RAINFOREST SHMAINFOREST

Original Air Date: April 7, 1999
Episode 301

THE STORY: The boys misbehave in class and are forced, as punishment, to join a touring musical group called Getting Gay With Kids. Led by the idealistic Miss Stevens, the group is dedicated to saving the rainforest.

The kids travel—via school bus—to Costa Rica to perform for a gathering of environmentalists who are against paving over the rainforest. They promptly get lost when their guide is killed, and then eaten, and then excreted, by a coral snake. They wander through the trackless green hell, encountering everything from giant insects to rebel guerillas to actor Tony Danza. They're finally captured by a tribe of natives called the Yanagopas, who inexplicably dress Miss Stevens in a cheerleader outfit and then tie her between two posts, to serve as a sacrifice to the Yanagopas' gigantic "god."

Suddenly Cartman, who wandered off on his own in search of help, bursts from the underbrush along with a gang of American construction workers. They make short work of the Yanagopas by crushing them with bulldozers.

The kids make it back to Costa Rica's capital of San Jose, where they sing a new song that includes the lyrics, "There's a place called the rainforest that truly sucks ass / Let's knock it all down and get rid of it fast."

MEMORABLE LINES

"Look how they live in peace with all living things. Gentle, noble—RUN FOR YOUR LIVES CHILDREN!!"
—*Ms. Stevens*

"The nightmare begins."
—*Cartman*

"Oh man, this is gonna suck donkey balls."
—*Cartman*

"Being an activist is totally gay."
—*Getting Gay With Kids*

"The rainforest sucks. I want to go home."
—*Kyle*

"I told you Jewish people don't have rhythm."
—*Cartman*

"Tom tilly ye!"
—*Yanagopas*

BODY COUNT

The choir group's Costa Rican guide is brutally eaten by a coral snake, and Jake (a student on the choir tour) is devoured by a giant Venus Flytrap-like plant. Also, most of the native Yanagopa tribe is killed by bulldozers as they rescue Ms. Stevens' class from capture.

Fortunately Kenny survives, thanks to his girlfriend Kelly.

NATIONS IMPUGNED

The government of Costa Rica was reportedly angered when it learned that an American TV show insinuated that the country's capital, San Jose, "smells like ass."

CELEBRITIES IMPUGNED

During a nighttime lightning storm Stan yells, "Oh my God dude, I just saw Tony Danza!" Sure enough, the next bolt reveals the star of TV's *Who's The Boss* sitting among the kids.

WHERE DID THE IDEA COME FROM?

The show is an extended rip on rainforests, inspired by a nightmarish vacation Trey took to Costa Rica. It was hot, dirty, smelly and very snake-and-spider intensive. All of Cartman's comments about the rainforest during the episode mirror Trey's own views.

POINTLESS OBSERVATION

Kenny's stint with Kelly here is his first taste of love. He doesn't find a girlfriend again until he meets Tammy in "The Ring." Also, we learn that Mr. Mackey speaks pretty fluent Spanish. Mbien?

POP CULTURE REFERENCES

Miss Stevens' attempted sacrifice to the Yanagopas' "god" is a direct lift from *King Kong*. When Cartman shows up with rescue, Ms. Stevens is shocked. He responds: "Who'd you expect, Merv Griffin?"

ORIGINAL SONGS

Two inspiring versions of the campy "Getting Gay With Kids" are performed by the activist group of the same name.

CHARACTER DEBUTS

Craig. He's been seen sitting outside Mr. Mackey's office, as well as in the classroom, but this is the first episode in which he's actually a main character. We also find out (and see) that he has a bad habit of flipping people off.

Ms. Stevens and Kelly (Kenny's girlfriend) also are introduced.

WHAT MISS STEVENS LEARNED

"Blast these stupid-ass rainforests!! This place fucking sucks!! I was wrong!! Fuck the rainforest!! I fucking hate it, I fucking hate it!!"

SPONTANEOUS COMBUSTION

Original Air Date: April 14, 1999
Episode 302

THE STORY: Kyle's dad can't perform sexually and things around the house are pretty grim. Kyle, misunderstanding the nature of the problem, visits various stores in an attempt to purchase a "nerection" for his father. During this fruitless search Kenny spontaneously combusts. Soon other townspeople catch fire too. The terrified survivors flock to church, where Stan, Kyle and Cartman agree to perform the Stations of the Cross. Cartman does it because he wants to play Jesus, and Kyle participates because he confuses the finale of the "resurrection" with the "nerection" he wants for his dad. After the service Stan and Kyle take Cartman, still bound to the cross, to the top of a deserted hill and leave him to die, so that he will get the desired "nerection."

Meanwhile, Stan's dad Randy is told by Mayor McDaniels to find a solution to the people-bursting-into-flames issue. Even though he's a geologist—and thus clearly unqualified—he gets the job because he's the only scientist in town. He theorizes that Kenny died because he had a new girlfriend (who he meets in "Rainforest, Shmainfor-

est," page 76), and was holding in his gas in her presence. This caused his body's methane levels to rise dangerously, triggering an explosion.

Randy believes that South Park will be safe if everyone farts freely—which everyone promptly does. Randy wins the Nobel Prize for his Break Wind Theory of Spontaneous Combustion.

But the town starts heating up because of all the methane released into the atmosphere. Randy is stoned and ridiculed by the populace.

However he saves the day when he realizes that spontaneous combustion and global warming can be avoided if people fart in moderation. Also, Kyle's dad finally manages to get a "nerection" when three beautiful women visit his law office and strip to show him possible skin cancer for which they want to sue Randy.

Much later, the boys remember that they left Cartman tied to the cross. They return to find him emaciated but still alive, having survived for three weeks on his Walrus-like stores of fat.

MEMORABLE LINES

"Lord, is it so much to ask that you not let us suddenly burst into flame for no apparent reason? I mean, come on. Amen."
—*Priest Maxi*

"On this blessed Friday, let us give thanks for stuff . . . and things."
—*Priest Maxi*

"You're too fat to be Jesus!"
—*Kyle*

"Dude! I think you pulled mud!"
—*Kyle*

"You're not too Jewish to worship Jesus are you?"
—*Priest Maxi*

"I just want a nerection so I can go give it to my mom!"
—*Kyle*

"As soon as I get my superpowers, I'm gonna smote you two assholes off the planet!"
—*Cartman*

"You die on that cross and get resurrected before I kick your ass!"
—*Kyle*

"Have you boys been sure to pass gas regularly so you don't spontaneously combust?"
—*Mr. Mackey*

BODY COUNT

Kenny, plus various other South Park residents who also spontaneously combust.

WHERE DID THE IDEA COME FROM?

The crucifixion of Cartman was a concept Matt and Trey long wanted to do. They dreamed it up even before *South Park* debuted.

BIBLICAL REFERENCES

The scene in which Stan's dad is forced to drag a statue of himself through town is a recreation of the Station's of the Cross. The statue is modeled after Michelangelo's *David*.

POINTLESS OBSERVATIONS

Kenny's dad and Mayor McDaniels are both seen reading a porn mag called *Guzunga's*.

Before Kenny explodes, Cartman nags Kenny for spending so much time with his "little girlfriend." This is actually a continuation of the storyline from "Rainforest Shmainforest" (page 76), in which Kenny gets a girlfriend named Kelly.

Although he loses the Nobel Prize to Randy, Dr. Mephesto finally created a 7-assed turtle.

ORIGINAL SONGS

The 70s-style, happy-go-lucky song "You and Me Girl" plays while Randy daydreams at the end of the episode.

POP CULTURE REFERENCES

Stan says that Jesus (the real one, not Cartman) told his followers that, "The needs of the many outweigh the needs of the few." In fact, Spock said this to Kirk in *Star Trek: The Wrath of Kahn*. Also Stan's dad lapses into a bizarre dream sequence, during which he and the boys are chased by someone in a mask and, incongruously, wind up playing in a pop band. It's an homage to similarly illogical scenes found in pretty much every episode of the various *Scooby Doo* cartoons.

Priest Maxi's entire sermon at Kenny's funeral is about the Denver Broncos. He starts, "Lord . . . though we have lost Neil Smith to free agency and Steve Atwater to the Jets. . . ."

CELEBRITIES IMPUGNED

Whoopie Goldberg, who hosts the 42nd Annual Nobel Prize Awards. Her "monologue" consists of repeatedly saying "Republicans are so stupid."

Nick Nolte also presents at the award show, giving a belabored, boring speech.

Also, Bob Dole, who shills for an impotency drug on the radio.

WHAT STAN LEARNED

"I learned something from the Stations of the Cross. At first Jesus was all like, 'Why me?' And he was all pissed off and stuff. Then he saw that what mattered most was everybody else. So he stopped thinking about his own misery and did what had to be done."

THE SUCCUBUS

Original Air Date: April 21, 1999
Episode 303

THE STORY: Cartman is forced to get enormous eyeglasses. Even worse, they're stapled to his head. Even worse than that, his opthamologist constantly makes fat jokes about him. Unsure about what to do, he and the other boys turn to Chef for advice. To their horror, they discover that their friend/spiritual advisor/life coach has a new girlfriend who's got him whipped. He's actually quit his job at the school cafeteria and signed on to work at an accounting firm. Unbelievably, the two even plan to marry.

Running low on male role models, the kids ask Mr. Garrison what to do. He says that Chef's girlfriend, Veronica, is a succubus—a female demon who sucks the life force from men.

The boy's try to warn Chef, to no avail. Instead they meet Chef's parents who are in town for the wedding. The couple is from Scotland and they regale them with stories of their bizarre encounters with the Loch Ness monster—a monster who keeps asking them for "tree-fiddy" ($3.50).

After much study, Stan, Kyle, Kenny and Cartman (now temporarily blinded by botched laser eye surgery) learn that a succubus controls men's minds by relentlessly playing a particular melody (in Veronica's case, "The Morning After" from the original *Poseidon Adventure*). On the bright side, playing the tune backwards can destroy the succubus.

At Chef and Veronica's wedding, Cartman plays the song backwards while Stan and Kyle sing the reversed lyrics. The succubus goes berserk, kills Kenny and gets sucked back into hell. Chef becomes his old self again.

Cartman solves his vision problems by taking Kenny's head to the opthamologist so he can swap out his dead friend's eyes for his own. Mysteriously, just before the operation begins, the doctor asks Cartman if he has $3.50.

MEMORABLE LINES

"Well aren't you crackers just cute as the dickens."
—*Chef's dad*

"Bitch, I hate that bitch!"
—*Cartman*

"I wasn't sleeping, I was just thinking really hard."
—*Cartman*

"Meaningless sex is fun for 20 or 30 years, but after that it starts to get old."
—*Chef*

"I ain't giving you no tree-fiddy you God damned Loch Ness monster!"
—*Chef's dad*

"How's my little piggy today?"
—*Dr. Lout*

"Ma'am, we're having a dude moment here, if you don't mind."
—*Cartman*

"She's a god damn succubus!!"
—*Chef's dad*

BODY COUNT

Kenny dies once, then gets resurrected and killed again. The first time he's seen waiting with the other boys for Chef, who has stood them up. They wait all day and through the night (during which Kenny, inexplicably, is seen dead and covered with rats). But when morning comes he's back on his feet. He dies the second time at the hands (or actually, feet) of the succubus.

Veronica is also banished back to the soul-sucking depths of Hell.

POINTLESS OBSERVATIONS

A sign outside one of the cubicles at the accounting firm where Chef works states that it belongs to I.P. Freely.

In the wedding vows, Priest Maxi asks Veronica if she would "take Chef to be her daddy."

WHERE DID THE IDEA COME FROM?

The running gag in which Chef's parents talk about their encounters with the Loch Ness monster—who always asks them for tree-fiddy—was something Matt and Trey developed while still in college. Originally Chef's character was supposed to be some kind of *X-Files*-type paranormal adventurer, the but concept was dropped—and moved to his parents.

CHARACTER DEBUTS

Chef's parents. Also Mr. Derp, Chef's replacement at the school cafeteria. "Derp" was a term Matt and Trey invented during the filming of the movie *BASEketball*. It was applied to extremely obvious jokes. Both Chef's parents and the term "Derp" will resurface in the episode "The Biggest Douche in the Universe."

Dr. Lout, Cartman's eye doctor, as well as Veronica, Chef's succubus girlfriend, make their debut.

POP CULTURE REFERENCES

During his eye exam, Cartman is told to choose between two slides. We see that they are actual pictures of Carmen Electra and Britney Spears.

Mr. Garrison gives a lecture on *The Facts of Life*. The sitcom, not actual life lessons.

BEHIND THE SCENES

Singing the song *The Morning After* backwards proved supremely difficult. Even worse, Matt and Trey found they couldn't get the backward version out of their minds.

CELEBRITIES IMPUGNED

When Cartman (wearing his giant glasses) visits the accounting firm where Chef has taken a job, the receptionist asks if he's "that cute little kid from *Jerry McGuire*."

WHAT MR. GARRISON LEARNED

"Never let poontang come between you and your friends."

JAKOVASAURS

Original Air Date: June 16, 1999
Episode 305

THE STORY: While camping at Stark's Pond the boys glimpse a strange creature which Jimbo and Ned help capture. Representatives from the Department of the Interior soon arrive and announce that it is a female "Jakovasaur"—a rare species thought to be extinct. The townspeople, hoping the female can be used to rebuild the breed, name it Hope—in spite of the fact that the Jakovasaur, which can talk, says that its name is Jun-Jun.

Soon a male Jakovasaur named Jakov is located, and the two are given their own home in South Park. Dr Mephesto artificially inseminates Jun-Jun, and the community is overrun by baby Jakovasaurs. The creatures turn out to be incredibly annoying—to everyone but Cartman, who finds them hilarious.

The townspeople get rid of the Jakovasaurs by having them play a rigged game show offering a trip to France for the winner and 50 of his closest relatives. The entire Jakovasaur crew is bundled onto a plane and sent to France, where they quickly gain Jerry Lewis-like fame.

MEMORABLE LINES

"I have semen? Where's their boat??"
—*Jakov*

"Oh come on. You all know that pigeon was a total slut."
—*Mr. Garrison*

"I'm glad you guys know all these pooping outside rules."
—*Cartman*

"Cool beans!"
—*Jakov*

"Jakov . . . please don't go. You make everything in South Park fun."
—*Cartman*

"I guess he finally found something that's as annoying as he is."
—*Stan*

"I hate you guys / You guys are assholes / Especially Kenny / I hate him the most."
—*Cartman's song "I Hate You Guys"*

"Jakovasaurs kind of piss me off, mkay?"
—*Mr. Mackey*

BODY COUNT

Kenny, eaten by a bear while impersonating a deer.

WHERE DID THE IDEA COME FROM?

The program was a critique of the character Jar Jar Binks from *Star Wars: The Phantom Menace*. Matt and Trey hated the movie in general and Jar Jar in particular. They wanted to make the Jakovasaurs the most irritating characters in television history. However, they feel the finished product still isn't as annoying as Jar Jar.

POINTLESS OBSERVATIONS

Cartman's home address is plainly visible on his backpack, which reads: 21208 E. Bonanza Circle, South Park, CO.

This is the one episode in which Ned doesn't have his normal voice box. He burp-talks a majority of the time, and also tries out an Irish voice box, as well as a "sucky" one.

We learn a lot about Jackovauars here: they don't have genitals, they only take four days to have babies (which come in huge litters), and they're really, really annoying. Also, Cartman absolutely loves them . . . even more than he loves ice cream.

We saw her on the cover of *Crack Whore* magazine in "Pinkeye" (page 22), but here we actually see Cartman's mom . . . being a crack whore.

Cartman is made an honorary "Department of the Interior Person" and given official authori-tah over South Park's fish and wildlife.

CHARACTER DEBUTS

The Jakovasaurs—loud, obnoxious woodland creatures that were thought to be extinct. Also, three Department of the Interior Guys make a cameo.

POP CULTURE REFERENCES

Originally Matt and Trey wanted to do a bit blasting Jar Jar for the *MTV Music Awards*, but the network didn't go for it. So they did an entire episode of *South Park* instead.

They parody cheesy 90s sitcoms with *JAKO-VASAURS*, a fake sitcom starring the Jakov family complete with laugh tracks and canned applause. Within this "sitcom," they joke about MTV: After hearing that something strange had happened, Jakov quickly responds, "You mean MTV played a video that WASN'T Will Smith?!"

CELEBRITIES IMPUGNED

Mr. Garrison refers to Chubby Checker as a member of the Beatles.

WHAT MAYOR MCDANIELS LEARNED

"Animal species come and go. It's all part of natural evolution."

TWEEK VS. CRAIG

Original Air Date: June 23, 1999
Episode 304

THE STORY: Stan, Kyle and Cartman join shop class. After seeing all the dangerous equipment in the school shop, Kenny takes home-economics instead. When the wood shop instructor, Mr. Adler, asks who the class's biggest troublemaker is, Stan and Kyle say it's Tweek, while Cartman maintains it's Craig. To settle the issue they provoke the two boys to fight. Craig learns sumo with Cartman, while Tweek gets boxing lessons from Jimbo and Ned. They finally engage in a bloody schoolyard brawl.

At the same time, Mr. Adler is in deep mourning for his dead girlfriend, who (we learn from live-action dream sequences) was killed in some sort of airplane/drowning incident. On the day of the Tweek/Craig matchup, Mr. Adler, distraught over her death (and that he's run out of nicotine gum)

lies down in front of a circular saw and prepares to cut himself in half.

Suddenly Tweek and Craig crash through a window, startling Mr. Adler out of his suicide plan. It also startles Kenny (recently booted from home economics and forced to take shop), who gets caught in some heavy equipment and hurled across the room into a box of rusty nails.

As Kenny is dying, he channels the spirit of Mr. Adler's dead girlfriend. The two reconcile, right in front of the crowd of children who were watching the fight.

Later the kids go to the hospital to visit the severely injured Tweek and Craig. They tell them their families were both on the TV news, calling each other names. And the brawl begins all over again.

MEMORABLE LINES

"In sumo, your body must be like a stone, and your mind like a meatloaf."
—*Craig's Martial Arts Instructor*

"What you got, bi-atch?!"
—*Ned*

"There is indeed great power in your ass, Eric."
—*Nishimura, Sumo Instructor*

"Stop screwing around!"
—*Mr. Adler*

"They wanna fight, they just don't know it yet."
—*Kyle*

"Fight back! Resist the ass!"
—*Craig's Martial Arts Instructor*

"I was just standing over by Tweek, and . . . he called you a big poop eater."
—*Cartman*

"I can't make love to you until we get a king-size bed."
—*Kenny*

"There is nothing in the world more 'man' than boxing. It is man at his most man."
—*Jimbo*

BODY COUNT

Mr. Adler's girlfriend, who dies (repeatedly) in flashbacks. Apparently she was flying a plane, which crashed. Or blew up. Then she fell in the water and drowned.

Also Kenny, who uses his last whim to channel the spirit of Adler's wife, grandma, and uncle. A 3rd grader named Tommy isn't killed, but loses his face to a belt sander in shop class.

WHERE DID THE IDEA COME FROM?

The character of Mr. Adler is based on one of Matt Stone's own shop teachers.

POINTLESS OBSERVATION

Mr. Adler's live-action girlfriend is played by *South Park* writer Pam Brady.

Token has his first lines of dialogue in this episode, a powerful: "Yeah, they left."

We learn a lot about Craig in this episode. Namely, that he watches *Red Racer* every day of the week, flips the bird more than he talks, and has a guinea pig named Stripe. His relationship with guinea pigs will be further explored in "Pandemic I & II."

The "Oppenheimer Technique," as we learn from Jimbo, is punching someone in the balls during a fight.

This episode features the iconic scene where Cartman dresses up in a Sumo outfit. We learn from his sumo instructor, Nishimura, that he has natural gift for the sport.

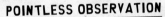

CHARACTER DEBUTS

Mr. Richard Adler, the shop class teacher with the band-aid permanently on his forehead.

Mrs. Choise, the Home-Ec teacher, makes her debut as well. We learn briefly that her and Adler are dating (unsuccessfully).

We also get to see Craig's parents and little sister, all of whom regularly flip each other off.

Nishimura (the Sumo Instructor) makes his first and only cameo.

WHAT MR. ADLER'S DEAD GIRLFRIEND LEARNED

"Saying goodbye doesn't mean anything. It was the time we spent together that really matters. Not how we left it."

SEXUAL HARASSMENT PANDA

Original Air Date: July 7, 1999
Episode 306

THE STORY: A costumed mascot called Peetie the Sexual Harassment Panda visits Mr. Garrison's class to teach the kids about sexual harassment. But he teaches them too much. When Stan calls Cartman an "ass sucker," Cartman sues him for sexual harassment and wins half his belongings. Kyle's dad, who serves as Cartman's attorney, then sues the school system for millions. He quickly makes a fortune representing both kids and adults in hundreds of similar court cases. He uses his new riches to turn his house into a mansion. Soon he's the most hated—and most feared—person in town.

The school system, impoverished by the huge payouts, is forced to fire Sexual Harassment Panda. Unable to find other work (and apparently suffering from the delusion that he really is a panda),

he winds up on the Island of Misfit Mascots, a sort of rest home/insane asylum for unwanted costumed characters. But the boys seek him out and convince him to help battle the wave of lawsuits—particularly a massive case called *Everyone vs. Everyone*, with Kyle's dad representing, literally, everyone.

The mascot, who now calls himself Peetie the Don't Sue People Panda, appears at the trial and advises everyone to stop suing each other because it's destroying society. The people agree that such suits are frivolous, then angrily turn on Kyle's dad and threaten to sue him. Not surprisingly, he instantly agrees that being overly litigious is bad and ditches the sexual harassment lawsuit business.

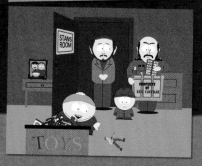

MEMORABLE LINES

"That makes me a saaaaad panda."
—Sexual Harassment Panda

"How would you like a big panda punch in your puss?"
—Sexual Harassment Panda

"I'm telling you guys, suing people kicks ass."
—Cartman

"This is freaking me out dude."
—Kyle

Mr. Garrison: "Does anyone know what sexual harassment means?"
Cartman: "When you're trying to have intercourse with a lady friend, and some other guy comes up and tickles your balls from behind?"

"You would think that, you little ass sucker."
—Stan

"Hey! Panda Bear!! We don't take kindly to your types in here!"
—Skeeter

BODY COUNT

Kenny, slain sort-of-inadvertently by "Jimmy The Don't Hold Onto A Large Magnet While Someone Else Uses A Fan Nearby Falcon," when he hands Kenny a magnet and switches on an enormous fan.

WHERE DID THE IDEA COME FROM?

The show was a statement about the large number of high-profile sexual harassment cases making the news at the time.

CHARACTER DEBUTS

A whole bunch of really awesome mascots, including "Willy The Don't Stare Directly Into The Sun Worm"; "Oinky The Run Around With Scissors Pig"; "Happy The Don't Do Stuff That Might Irritate Your Inner Ear Badger"; and "Jimmy The Don't Hold Onto A Large Magnet While Someone Else Uses A Fan Nearby Falcon."

Judge Julie, the honorable Judge that oversees the sexual harassment cases.

Skeeter, an orange-haired redneck, and a couple of his Redneck buddies. They frequent South Park's Bar, and will be seen in many future episodes, including "I'm A Little Bit Country."

The Newscaster. He is introduced as Kevin McCarty here, but will be seen again in "Two Guys Naked in a Hot Tub" (page 90) as Derek Smalls.

POINTLESS OBSERVATIONS

On the Island of Misfit Mascots there's a brief glimpse of a whale with the words "Use Lambskin Condoms" on it. He's playing badminton.

Principal Victoria, while on the witness stand, admits to committing a pretty gruesome murder. Luckily, the question was about sexual harassment, so no one cared.

In the commercial for Kyle's dad's legal representation, we learn that he got Bebe $1.6 million and Clyde $1.4 million. Later in the courtroom, Pip gets $1.6 million, Craig gets $2.1 million, and Mr. Mackey gets $2 million.

BEHIND THE SCENES

At the time this episode was produced, Matt and Trey had been working seven days a week for eight months, producing both new *South Park* episodes and the theatrical release *South Park: Bigger, Longer & Uncut*. They don't remember much about the shows from this period—especially this one.

ORIGINAL SONGS

Peetie the Panda sings the very informative theme song, "Sexual Harassment Panda."

POP CULTURE REFERENCES

The Island of Misfit Mascots refers to the Island of Misfit Toys on the TV special *Rudolph the Red-Nosed Reindeer*.

CELEBRITIES IMPUGNED

The judge presiding over the myriad lawsuits is named Judge Julie, in a reference to TV's *Judge Judy*.

WHAT PEETIE THE DONT SUE PEOPLE PANDA LEARNED

"When you sue somebody it hurts everyone. You sue for money, but where do you think that money comes from? From the schools, from taxes, from the state. From you. There's no such thing as free money. When you sue somebody you take money away from parks and schools and charities and put it in your own pocket. And that makes me a sad panda."

CAT ORGY

Original Air Date: July 14, 1999
Episode 307

THE STORY: Cartman's mom attends a meteor shower viewing party at Mr. Mackey's house, leaving her son in the care of Stan's sister, Shelly. She verbally and physically abuses Cartman, then invites over her 22-year-old boyfriend, Skyler. Cartman, enraged, takes a photo of the two of them making out and tries to smuggle it to his mom by tying it to his cat, Kitty, and tossing her out a window. However, Kitty immediately returns to the front door of the house, where Shelly intercepts the photo.

But his cat has problems of her own. In heat and looking for a mate, she escapes the house and wanders South Park. She finally locates a group of interested males, who all attempt to "service" her at the same time.

Back at the house, Shelly allows Cartman out of his room to watch the meteor shower. But Skyler gets angry when Shelly (who is, after all, 12) won't put out, and breaks up with her. Distraught, she turns to Cartman for help. The two go to Skyler's house, where Cartman lures him outdoors while Shelly destroys his cherished guitar.

When the two return home they discover Kitty and her "friends" in the midst of a cat orgy. Skyler shows up seeking revenge, but Cartman dusts him with catnip, causing the hoard of felines to attack him. Cartman's mom returns before the orgy-related mess is cleaned up, but is too drunk to notice.

MEMORABLE LINES

"Wild Wild West! Yo!
A wiki wiki scratch!
A wiki wiki scratch!!"
—*Cartman*

"You're a stinking, dried-up, stupid turd. Got it?"
—*Shelly*

"Luckily for us my mom is a total lush."
—*Cartman*

"And if he gets cranky just play Tummy Rub-Rubs with him. And make sure he wipes good after he makes bears."
—*Cartman's mom*

"As far as turds go, you're okay."
—*Shelly*

"I cherish you. Almost as much as I cherish my guitar."
—*Skyler*

"Dude, that's not cool."
—*Cartman*

BODY COUNT

Nobody. Kenny didn't appear in this episode.

WHERE DID THE IDEA COME FROM?

This episode is the first of three stories that all take place on the same night, each involving a different set of characters. Called the *Meteor Shower Trilogy*, it was born of expediency. The team was exhausted after working for so long on both the series and the *South Park* movie, and decided to do a three-parter to close out their production obligations so they could take a well-needed rest. In the middle of the trilogy, they realized that doing three intertwined episodes wasn't the easiest way to go.

ORIGINAL SONGS

Cartman and Clyde Frog's hip hop rendition of "Wild Wild West" from this episode is one of *South Park's* all-time classics. Also, Skyler's band plays the hard-rockin' tune "Shelly," as well as the happy-go-lucky song "Turds," on which Shelly steps in to sing lead vocals.

POINTLESS OBSERVATION

The grotesquely fat orange-and-black tomcat that Kitty tries to mate with in an alley looks an awful lot like Garfield.

Polly Prissypants, while "playing" Selma Hayek, says that she needs to "eat some tacos and burritos. *Mi gusta tacos mucho.*" This eloquent portrayal of Mexican culture will be used again by Cartman's hand (as J-Lo) in "Fat Butt and Pancake Head."

Shelly's babysitting rates (especially her use of the term "golden time") is a subtle joke that references pay rates for union workers in the entertainment business.

Cartman gets an atomic wedgie three separate times in this episode.

This episode contains the first use of Wellington Bear—seen here on Cartman's Speak-and-Record toy. Wellington's happy bear face can be seen on Cartman's clothes and toys in future episodes.

CHARACTER DEBUTS

Skyler and his bandmates (Mark on the drums and Jonesey on bass) make their rocking debut. Mark can actually be seen partying in the background of "Clubhouses" (page 60) with his signature Zildjian shirt, but isn't introduced until here. All three band members will join forces with Timmy to form the super-group Timmy and the Lords of the Underworld in "Timmy 2000" (page 116).

POINTLESS OBSERVATION ABOUT SHELLY'S USE OF THE WORD "TURD"

Stan's sister uses the t-word in a masterful set of insults, referring to Cartman variously as, "the Turdman of Alcatraz," "Turd Rock From the Sun," "Richard the Turd," and "Turdledove."

CELEBRITIES IMPUGNED

The show contains numerous references to *Wild Wild West*, a movie starring Will Smith and Selma Hayek released on the same weekend as *South Park: Bigger, Longer & Uncut*. In fact, Cartman reenacts the movie with his stuffed animals: Clyde Frog (referred to as "Artimus Clyde Frog") plays U.S. Marshall Artemus Gordon, Cartman plays James West, Polly Prissypants plays Selma Hayek, and Rumper Tumpskin is Dr. Loveless. Selma Hayek gets most of the attention, however, with Clyde Frog saying, "If we save her, I'm going to take off her pants and play slip and slide."

POP CULTURE REFERENCES

Cartman watches the movie *Aliens,* mimicking the line "They mostly come out at night. Mostly." Shelly turns off *Aliens* instead to watch *Friends*. Also, when Cartman takes a picture of Skyler and Shelly making out, he shouts "Ha ha, charade you are!" It's a line from the Pink Floyd song "Pigs (Three Different Ones)."

Wild Animal World, a TV show featuring live-action footage of lions having sex, is a parody of the many Discovery Channel and National Geographic-type shows that document the beauty of . . . animals having sex.

WHAT SHELLY LEARNED

"It's kind of cool that two people who hated each other can be friends."

TWO GUYS NAKED IN A HOT TUB

Original Air Date: July 21, 1999
Episode 308

THE STORY: The second installment in the *Meteor Shower Trilogy*. Stan is forced by his parents to attend Mr. Mackey's meteor shower party, where he's locked in the basement along with the town's biggest "Melvins": Pip; a first-grader named Dougie; and Butters (his first appearance in which he actually has lines). Meanwhile Stan's dad Randy and Kyle's dad Gerald climb naked into Mr. Mackey's new hot tub and discuss their mutual desire to watch another man masturbate. A desire they promptly fulfill.

Stan tries to escape the basement, but the Melvins decide to dress up in women's clothing and play *Charlie's Angels*. They ask Stan to be Bosley, and he gives them the "mission" of finding a way out. They exit via an air duct, locate a TV and discover that agents from the Federal Bureau of Alcohol, Tobacco and Firearms have surrounded the house. The ATF believes the party guests are cult members planning to commit suicide. To counter this crazed cult suicide, the ATF prepares to storm the house and kill everyone.

But the boys, still in their *Charlie's Angels* outfits, make a video proving that there's nothing going on in the house, then smuggle it out to the press. Disaster is more-or-less averted.

While the life-or-death struggle with the ATF plays out, Randy spends the party moping around, freaked out by the masturbation session in the hot tub. But he feels better when he learns that pretty much every other male at the gathering has done something similar.

Is it gay? "Well, maybe a little," Jimbo says. "But we're all a little gay."

MEMORABLE LINES

"Well, it's not like you're the only guy who's ever watched another guy masturbate."
—Mr. Mackey

"You can't just hang out with your buddy Kyle all the time. People will think you're . . . you know . . . funny."
—Stan's dad

"Did I do a nice job, really?"
—Pip

"Well, it is a night for experimenting.'"
—Stan's dad

"Those sick cult-fanatic bastards!"
—Newscaster

"All right, let's get ready to kick some religious fanatic ass."
—ATF Commander

"This sounds as fun as Wickershams and Decklers!"
—Pip

BODY COUNT

Eight partygoers gunned down by the ATF as they try to leave Mr. Mackey's house. Four homes blown up.

WHERE DID THE IDEA COME FROM?

Inspired by Trey and Matt's chance viewing of an HBO documentary about the ATF attack on the Branch Davidian compound in Waco, Texas.

POINTLESS OBSERVATION

In an early scene Cartman's mom is shown at the party talking on the phone to her son—a direct reference to events in the first installment of the *Meteor Shower Trilogy*, "Cat Orgy" (page 88).

The instrumental version of "Wild Wild West" from "Cat Orgy" (page 88) can be heard playing in the background of the party during the scene where Dougie is taping his report. Later, an instrumental version of "Stinky Britches" from "Chef Aid" (page 64) plays.

Usually, negotiators try to find compromise in dangerous situations. Here, "the Negotiator" is just a large cannon, which the ATF points directly at Mackey's house.

Pip was Archery class esquire at Stratfordshire. That probably means he was good.

CHARACTER DEBUTS

Dougie, the first-grader, who would surface again three years later as Professor Chaos' sidekick, General Disarray, in "Professor Chaos." Also Butters, because this was the first time he actually got to say anything. His halting speech pattern was modeled after that of *South Park's* Director of Animation Eric Stough.

Cameron, the big burly guy who's friends with Jimbo.

POP CULTURE REFERENCE

Reporter Derek Smalls, who saves the house from destruction by telling the world about the boys' video, is named after a character from *This Is Spinal Tap*.

After finding women's clothes, the Melvins immediately decide they should play *Charlie's Angels*. Butters and Pip both want to be Jacquelin Smith. But eventually, Butters wins out, leaving Pip to play "Sabrina Duncan." By default, that would make Dougie "Kris Munroe."

CELEBRITIES IMPUGNED

Cher, whose music is used by the ATF to try to drive the "suicide cult" from its lair. The sad truth is that the ATF actually *did* blast Cher songs at the Branch Davidians during the siege.

Randy freaks out when he overhears two townspeople gossiping about who they heard "was gay." Turns out, it was just Ricky Martin.

WHAT STAN LEARNED

"I used to call you guys Melvins. But you're just kids like me. We separate you in school because you talk different and study too hard, and you've proven tonight that we can all get along." Seconds later Stan disavows this statement and abandons his new friends when Kyle shows up.

JEWBILEE

Original Air Date: July 28, 1999
Episode 309

THE STORY: The third installment in the *Meteor Shower Trilogy*. Kyle's parents, before going to Mr. Mackey's party, bundle Kyle and his brother Ike off to Jew Scouts for an event called Jewbilee. Kenny, who promises to "act Jewish," tags along. Once there, Ike is sent off to the Squirts, which is the Jew Scout section for very young kids. The Squirts work on macaroni pictures while Kyle and Kenny carve soap sculptures.

Later that evening, to Kenny's amazement, Moses is conjured up from a campfire. The Jew Scouts present their soap carvings to him. But when Kenny does, he's instantly detected as "impure" and ejected from the camp.

The Squirts are AWOL, having gone on an ill-advised expedition to kill a bear seen lurking around the camp. The bear makes matters worse by picking off the toddlers one by one. But instead of killing them, it takes them back to play with its cub. Kenny is also rounded up, and he leads the kids (and the bears) back to camp.

Their timing couldn't be better, because Elder Garth, leader of the Anti-Semitic Jews, has captured Moses in a conch shell, locked up the other adults, and is busily conjuring up the evil Haman to replace Moses as leader of the Jews. The Squirts free the adults and Kenny smashes open the conch imprisoning Moses, killing himself in the process. Moses smites both Haman and Elder Garth, then declares that the Jews shall meet every year on that day to celebrate Kenny—by making macaroni pictures, paper plate bean shakers and other knick knacks.

MEMORABLE LINES

"No cake for the impurity."
—*Moses*

"Kenny will believe whatever you want him to."
—*Kyle*

"I desire . . . macaroni pictures."
—*Moses*

"I pledge to be a Jew Scout. My honor wide and true. I am proud to be a Jew Scout. Otherwise, I'd just be a Jew."
—*Jew Scout Pledge*

"You must leave before the great eating of carrot cake."
—*Jewish Elder*

"If you guys love Moses so much, why don't you marry him?"
—*Elder Garth*

BODY COUNT

Kenny and Elder Garth.

WHERE DID THE IDEA COME FROM?

This was the last show Matt and Trey, exhausted after doing the *South Park* movie, had to complete before they could take a long vacation. In the spirit of expediency, they decided to deliberately fashion an episode that was as dumb and weird as possible. "We shit this out of our ass," said Trey on the episode's DVD commentary. Yet they both consider it one of their favorites.

POINTLESS OBSERVATIONS

When Kenny is tossed out of camp he walks dejectedly beside the highway, trying to thumb a ride. Suddenly a convoy of ATF vehicles streams by. They're on their way to Mr. Mackey's party, as seen in "Two Guys Naked In A Hot Tub" (page 90).

Kyle, Ike, Kenny, and all the other Jew Scouts wear "peyos"—long, curly sideburns that hang freely. These are usually seen on Orthodox Jewish men. Furthermore, the main hall at Jewbilee is called Mashugana Hall. "Mashugana" is Yiddish for "crazy." Also, within the Chamber of Elders, the Elders are actually speaking Hebrew.

In order to fit in, Kenny's name in this episode is Kenny McHeimerberg.

Ike makes a macaroni picture of the Last Supper. He will again be involved in a Last Supper recreation in "Margaritaville."

CHARACTER DEBUTS

The Squirt Leader, Shlomo, is also a minor character in *South Park: Bigger, Longer & Uncut*, where he's the ticket taker at the town's movie theater.

Moses. He will appear again in "Super Best Friends" (page 152).

BIBLICAL REFERENCES

The Haman to whom Elder Garth refers was a 4th Century B.C. Persian official who schemed to have all the Jews residing in the Persian Empire killed. The plot was foiled by one of the Persian king's wives, Esther, who was Jewish. Haman was hung on the gallows he had prepared for the leader of the Jews. The feast of Purim commemorates his demise.

WHAT KYLE LEARNED

"It's fine to have your own beliefs and your own traditions, but as soon as you start excluding people from your ways, only because of their race, you become separatist. And being a separatist sucks ass."

WHAT MATT AND TREY LEARNED

"Don't sit around a table and figure out your plot for very long. Just be stupid and have fun."

POP CULTURE REFERENCES

When Moses appears, he looks like the Master Control Program from 1982's *Tron*.

The Jew Scouts all sing "Koom By Ya" around the fire. Ned also sings this tune around a campfire in "Volcano" (page 14).

KORN'S GROOVY PIRATE GHOST MYSTERY

Original Air Date: October 27, 1999
Episode 312

THE STORY: It's Halloween again, and the band Korn has been booked to play at a big festival at the South Park Docks. But the musical group's van (which looks suspiciously like the Mystery Machine from the *Scooby Doo* cartoons) is forced off the road by what appear to be ghost pirates.

When Korn finally makes it into town, the group encounters Stan, Kyle, Cartman and Kenny, who have problems of their own. In order to scare some fifth graders, they dug up the moldering corpse of Kyle's grandmother and then they promptly misplaced it.

The townspeople quickly learn of the grave robbing. Not knowing the true fate of the body, they fear it was taken by necrophiliacs. During a town meeting about the "problem," they're attacked by ghost pirates who slay several residents, then warn that they'll come back to finish the job if the Halloween festivities continue.

The townspeople decide that Korn is responsible for the outbreak of Satanic events, cancel their concert and roll their van for good measure. Meanwhile, the musical group and the boys endeavor to solve the mystery. After what can best be described as "hijinks," they discover that Father Maxi, who loathes Halloween, is behind everything. He created the pirates using "a flashlight and some cotton swabs," and their ship using "some candles, a mirror and two squirrels." Kyle's grandma's corpse is also recovered when the dog that ate it regurgitates it in front of a crowd of horrified onlookers.

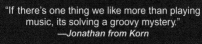

MEMORABLE LINES

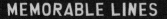

"People stealing bodies to have sex with them, pirate ghosts destroying the town—when did everything go so wrong?"
—*Kyle's mom*

"Somebody wanted to have sex with her dead body."
—*Night Watchman*

"LYNCH MOB!!"
—*Stan's dad*

"If there's one thing we like more than playing music, its solving a groovy mystery."
—*Jonathan from Korn*

"Aw, nuts! Come on Ned, this ain't a whore house, it's a hor-ROR house!"
—*Jimbo*

"You son of a bitch chicken from outer space!! Come back here!"
—*Cartman*

"Dude, we're not digging up my Grandma! I'll get in trouble!"
—*Kyle*

"Screw Halloween, I already got my Christmas present!"
—*Cartman*

"You best clear out of here. There's pirate ghosts and they'll kill you."
—*Announcer*

BODY COUNT

Several residents killed by pirates. Also Kenny, shot to pieces by tiny Rebel snowspeeders from *Star Wars: The Empire Strikes Back*—perhaps because the Halloween costume he's wearing at the time looks like an Imperial Walker. See *Pop Culture References* for the details.

WHERE DID THE IDEA COME FROM?

The band Korn approached the show about debuting the first single from their new album on *South Park*. The writers thought it would be funny if they used them as clueless "mystery" investigators, a la *Scooby Doo*.

POP CULTURE REFERENCES

Kenny's Halloween costume is a faithful reproduction of the ED-209 law enforcement robot from the movie *Robocop*. Ironically, in that film the ED-209 malfunctions and kills a man named "Kinney." Also Korn makes use of many *Scooby Doo* props, including driving around in a tricked-out van.

POINTLESS OBSERVATIONS

When Cartman flips through a toy catalog, one can see ads for Alabama Man from "Chinpokomon" (page 96) and for a Mr. Hankey Play Set from "Mr. Hankey, the Christmas Poo" (page 26). Also Wendy wins the town's Halloween costume competition by wearing the same Chewbacca outfit she wore in "Pinkeye" (page 22) two seasons earlier. Finally, at the graveyard where they dug up Kyle's grandma, one of the gravestones reads "Kenny-1999."

Much like the *Power Rangers*, each member of Korn has the super ability to turn into various corn products (popcorn, creamed corn, corn on the cob). It doesn't help out.

BEHIND THE SCENES

Matt and Trey remember this as one of their most difficult episodes to produce, because it was the first one after a months-long break to rest and recuperate after the *South Park* movie. It took a while to get their groove back. Also, the argument during the episode about whether the evil spirits were "pirate ghosts" (ghosts that had become pirates) or "ghost pirates" (pirates that had become ghosts) actually raged for a while between Matt (who favored "pirate ghosts") and one of the show's writers.

CHARACTER DEBUTS

Korn, the musical group, as well as Niblet, an annoying yellow canary/chicken that serves as Korn's mascot.

The Fifth Graders, who will continue to bully the boys from here on out. The Leader of the Fifth Graders is best known for his muttonchopped brown hair and green t-shirt with a picture of himself on it. (General note: After "Fourth Grade" (page 132), they will be referred to as "Sixth Graders," as everyone moved up a grade. Derp.)

We "meet" Kyle's grandmother, Cleo Broflovski. She's dead, pretty badly decomposed, and then eaten by a dog.

POINTLESS GEOGRAPHICAL OBSERVATION

Much of the action takes place on the South Park Docks. However South Park (being part of Colorado) is landlocked.

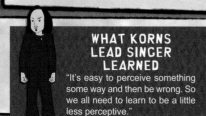

WHAT KORNS LEAD SINGER LEARNED

"It's easy to perceive something some way and then be wrong. So we all need to learn to be a little less perceptive."

CELEBRITIES IMPUGNED

Cartman's mom gets a "Lifesized Blow-Up Antonio Banderas Love Doll With Realistic Genitalia" in the mail. Cartman thinks it's a Christmas gift for him, blows it up and carries it around.

CHINPOKO MON

Original Air Date: November 3, 1999
Episode 310

THE STORY: The boys (along with every other kid in town) become fascinated with a Japanese cartoon, Chinpokomon. In spite of the fact that the show has no discernable plot and the dialogue makes little sense, South Park's kids flock to the toy store to purchase action figures and the Chinpokomon video game.

Kenny suffers a massive seizure while playing the game but the rest of the children all attend a special Chinpokomon camp, where the real reason behind the craze is revealed—by none other than Emperor Hirohito himself. The kids are being fed military tactics through the toys and games. Soon they will be used as pawns to pilot jets to bomb Pearl Harbor. Whenever any adults get suspicious, the Japanese distract them by telling them how large their American penises are.

In the nick of time, South Park's grownups figure out how to counter the Chinpokomon threat. As the kids board their fighter jets to attack Pearl Harbor, their parents inform them that they now like Chinpokomon too. This kills the thrill for the boys, who immediately abandon the plan.

MEMORABLE LINES

"But Moooom! I have to get a Chinpokomon doll before anyone else
does because then I'll be cooool!"
—*Cartman*

"We are very simple people, with very small
penis. Mr. Ose's penis is especially small."
—*Emperor Hirohito*

"Thank you for stopping by with your
gargantuan penis."
—*Emperor Hirohito*

"I love you! Let's be friends . . .
and destroy the capitalist American
government!"
—*Chinpokomon doll*

"Jesus tap dancing Christ! Get
with the program, Kyle."
—*Cartman*

"The Primary Main Objective is to
destroy the evil power!"
—*Stan*

BODY COUNT

Kenny has a violent seizure while playing the Chinpokomon video game and stays comatose for the rest of the episode. Finally, at the very end, his body bursts open, revealing that he's filled with rats. So he'd probably been dead for awhile.

WHERE DID THE IDEA COME FROM?

The story was an extended critique of the *Pokemon* phenomenon.

POP CULTURE REFERENCES

After the kids' parents get them to stop liking Chinpokomon by pretending to like it too, Stan's mom tells Mr. Garrison to, "Get on the wire to every parent around the country and tell them how to bring those sons of bitches down." The line comes from the movie *Independence Day*.

When talking about how stupid TV shows can destroy a child's mind, Sharon begs Randy to "remember what *Battle of the Network Stars* did to an entire generation." This is a reference to the long-running TV series that pitted popular television performers against one another in athletic events.

Kyle uses the phrase "ay-eet," trying to say it the way Lauren Hill does, but it turns out that stopped being cool eight days ago.

CHARACTER DEBUTS

A whole bunch of Chinpokomon: Furry Cat, Donkeytron, Pen-Gin, Shoe, Lambtor, Roo-STOR, LAMtron, and Chu-Chu Nezumi. Collect them all, and you just might become Royal Crown Chinpoko Master.

Red Harris, owner of Luau's Toys. You can see him again in "A Very Crappy Christmas" (page 144).

Hirohito, President of the Chinpoko Toy Corporation, and his associate, Mr. Ose, who we learn has a microscopic penis.

POINTLESS OBSERVATIONS

Trey Parker studied Japanese. Thus the Japanese names and dialogue in this episode are right on the money. Emperor Hirohito was played by an old friend of his, Junichi Nishimura—who also supplied the narration for Trey's college short film, *American History*. You can see a young, animated Junichi briefly in "Jewbilee" (page 92).

Cartman shows off his ability to play guitar in this episode, as he sings on the sidewalk for people to give him money for more Chinpokomon.

We see two live-action commercials for toys developed to subvert the Chinpokomon phenomenon: Alabama Man, a plastic doll which spends a lot of time bowling, drinking and beating its wife; and Wild Wacky Action Bike, "the bike that's hard to ride!"

JAPANESE CULTURE REFERENCES

The word chinpoko means "small penis" in Japanese. The phrase Chinpokomon means "small penis monster." Also, Kenny's seizure is a reference to an incident in Japan in which the viewing of a *Pokemon* episode called "Electric Soldier Porygon" caused a similar problem with Japanese children. It was never aired in the United States.

WHAT STAN LEARNED

"This whole Chinpokomon thing happened because we all followed the group. We only liked Chinpokomon because everyone else did. And look at the damage it caused."

HOOKED ON MONKEY PHONICS

Original Air Date: November 10, 1999
Episode 313

THE STORY: Cartman's mom buys him a study aid called Hooked on Monkey Fonics. It comes with an actual monkey, which taps out a beat on a tiny set of drums and makes learning to spell easier. Cartman figures the monkey makes him a shoo-in to win The 15th Annual South Park Spelling Bee. But on the big day the monkey, instead of playing his drums, begins masturbating furiously. Cartman, flustered, misspells "chair" as "chare."

The spelling bee championship is, to Kyle's amazement, shared by two home-schooled kids, Mark and Rebecca. Mark becomes fascinated with the bizarre interactions of the public school kids, while Kyle becomes infatuated with Rebecca. Mark enrolls at South Park Elementary, where he's relentlessly ripped on by his classmates. Meanwhile Kyle pursues Rebecca, asking her to attend the South Park Bay of Pigs Memorial Dance. She agrees—and kisses him to boot.

Unfortunately Rebecca's first kiss has some undesired effects. She shows up at the dance dressed like a hooker and kisses every boy she sees. Mark, enraged, beats Kyle to a pulp—giving him instant "street cred" with the other kids, who suddenly accept him. Mark realizes that keeping him and his sister from the "real" world of public school turned his sister into a whore, and him (almost) into a social cripple.

MEMORABLE LINES

"If your monkey arrived in the box dead, call 1-800-555-4500 to get a new monkey."
—*Hooked on Monkey Fonics Instructional Tape*

"Please hit me."
—*Pip*

"All right children, let's just try to pretend there isn't a little boy in a huge plastic hamster bubble here and go on with our studies."
—*Mr. Garrison*

"Oh God, that kid's gonna last about five seconds out on the playground."
—*Stan*

"Put your hand down, cream puff."
—*Mr. Garrison*

"You bitch! I'm gonna whip your bitch ass!"
—*Mark*

"You made my sister into a slut!! I'll kill you!!"
—*Mark*

"Screw you guys, I'm gonna be home schooled."
—*Cartman*

"No fonics monkey! That's a bad fonics monkey!"
—*Cartman*

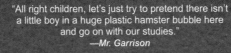

BODY COUNT

Kenny, killed by Fonics Monkey in a fight over a cupcake.

WHERE DID THE IDEA COME FROM?

Matt and Trey have a mutual friend who home schooled his kids, so this seemed like a perfect opportunity to "investigate" the issue. Also they'd seen a spelling bee on TV and thought the kids (most of whom were home-schooled) seemed seriously stunted. Matt thinks this episode sums up South Park's attitude toward children. Most people see them as kind little creatures, but "we just view kids as just evil little bastards."

CELEBRITIES IMPUGNED

Heavy metal icon Ronnie James Dio, who apparently has fallen so far down the food chain that he's hired to play at the South Park Bay of Pigs Memorial Dance. He serves up his anthem "Holy Diver."

When Mark rolls into Mr. Garrison's class in his hamster ball, Cartman says "Dude, what's wrong with you? Do you have some kind of John Travolta disease?"

POP CULTURE REFERENCES

The encounter between Kyle and Rebecca in her father's garden is a parody of the *Star Trek* episode "The Gamesters of Triskelion," in which Captain Kirk sweet talks an alien woman.

Hooked on Monkey Fonics is a clear parody of the learn-to-read series "Hooked on Phonics," which gained popularity in the 90s.

CHARACTER DEBUTS

The Fonics Monkey makes his drumming debut. Rebecca, Mark, and their over-protective parents, Mr. and Mrs. Cotswold.

POINTLESS OBSERVATIONS

During the school dance, an instrumental version of Chef's song "Stinky Britches" briefly plays. It can also be heard in the background of "Two Guys Naked in a Hot Tub" (page 90).

The word Kyle has to spell in the Spelling Bee Finals is "Kroxldyphivc," which is not an actual word.

This episode features Kyle's first crush, and his second kiss. It's quite a dramatic change from his first smooch with Bebe in "Clubhouses" (page 60), after which he runs away screaming.

Rebecca has a flag of Slovenia on the back of her bedroom door.

ORIGINAL SONGS

Kyle picks up a guitar and sings his heartfelt, acoustic song "Rebecca" outside of his love's window.

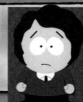

WHAT MARK THE HOME-SCHOOLED KID LEARNED

"Public schools may be a bit lacking in education, but it's the main place where children learn all of their social skills. You can't teach a child social skills. They have to learn them themselves. And the only place to do that is on the playground and the cafeteria and so on."

STARVIN' MARVIN IN SPACE

Original Air Date: November 17, 1999
Episode 311

THE STORY: When an alien lands in Ethiopia to make first contact with Earth's intelligent life, the pilot is immediately eaten by lions. The next morning, the starving locals (who attend a missionary school in the mistaken belief that they'll get food) find the alien's ship. The crowd includes Starvin' Marvin (first seen in "Starvin' Marvin," page 24). He climbs aboard and takes the ship on a world-spanning joyride.

Meanwhile, back in South Park, CIA agents round up Stan, Kyle, Cartman and Kenny and torture them until Cartman reveals where Marvin's village is located. Later that same day the starship crashes into Cartman's house, and Marvin takes the boys for a ride.

They fly through a wormhole to the ship's home—the distant planet of Marklar, where the word "Marklar" is used in place of all nouns. Marvin is delighted when the Marklars allow his starv-ing tribe to move to their planet.

But when he and the boys return, their ship is seized by the CIA. The boys create a distrac-tion by posing (together) as Tom Brokaw, allow-ing the Ethiopians to board the ship and take off. The boys make it aboard too—except for Kenny, who's recaptured.

The CIA wants the ship's technology, and en-lists Sally Struthers (now swollen to Jabba the Hutt-like proportions) to help retrieve it. As part of the deal, the agents give her Kenny, who she imme-diately encases in a block of carbonite. Also in hot pursuit is a starship piloted by missionaries from Pat Robertson's *600 Club*. After an epic space bat-tle, the three vessels land on Marklar, where the Marklars take in the Ethiopians and tell everyone else to leave. The boys catch a ride home with Sal-ly Struthers, who has had a last-minute conver-sion from the Dark Side.

MEMORABLE LINES

"Here at the 600 Club we need your money to spread the word of Jesus and build more advanced deflector shields for our galactic cruiser."
—*Pat Robertson*

"Remember . . . Reading Bible + Accepting Jesus = Food!"
—*Missionary Woman*

"Here on Marklar we refer to all people, places and things as Marklar."
—*Marklar*

"Ooh! Kyle's making mud pies, you guys want one?!"
—*Cartman*

"Back away from the spacecraft, children!"
—*CIA Guy*

"Young Marklar. Your Mark-lars are wise and true."
—*Marklar*

BODY COUNT

The explorer from Marklar who was eaten by lions. And possibly Kenny. When we last see him he's encased in a block of carbonite, just like Han Solo in *Star Wars: The Empire Strikes Back*. But as we know from that film, this isn't necessarily fatal.

WHERE DID THE IDEA COME FROM?

The show was a both a chance to reacquaint everyone with Starvin' Marvin, and to take a dig at Pat Robertson's *700 Club* (a Christian TV program, referred to as "*The 600 Club*" here). The show doesn't open with South Park's usual credits, the feeling being that this was, in fact, an episode of "Starvin' Marvin In Space."

POINTLESS OBSERVATIONS

At the beginning of the episode Cartman and Kyle both accuse each other of "going number two" in a school urinal. The matter will serve as a subplot in "Mystery of the Urinal Deuce." Also, the song "I Am Chewbacca", which plays over the closing credits, is performed by Matt and Trey's band, DVDA.

The boys experience a new, brutal torture method at the hands of the CIA: the balloon rub.

POP CULTURE REFERENCES

The Christian Broadcasting Channel (CBC) featured here is a take off on the Christian Broadcasting Network, a real TV channel that hosts shows such as Pat Robertson's *The 700 Club*.

Sally Struthers massive slug-like form is a parody of the greasy, torture-loving Jabba the Hutt from the *Star Wars* films; most notably in *Return of the Jedi*.

CHARACTER DEBUTS

The Marklars, with their awesome habit of using the word "Marklar" for every single noun.

CELEBRITIES IMPUGNED

Sally Struthers, now even bigger and more hideous than she was in "Starvin' Marvin" (page 24). However, it must be said that at the end of the episode she has a change of heart and becomes a force for good.

Tom Brokaw, who the boys poorly impersonate with a crappy mustache and grey toupee.

COUNTRIES IMPUGNED

The CIA worries what "sadistic, backwards third world country" will get their hands on the Marklar spaceship, and it turns out to be . . . Australia. Although they're inviting, the Australians are portrayed as less than intelligent.

ORIGINAL SONGS

The inspirational little song snippet "Soaring So High" plays throughout the episode when Starvin' Marvin is flying the space ship.

WHAT KYLE LEARNED

"Marklar, these Marklars want to change your Marklar. They don't want this Marklar or any of his Marklars to live here, because its bad for their Marklar. They use Marklar to try and force Marklars to believe their Marklar. If you let them stay here they will build Marklars and Marklars. They will take all your Marklars and replace them with Marklars. These Marklars have no good Marklar to live on Marklar, so they must come here to Marklar. Please, let these Marklars stay where they can grow and prosper without any Marklars, Marklars or Marklars."

THE RED BADGE OF GAYNESS

Original Air Date: November 24, 1999
Episode 314

THE STORY: As South Park prepares for its annual reenactment of the Battle of Tamarack Hill, friction builds between Cartman, Stan and Kyle. On the day of the reenactment, Cartman arrives dressed as Confederate commander Robert E. Lee. He bets Stan and Kyle, who fight on the Union side, that the South will win the war. If he's right, they have to be his slaves for a month. If he's wrong, he's their slave.

As the day goes on, the "Confederate" reenactors become progressively more drunk on the event's alcohol sponsor, Jagerminz S'More Flavored Schnapps. So drunk, in fact, that Cartman convinces them to beat the Union reenactors for real. Which, to everyone's amazement, they promptly do.

At the party after the battle, everyone gets drunk on schnapps. Soon Cartman convinces

them to start a rampage across North America, capturing city after city—in spite of the fact that they're only armed with blanks. Kyle and Stan briefly stop the rampage by stealing the "armies" alcohol supply, but Cartman manages to secure more. Soon everyone's drunk again and the onslaught continues.

The troops take Washington, D.C. and force President Bill Clinton to allow the South to form its own nation, effectively "winning" the Civil War. But at the last moment Kyle and Stan, dressed as Lincoln and Jefferson Davis, reenact the real surrender of the South. The army of drunken pretend soldiers promptly melts away.

It seems that Kyle and Stan can now use Cartman as their slave for a month. But as he points out, if the North wins, slavery is abolished. So they have no claim to him, and so everyone's screwed.

MEMORABLE LINES

"Dear guys . . . Words cannot express how much I hate you guys." —*Cartman*

"I say we take Topeka!" —*Cartman*

"Get me more S'more Schnapps, I'm gonna be sick!" —*Jimbo*

"You can't just hit a drum. You have to beat the shit out of it." —*Cartman*

"Come, Kenny. Come fight for us and I'll make sure you get lots of plunder and womens." —*Cartman*

"Confederate messenger Butters reporting, sir." —*Butters*

BODY COUNT

Just Kenny, killed by a "warning flare" fired by the National Guard. However, a number of innocent townspeople in Topeka, Chattanooga, and Fort Sumter are beaten and bludgeoned without mercy by the approaching Southern "army."

CHARACTER DEBUTS

Suzette, the S'More Schnapps Girl.

WHERE DID THE IDEA COME FROM?

This episode, along with the rest of Season 3, was born of tragic expediency. When Mary Kay Bergman, who voiced nearly all of South Park's female characters, died unexpectedly, stories had to be created that didn't rely on her work. No one, out of respect for Bergman, was keen on rushing out to hire replacements. Which is why in this episode the only recognizable female who gets screen time, Kenny's mom, never opens her mouth.

CELEBRITIES IMPUGNED

Bill Clinton, whom the boys call a "dick." Vice president Al Gore gets off comparatively lightly, especially considering the hammering he'll take in "Manbearpig" and "Imaginationland Episode III." Furthermore, Cartman blackmails President Clinton to declare the Confederacy its own nation by saying, "If you do not meet our demand, we will be forced to show the video tapes we have of you with Marisa Tomei." It works.

We catch the end of a news report that informs us Courtney Love ". . . was forced to live off her own feces for several days."

POP CULTURE REFERENCES

Cartman writes a letter to Kenny's mother stating that her son was killed at "Ruby Hills Funland in Chattanooga." It's a reference to a real Chattanooga tourist trap called Ruby Falls. Also, the episode's title is a play on the Civil War novel *The Red Badge of Courage*.

POINTLESS OBSERVATIONS

The alcohol company Jagerminz is a parody of the all-too-real alcoholic beverage Jagermeister—a.k.a. the Devil's Mouthwash or Hell's Pancake Syrup. Also, when the boys pull off Cartman's fake Civil War beard, his scream of pain is heard on the planet Marklar, which we first see in "Starvin' Marvin In Space" (page 100).

WHAT KYLE THINKS CARTMAN LEARNED

"You've learned that you can't rewrite history. You see, history is forever, and everything happens for a reason." In the middle of this speech, Cartman walks away to procure more schnapps for his "army." He does, and the campaign to rewrite history continues.

MR. HANKEY'S CHRISTMAS CLASSICS

Original Air Date: December 1, 1999
Episode 315

THE STORY: A collection of timeless holiday songs, *South Park*-style—each hand-picked from *South Park's* musical album also called *Mr. Hankey's Christmas Classics.* The lineup features Kyle and his family, plus Cartman, offering a heavily revised version of "Dreidel, Dreidel, Dreidel." Other highlights include Hitler singing "O Tannenbaum," Satan knocking out a surprisingly high-spirited "Christmas Time In Hell," and Jesus and Santa performing a slightly strained medley of holiday favorites. Mr. Hankey serves as the narrator, sitting in a tiny chair in front of a fireplace. Kenny doesn't appear until the closing number, during which he's killed by a falling light fixture.

MEMORABLE LINES

"Oh holy night! The something something something. And is the night with Christmas trees and pie."
—*Cartman*

"Stick me in your mouth and try to say 'Howdy Ho, Yum Yum Yum!' "
—*Mr. Hankey*

"Ah, fuck you, Jesus."
—*Santa Claus*

"Joy to the world, for I have come. Let earth receive . . . me."
—*Jesus*

"Let's not forget that for some people, Christmas is about the birth of Jesus."
—*Mr. Hankey*

"Jews . . . Play stupid games. Jews . . . That's why they're lame!"
—*Cartman*

WHERE DID THE IDEA COME FROM?
Matt and Trey were still producing episodes without the services of Mary Kay Bergman. In this case they got around the problem because the pre-recorded songs included her numerous characters.

BODY COUNT
Just Kenny

POP CULTURE REFERENCES
Cowboy Timmy, the mailman that sings the opening song "Mr. Hankey the Christmas Poo," is an homage to the classic animated character Postman Pat.

Kyle's dad joins in the collaborative performance of "Dreidel, Driedel, Dreidel" by singing "Coutrney Cox, I love you. You're so hot, on that show." He's referring to *Friends*.

During Jesus and Santa's duet, they slip in a little Duran Duran, with their cover of the band's hit single "Rio."

POINTLESS OBSERVATION
In their most obscure reference of all time, Matt and Trey included a live-action news anchor at several points in the show who says, enigmatically, "Fighting the frizzies at 11." It refers to a bootleg copy of the 1978 *Star Wars Christmas Special*, a bizarre CBS production that's unavailable in any format, save for a much-duped videotape that someone made while the thing aired for the first (and only) time. It comes with commercials intact, including a news anchor saying, "Fighting the frizzies at 11," on several occasions. Matt and Trey went one better by showing their anchor actually fighting a frizzy monster at the end of the show.

Much like "Chickenlover" (page 42), this is another classic "Robert T. Pooner" production. This alias has been used various times by Parker and Stone, including in their pre-*South Park* short *The Spirit of Christmas*.

During the opening song, the Postman can be seen holding two pieces of construction paper that correspond to the colors he's singing about ("brown" and "greenish brown"). This is a reference to *South Park's* animation style, as all textures and colors are based off of scanned pieces of construction paper.

CELEBRITIES IMPUGNED
During "Christmas Time In Hell," John F. Kennedy, Princess Diana, Michael Landon, Jimmy Stewart, and film critic Gene Siskel are all shown burning in the fires of perdition, alongside world leaders Hitler, Ghengis Khan, and Kim Jong-il. Also Andy Dick, who (at the time this episode aired) isn't even dead.

In the final, joy-filled moments of this episode, Hitler and John F. Kennedy share a hug.

ORIGINAL SONGS
When it comes to *South Park* musical numbers, this episode is—as Cartman would say—the "tits". The entire show is stuffed to the brim with a tasty assortment of holiday treats, performed by everyone from Satan to Kyle's mom.

It kicks off with Postman Pat and a chorus of South Park kids caroling to "Mr. Hankey the Christmas Poo" (along with Mr. Hankey himself); Kyle and his clan get kosher with a sweet new version of "Dreidel, Dreidel, Dreidel"; and a somber Hitler performs "O Tannenbaum" before Satan warms his heart with "Christmas Time in Hell".

Also, Mr. Mackey sings a Mkay-filled "Carol of the Bells"; Cartman shows off his softer side with a crappy rendition of "O Holy Night"; Mr. Garrison belts out his totally non-denominational holiday classic "Merry Fucking Christmas"; and Shelly gets classy with her piano ballad "I Saw Three Ships", before beating up a few turds.

Santa and Jesus get together for the first time on stage—duetting a mashup of holiday classics. And for the finale, Mr. Hankey and the boys fill our hearts with peace, love, and poo with their tender song "Have Yourself A Merry Little Christmas".

POIGNANT OBSERVATION
During the final number, "Have Yourself a Merry Little Christmas," most of the major characters portrayed by Mary Kay Bergman are shown singing together. It marks the final episode in which Bergman's voice appears.

ARE YOU THERE GOD? IT'S ME, JESUS

Original Air Date: December 29, 1999
Episode 316

THE STORY: It's almost Y2K, and Cartman is very excited . . . for reasons that have nothing to do with Y2K. He's bleeding from his anus, and convinced he's getting his period, thus entering puberty. The other boys are horrified to think that Cartman is the first of them to hit maturity, and start watching for their own "periods." However, the bleeding is actually caused by a viral infection. Kenny promptly contracts it, while Kyle simply lies about having it. The three form a post-puberty "clique," excluding Stan, who in desperation overdoses on growth hormones supplied by Dr. Mephesto. He promptly develops a beard, a lower voice, and breasts.

Meanwhile, the approach of the new millennium makes Jesus hugely popular. His followers demand some sort of sign, so he decides to organize a huge Las Vegas concert featuring Rod Stewart. Unfortunately his followers also expect God to appear, and when he doesn't (and Stewart proves a bust) they prepare to crucify Jesus again. Jesus, horrified, realizes he let his newfound fame go to his head.

God, apparently satisfied that his son learned his lesson, then descends from heaven and reveals himself to the astonished crowd. His true visage, it seems, is that of a three-foot-tall hippopotamus thingy. God allows his followers to ask him one question. While the adults debate what they want to know, Stan asks why he doesn't have his period yet. God says it's because he's a boy, and that his friends don't have them either. Then God ascends back up to heaven, promising to answer another question in 2000 years.

The final credits roll over what sounds like Stan being lynched.

MEMORABLE LINES

"I'm 2,000 years old but I feel like I'm 28 again."
—*Jesus*

"Yea, like John Travolta before you, you are experiencing a second revival."
—*God speaking to Jesus*

"Pooped my pants."—*Rod Stewart*

"You will hit puberty when the time is right, but you will never have a period because you are a man . . . with titties."
—*God*

"I'm just here to tell you that my puberty is gonna be bigger than any of you guys!"
—*Stan*

"There comes a time in every child's life when they grow up, and nature starts to take its course by having you bleed out your ass for a few days a month."
—*Cartman*

"Whoa, dude. I've got boobs."
—*Stan*

"I was just hanging out in my room and then I perioded all over the place."
—*Kyle*

"As we all know, if Jesus comes out of his house and is not scared by his shadow, it means the next thousand years will be full of peace and love."
—*Newscaster*

BODY COUNT

Kenny, when a tampon he crammed up his butt causes him to "burst from the inside out like a ruptured septic tank."

WHERE DID THE IDEA COME FROM?

It was the end of the millennium, and everyone was doing Y2K episodes. Comedy Central wanted *South Park* to do one. So they did.

FEMININE HYGIENE REFERENCES

Cartman considers several different products to use for his "period," including items called Winged Span, Plug-ups, Breeze, Cotton Cork, and Beaver Dam.

CHARACTER DEBUTS

God—a furry half-cat, half-hippo looking being with crooked teeth and a booming voice.

POINTLESS OBSERVATIONS

In news shots of people around the world partying (actually, rioting) before Y2K, one briefly glimpses the Paris café where the Jakovasaurs (see page 82) were dumped. Jakov is still there, furiously waving his arms. Also Jesus has a picture of himself and Santa Claus singing together from "Mr. Hankey's Christmas Classics" (page 104).

Kyle, Kenny, and Cartman all gather for their "period meeting" in Cartman's big, crappy clubhouse (aka Ewok Village 2000). He and Kenny built this in "Clubhouses" (page 60).

POP CULTURE REFERENCES

The episode's title is a reference to the Judy Blume novel called *Are You There God? It's Me, Margaret*. This is also referenced in "Merry Christmas Charlie Manson!" (page 68).

Cartman says his mom gave him the book *Women Who Run With the Wolves*, a best selling novel by Clarissa Pinkola Estes. He uses the book to help find out about his inner Goddess powers.

Stan closes out the episode with his *a capella* version of "Auld Lang Syne," but is attacked by an angry mob before he can finish it.

BEHIND THE SCENES

There was much discussion as to what God, who reveals himself to the faithful during this episode's climactic scene, should look like. After several long, theology-laden discussions, it was decided to make him look "sort of like a midget hippopotamus, lizard thing."

CELEBRITIES IMPUGNED

Rod Stewart, portrayed as a senile, liver-spotted, wheelchair-bound has-been.

ORIGINAL SONGS

Chef teaches Stan about the joys of womanhood with his exploratory jam "The Menstrual Cycle." Also, Rod Stewart rocks out to the mostly unintelligible "Poop'd 'Em."

WHAT JESUS LEARNED

"I was overcome with my new popularity and I let pride get in the way of good judgment."

WORLD WIDE RECORDER CONCERT

Original Air Date: January 12, 2000
Episode 317

THE STORY: South Park Elementary's entire third-grade class is roped into appearing at a live, worldwide recorder concert put on by the Pox network. But Mr. Garrison is horrified to learn that it will take place in his home state of Arkansas.

His reluctance to go there stems from child molestation. Or rather, the lack thereof. Apparently Mr. Garrison has never gotten over the fact that his father *didn't* molest him. He feels, somehow, that it was because he wasn't desirable. Encouraged by Mr. Mackey, he confronts his parents about the issue. Not surprisingly, his father thinks he's insane.

Meanwhile, the boys try to fit in at the recorder concert, called the "4 Million Child Blow 2000." Cartman is obsessed with locating "the brown note," a legendary audio tone that causes anyone who hears it to spontaneously poop

their pants. Incredibly, he actually finds it. The boys use it to take revenge on a group of New York kids who make fun of them. They change the kids' sheet music to include the brown note, hoping they'll poop their pants on live TV. Unfortunately, a manager for the show finds the new music and alters it for *all* the kids.

The concert finally takes place, with all four million kids hitting the brown note in unison . . . and *everyone* around the world poops themselves. But there's a happy ending. In light of this horrendous act, the New York children develop a new respect for the South Park kids.

Mr. Garrison is happy too, because his father finally "molested him." Except that he didn't. We learn that it was actually Kenny G, who was paid $100 to do the job.

MEMORABLE LINES

"You guys are nothing but MUNG!"
—*Stan*

"Would you have sex with your son to save his life?"
—*Mr. Garrsion's father*

"It's been just under 20 hours since everyone on earth pooped their pants. And people still roam their damaged homes with disbelief and loss."
—*Newscaster*

"Everybody on earth shat themselves 'cause of you. . . . That's pretty amazing."
—*Smitty, the New Yorker Kid*

"You kiss just like my dad."
—*Mr. Garrison*

"What's Arkansas? Is that a state?"
—*Stan*

"I'm gonna kick your ass, mkay?"
—*Mr. Mackey*

"God dammit! I don't think you children have been working on your fingering!"
—*Mr. Garrison*

"Well, you look like a bunch of queefs to me!"
—*Smitty, the New Yorker Kid*

BODY COUNT

Kenny, who pooped himself to death.

WHERE DID THE IDEA COME FROM?

Matt and Trey both proudly state that this is "one of the most fucked-up things we've ever done," describing its horrendous take on child molestation as like a "reverse Afterschool Special from hell."

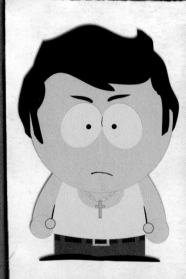

CHARACTER DEBUTS

Smitty, the leader of the New York kids.
Mr. Garrison's Parents.

POP CULTURE REFERENCES

When asked where to go by Ms. Crabtree, Mr. Garrison says, "Second star to the right, then straight on 'til morning." It originally comes from the 1904 play *Peter Pan*, but is actually referencing its reuse in *Star Trek VI: The Undiscovered Country*.

Cartman mentions his affinity for the medical drama *Chicago Hope* in this episode, saying, "they should bring back another season of *Chicago Hope*, though. Seriously." When this aired, the hospital drama was in its final season.

POINTLESS OBSERVATIONS

The Pox network is, of course, a parody of the Fox network.

Mr. Hat beats up Mr. Mackey in this episode. This, along with his daring jailhouse breakout in "Chef Aid" (page 64), offers further evidence that Mr. Hat is his own man.

The New York kids call the boys "queef," and they are pissed that they don't know what it means. Ten seasons later, they find out first-hand in the episode "Eat, Pray, Queef."

CELEBRITIES IMPUGNED

Kenny G, who according to the episode can be hired to deflower middle-aged men. Also Yoko Ono, who is the incomprehensible "special guest conductor" of the 4 Million Child Blow 2000.

Cartman threatens to find the brown noise and make Kyle crap himself "until he looks like Karen Carpenter," lead singer of the popular 70s duo The Carpenters.

WHAT STAN LEARNED

"We were so worried about how cool we looked to those New Yorker kids that we forgot we're already totally cool. Even if we don't know what queef means."

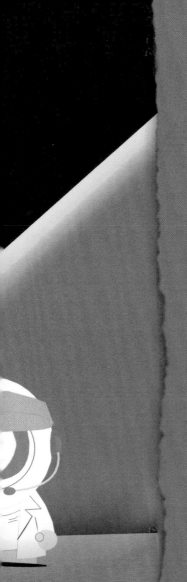

SEASON

4

THE TOOTH FAIRY'S TATS 2000

Original Air Date: April 5, 2000
Episode No. 402

THE STORY: The boys try to make extra cash by rounding up stray teeth and leaving them under Cartman's pillow for the Tooth Fairy. But they leave so many (112, including 15 in one night), that his mom is forced to admit she's the one handing out the money. The news that the Tooth Fairy doesn't exist stuns the boys. Kyle begins to question if *anything*, including himself, is real.

Nevertheless, they soon come up with a new scam—placing teeth under the pillows of other kids, then collecting the money their parents leave. But they soon run afoul of a kid named Loogie who masterminds a shadowy Tooth Fairy syndicate based on the same principle. The boys agree to handle Loogie's South Park operation in exchange for 2 percent of the profits—and not having their penises cut off. Kyle is now consumed by the possibility of infinite alternate realities.

Cartman gets greedy and decides to cut Loogie out and keep all the money. The American Dental Association is on to the Tooth Fairy racket and sets a trap. Cartman, Stan and Kyle show up at the home of a kid with leukemia they saw on TV. The leukemia kid is supposed to get $600 from the Tooth Fairy for a bone marrow transplant. The ADA lies in wait and so do Loogie and his goons. Just as the boys are about to be beaten to a pulp or arrested, Kyle winks out of existence, only to return as an all-powerful being that can bend reality to its will (which, for a moment, is a half-chicken half-squirrel monster). The dentists flee in terror. Loogie's criminal empire is destroyed. Kyle returns to our plane of existence, satisfied that though the thing we call "reality" may be ephemeral, the fact of our consciousness is not.

MEMORABLE LINES

"I don't know why the Tooth Fairy's being so cool to me. Maybe she's hot for me. I don't know."
—*Cartman*

"This is so tits!"
—*Cartman*

"I am nothing and everything!"
—*Kyle*

"Give it up kids. You're surrounded by dentists."
—*Tom Foley, D.D.S*

"Do not open your eyes until morning, or else I will kick you in the nuts. . ."
—*Cartman as the Tooth Fairy*

"No, honey, mommy's gotta save her throat. I have to work tonight."
—*Cartman's mom*

BODY COUNT

Kenny, plus a few random dentists picked off during Kyle's brief transformation into a pan-dimensional deity. Kenny bought it when his feet were encased in cement and he was thrown off a bridge into a river. The water where he landed was only a few inches deep, but when he tried to hop to the shore he stumbled into a much-deeper sinkhole and drowned.

CELEBRITIES IMPUGNED

Kyle, in the midst of his existential crisis, questions whether Dan Rather is real. To which Cartman replies, "No man, that's just a TV show."

When arguing about who's got the better Tooth Fairy outfit, Cartman yells, "It's better than your dress! You look like a bad Jennifer Lopez nightmare!!!" This insult instigates a tooth fairy brawl.

A picture of Hillary Clinton is seen on screen as the newscaster finishes his story: "To which Ms. Clinton replied: 'I don't even like vagina.'"

POINTLESS OBSERVATIONS

This is the first episode in which you can see Kenny without his hood. He is hurled out of his parka by Timmy's wheelchair, and thrown totally naked into the snow. Although his face remains unseen, you get a clear view of his signature blond hair.

Cartman yells at Stan and Kyle to move him "camera left," a reference to stage direction in television and film productions.

This episode features two iconic wardrobes for the boys: Cartman in the Tooth Fairy outfit, and all four boys dressed up as pimp/gangsters.

Cartman calls the bear on his shirt "Willikins Bear" here. He will refer to it mostly as "Wellington Bear" in the future.

During the montage, we see that Timmy was actually part of Loogie's tooth racket long before the boys got involved. He can be seen dressed as a tooth fairy hanging from a string (still in his wheelchair).

CHARACTER DEBUTS

Timmy. Matt and Trey needed an amusing way to extract a tooth from Kenny. What could be funnier than tying a line to the tooth and the other end to the electric wheelchair of a handicapped kid?

Dr. Roberts, Cartman's dentist and the head of the American Dental Association.

Mr. Tom Foley, the person with a real idea of what's going on for the ADA.

Also, Loogie, head of the Tooth Fairy crime syndicate.

POP CULTURE REFERENCE

Kyle's transformation is a parody of the closing sequence of *2001: A Space Odyssey,* and also references the 1982 Pink Floyd movie, *The Wall.*

The boys' motivation for the whole teeth-for-cash racket is buying a Sega Dreamcast. The gaming system had just been released in the U.S. several months earlier.

When the boys go to Cherry Creek (the richest neighborhood in Denver), they sneak into a kid's window that has Mega Man stickers on it. Cartman badly wanted Mega Man toys for his birthday in "Damien" (page 28).

Loogie, the mobster head of the Tooth Fairy syndicate, is based on Marlon Brando's iconic character in *The Godfather.*

BEHIND THE SCENES

Richard Belzer (who voiced Loogie, the kingpin of the Tooth Fairy syndicate) had to be impersonated in one scene because they couldn't get him to come in at 4 a.m. to redo some lines.

A "2000" was added to the title because at the time everyone was doing this sort of thing. Matt and Trey considered attaching 2000s to every fourth-season episode, but the joke ran out of gas after the first four.

ORIGINAL SONGS

In Chef's childhood flashback, we get to hear an eight-year old Chef turn down drugs and instead sing a little tune to his lady friend: "Make Love to You, Amanda."

WHAT KYLE LEARNED

"The basis of all reasoning is the mind's awareness of itself. What we think, the external objects we perceive, are all like actors that come on and off stage. But our consciousness, the stage itself, is always present to us."

FRENCH CULTURE REFERENCE

Though he never mentions the title of the book, it's obvious that Kyle is reading *Meditations on First Philosophy* by Rene Descartes. He paraphrases Descartes' famous statement, "I think, therefore I am," by saying, "This book says I don't exist unless I think I do."

CARTMAN'S SILLY HATE CRIME 2000

Original Air Date: April 12, 2000
Episode No. 401

THE STORY: Cartman beans a classmate named Token on the head with a rock. Unfortunately for him, Token is South Park Elementary's only African American student. Cartman is charged with a hate crime and sent to Alamosa Maximum Security Juvenile Hall. Stan, Kyle, and Kenny are heartsick, because Cartman was supposed to anchor their sled team in a race against a girls' team down Phil Collins Hill. Without the extra speed provided by their associate's enormous bulk, they can't win.

In prison Cartman befriends his cellmate, a hardened con named Romper Stomper. After proving his worth by smuggling contraband into their cell via his rectum, Cartman convinces Romper Stomper to help him escape. The boys make it outside, but are quickly cornered by the police—who inform Cartman that, thanks to an impassioned plea to the governor by his friends, he's been pardoned. No such luck for Romper Stomper, who's dragged back to his cell. Cartman makes it back to South Park just in time to anchor the boys' entry in the sled race, which they win by cheating. Later, after making sure that attacking British people isn't considered a hate crime, Cartman beans Pip with a rock.

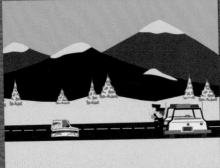

MEMORABLE LINES

"They're gonna put me in jail for a hate crime! You have to take me to Mexico!!"
—*Cartman*

"Why, us men will show those skanky hos who's who!"
—*Butters*

"Hey! I'm not fat, you guys. I'm just kind of big boned!"
—*Clyde*

"I am making an example of you. To send a message out to people everywhere that if you want to hurt another human being, you better make damn sure they're the same color as you are."
—*Judge*

"Why don't you chicks go wash some dishes or get pregnant or something?"
—*Cartman*

"We killed Kenny. We're bastards"
—*Stan*

"What the hell is a hate crime?"
—*Cartman*

"You know something guys? I think we all took Cartman's ass for granted."
—*Stan*

WHERE DID THE IDEA COME FROM?

This show is a statement against hate crime legislation, which Matt and Trey think is silly.

BODY COUNT

Kenny, killed during a sledding accident. Possibly the entire girls' sledding team after they plunge over a cliff. All are shown lying motionless on the ground, and one is actually dragged off by a bear.

CELEBRITIES IMPUGNED

This episode marks the beginning of a sustained assault on Phil Collins, who that year won the Academy Award for Best Song over *Blame Canada* from *South Park: Bigger, Longer & Uncut*. Which didn't go over too well at the *South Park* offices. The relatively tame insults leveled here are just a prelude to what's coming.

POINTLESS OBSERVATIONS

At reform school Cartman is given the prisoner number 24601—the same as Jean Valjean in *Les Miserables*. However the number that's actually on his uniform is 26354—Rick Deckard's (Harrison Ford's) police ID in *Blade Runner*.

According to everyone at school, Clyde is the next fattest kid in South Park after Cartman.

Kyle and Stan both show a surprising proficiency in Pig Latin; they speak it while trying to sneak stuff to Cartman in prison: "Listen Ag-got-Fay! An AIL-NAY ILE-FAY so you can REAK-BAY out of RI-SON-PAY."

Cartman smuggles a Tic-Tac-Throw game in. It's not a real game, but Romper Stomper and his prison clan really seem to like it.

The "Free Eric Cartman Now Committee" is Stan, Token, and Kyle. They give a rather moving and articulate presentation on "Hate Crime Laws: A Savage Hypocrisy." It works.

CHARACTER DEBUTS

Although Token had one line of dialogue in "Tweek vs. Craig" (page 84), this is the first episode where he's a main character. His voice was furnished by the head of *South Park's* Storyboard Department, Adrien Beard, because he was the only black guy in the building at the time. We also meet Token's parents, and see their huge, luxurious home.

Lizzy, a 3rd grade girl who wears a Kenny-esque pink hoodie. She leads the charge against the boys in the sledding competition, and unfortunately, gets taken away by a grizzly bear at the end.

Romper Stomper, Cartman's cellmate in prison, also makes his debut.

WHAT-THE-FUCK MOMENT

During the episode Cartman smuggles contraband to Romper Stomper by hiding it in his butt. After his release he visits his friend in prison and makes his dream of visiting Disneyland come true by pooping out the entire park—mercifully, off-screen.

POP CULTURE REFERENCES

The show is a tour de force of prison movie allusions. The theme from the HBO series *Oz* plays when Cartman enters reform school, and his prison break is lifted from the 1983 film *Bad Boys*. Also, when Cartman tries to escape to Mexico to avoid prison, he does so in Kenny's battery-powered Go-Go Action Bronco—a reference to O.J. Simpson's infamous run for daylight.

TrialTV is a parody of *CourtTV*, a popular law-themed cable channel.

Romper Stomper says there are two kinds of kids in the world: "Kids who like *Animaniacs*, and kids who don't like *Animaniacs*. You're either with us or against us." It's a tough choice, but Cartman chooses that he doesn't like it. Neither do they. *Animaniacs* is a popular Spielberg-produced animated series that ended in 1998.

Romper Stomper—the name of Cartman's cellmate in prison—is also the name of a 1992 film about a neo-Nazi skinhead group in a suburban Australian town, starring Russell Crow.

WHAT CARTMAN LEARNED

"I'm never going to take my friends for granted ever again!" (A moment later he throws a rock at Pip, knocking him unconscious.)

TIMMY 2000

Original Air Date: April 19, 2000
Episode No. 404

THE STORY: A handicapped child named Timmy joins Mr. Garrison's class, where he's quickly diagnosed with Attention Deficit Disorder (ADD), given Ritalin and excused from all homework. The other kids promptly complain that *they* have ADD, and get exactly the same deal.

Meanwhile, a local garage band called Lords of the Underworld (first seen in "Cat Orgy," page 88) struggles to prepare for a battle of the bands contest. The winner will open for Phil Collins at a music festival called Lalapalozoda. Timmy joins the group as the front man. They win the contest and become an overnight sensation—to the horror of Collins, who is soon replaced by Timmy and the Lords of the Underworld as the headliner at Lalapazoola.

Collins manages to break up the band by telling its former leader, Skyler, that the others are holding him back. The South Park kids are on so much Ritalin that they actually think Phil Collins is cool and attend his show. However Chef convinces the town's pharmacists to provide a Ritalin antidote, which he distributes at Lapislazuli. The boys wake up from their drug-induced stupor and boo Collins off the stage. Timmy and the Lords of the Underworld reunite and perform, to the joy of the drug-free (or, at least, Ritalin-free) crowd.

MEMORABLE LINES

"Hey wait . . . I think maybe I have Attention Defunction Disorder!"
—*Kyle*

"Timmy gets all the applause! Timmy gets all the chicks!"
—*Skyler*

"Thanks to you, we have children in our town that like Phil Collins!"
—*Chef*

"Wait a minute! Phil Collins sucks ass!"
—*Stan*

"I can't handle you little bastards being so mellow!"
—*Mr. Garrison*

"No dude, you gotta try it. It makes you feel goooood."
—*Cartman*

"Timmy!"
—*Timmy*

"Timmy! Livin' a lie!"
—*Timmy*

"That does it!! The Ritalin has affected your little cracker brains too deeply!!"
—*Chef*

"Kyle gets so hyper sometimes he runs around and screams like a little eight-year-old."
—*Kyle's mom*

BODY COUNT

Kenny. Cartman spots a "pink Christina Aguilera monster" (an hallucinatory side effect of the Ritalin he's taking) on Kenny's face and hits him with a frying pan.

CHARACTER DEBUTS

Timmy's parents, Richard and Helen. They're also confined to wheelchairs and can only say, respectively, "Richard!" and "Helen!"

ORIGINAL SONGS

Timmy screams his heart out on the rockin' self-titled hit from his band, Timmy and the Lords of the Underworld.

BEHIND THE SCENES

Timmy was an instant hit—and an instant problem. How, exactly, does one write shows about a character who can't speak? Especially when you already have a character (Kenny) with pretty much the same limitation?

WHERE DID THE IDEA COME FROM?

The show is a blast against the overmedication of kids. Isaac Hayes was waaay into this episode because he was a Scientologist, and Scientologists have a big problem with the psychiatric profession's use of mood-altering pharmaceuticals. It was also a chance to showcase Timmy, whom Matt and Trey became infatuated with after his debut in "The Tooth Fairy's Tats 2000" (page 112). The network hated the idea of having a handicapped kid in the show—until Timmy became one of the most popular characters ever.

POP CULTURE REFERENCES

The boys are portrayed as so zonked out on Ritalin that they start watching VH1. The episode isn't much nicer to *MTV News*, called the "cool brainwashing 12-year-old and younger station that hides behind a slick image." Host Kurt Loder is even caught saying, "Why am I still doing this? I've got to be the oldest person on this network by at least 40 years."

The Psychologist tests out children's attention spans by reading them passages from *The Great Gatsby* by F. Scott Fitzgerald and *A Farewell to Arms* by Ernest Hemmingway. Of course, none of the kids pay attention, and they all wind up being prescribed Ritalin.

The Charlie Rose Show (as it is shown here) is an actual show on PBS, where he interviews famous people . . . like Phil Collins.

POINTLESS OBSERVATIONS

The concert Timmy and Phil Collins are supposed to play at is a satire of the '90s phenom Lollapalooza. No one on the show pronounces the name the same way. A banner at the actual event "definitively" spells it as "Lalapalalapaza." Also, Mr. Derp, last seen in "The Succubus" (page 80) serves drinks at a concession stand at the music festival.

During the *MTV News* segment with Kurt Loder, music acts from past *South Park* episodes play on the various TV screens—Ozzy Osbourne, Elton John, and Rick James from "Chef Aid" (page 64); Robert Smith from "Mecha-Streisand" (page 32); and Korn from "Korn's Groovy Pirate Ghost Mystery" (page 94). A poster of Rick James can also be seen as Timmy's band enters the concert hallway.

Chef tries to convince the parents to use a non-drug alternative to Ritalin, a program called "You Can Either Calm Down, Or I Can Pop You in the Mouth Again." Unfortunately, they don't go for it.

CELEBRITIES IMPUGNED

Phil Collins, who is masterfully and comprehensively boned. He talks and sings as if he just sustained a massive stroke; bystanders laugh at him and hurl insults. He is portrayed as a ruthless glory hound, clutching tightly onto his Academy Award at all times (which eventually gets shoved up his ass). Collins also performs two crappy songs: "Boo-Bodio" and "You'll Be in Me," parodies of "Sussudio" and "You'll Be in My Heart."

Christina Aguilera. A photo of her face is attached to the creepy, cockroach-like "Christina Aguilera Monster," which haunts drugged-up Cartman.

WHAT STAN LEARNED

"Yeah sure we laugh at Timmy, but what's wrong with laughter? Just because we laugh at something doesn't mean we don't care about it. Timmy made us smile. And playing made Timmy smile. So where was the harm in that? The people that are wrong are the ones who think that people like Timmy should be protected and kept out of the public's eye. The cool thing about Timmy being in a band was that he was in your face and you had to deal with him, whether you laughed or cried or felt nothing. That's why Timmy rules!"

QUINTUPLETS 2000

Original Air Date: April 26, 2000
Episode No. 403

THE STORY: The boys are forced to watch an extremely artsy, extremely dreary "adult" circus called Cirque du Cheville. The only good part is a group of female Romanian acrobats called the Vladchick Contorting Quintuplets. That night the quints and their grandmother flee the circus and turn up at Stan's house, seeking refuge from Romania. Their grandma makes love to Grandpa Marsh, and then dies from the exertion—leaving Stan's family in charge of the girls.

Their story quickly becomes national news and people from all over the country flock to South Park to see the Quints. The boys charge admission. The boys enlist the quint's help to start their own circus, and tell Kenny he must learn to sing better. He travels to Europe, eventually landing in Romania, where he becomes a famous performer.

When the girls' Romanian father demands their return, Janet Reno, dressed as the Easter Bunny, takes them by force from Stan's home on Easter Sunday. But instead of returning to their homeland, the Quintuplets escape Reno's forces and drive off to do the *Oprah Winfrey Show* where they reveal everyone (including the boys) who attempted to exploit their misfortune and begin a book tour.

Shortly thereafter, Kenny is forcibly removed from Romania during another U.S.-sponsored raid. Not surprisingly, he's killed when an agent's gun goes off by accident.

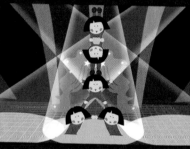

MEMORABLE LINES

"I want to assure you, and the Romanian people, that we are going to do everything in our power to make this all as confusing as possible."
—*Janet Reno*

"Wow, what a great country! Everybody's poor like us!!
—*Kenny's mom*

"We gotta get all the Frenchie-poo fag nasties out of you."
—*Grandpa Marsh*

"Hello Girls! I'm the Easter Bunny!"
—*Janet Reno*

"Close your eyes and cover your ears, Billy! Remember YOU'RE A MAN!!
—*Grandpa Marsh*

"Dammit! How come every time we get a sweet idea, the government has to screw it up!"
—*Kyle*

"We've just got to convince these chicks that America kicks the ass out of every other country."
—*Stan*

"I knew it! They turned you into poofters!
—*Grandpa Marsh*

"Let the quints stay! Romania is gay!"
—*Protesters*

"Yes luckily for them, these quintuplets no longer have to live in Romania, the asshole of the world."
—*Newscaster*

WHERE DID THE IDEA COME FROM?

It's a take on the story of Elian Gonzalez, the Cuban boy brought to Florida by his mother, who perished on the trip. After a long legal battle and public relations war, he was taken at gunpoint by Federal authorities and shipped back to his father in Cuba.

BODY COUNT

Two Romanian agents and two canoe-paddling Native Americans are blown to pieces during the quintuplets daring escape from Cirque du Cheville. Unfortunately, the Quintuplet's Grandmother meets her death after a passionate love-making session with Grandpa Marsh.

A large number of bystanders and army people are killed during the raid on the Marsh home and in subsequent riots. Kenny too.

WHAT-THE-FUCK MOMENT

The agonizing, wrinkle-covered sex scene between Grandpa Marsh and the Quintuplets' Grandmother is an awesomely disturbing sight to behold, especially after we learn that the Grandmother, despite her old age, is still quite the contortionist.

POINTLESS OBSERVATIONS

Kenny and Stan are shown as next-door neighbors—even though it's been stated before (and after) that Kenny lives in a different, poorer part of town. Stan's house also gets blown up here by the government.

The boys charged a $5 admission to see the quints, and for a few more dollars, you could feed them fishsticks. The importance of these breaded, frozen fish snacks will be fully explored in "Fishsticks."

CELEBRITIES IMPUGNED

Janet Reno, who dresses up as the Easter Bunny (an Easter Bunny armed with an automatic rifle and a teargas-filled Easter egg) to infiltrate the Marsh's home and seize the quintuplets.

POP CULTURE REFERENCES

Cirque du Cheville is a parody of the popular *Cirque du Soleil*.

Grandpa Marsh sits Stan down and makes him watch *MacGyver* to "get all the Frenchy poo fag nasties" out of him.

Kenny learns to sing from the book *Singing Like Bocelli For Dummies*; this is a take off on the famous "For Dummies" instructional series. The song he's belting out is "Con Te Partiro," a mumbled version of Bocelli's hit song of the same name. It plays romantically over Grandpa Marsh and the Grandmother's tender love scene.

BEHIND THE SCENES

Just days before the air date, Matt and Trey had the first half of an episode (quintuplets visit South Park) but no back half. Then Elian Gonzalez was taken from his Florida relatives and sent back to Cuba, providing the ending. The show was broadcast just two days after the actual event, causing media critics to gasp at Matt and Trey's ability to produce something so "topical" and "relevant."

WHAT ONE OF THE QUINTUPLETS LEARNED

"You know nothing about Romania and yet you assume America is so much better. Maybe Romania isn't as nice as America, but it is our home. You can all kiss our little white Romanian asses!"

CARTMAN JOINS NAMBLA

Original Air Date: June 21, 2000
Episode No. 406

THE STORY: Cartman decides he wants more mature friends and starts trolling for older male buddies on the Internet. He's soon involved with one prospective child molester after another—each of whom is arrested by the FBI shortly after they meet with him. Still friendless, Cartman consults with Dr. Mephesto, who tells him he's a perfect fit for an organization he belongs to—North American Marlon Brando Look Alikes.

Kenny faces an even more pressing crisis: His parents want to have another baby. Kenny does everything in his power to prevent the pregnancy. He shatters his father's testicles with a well-placed baseball; mixes up a "special" cocktail for his mom made mostly of abortion pills and vodka (which his father mistakenly drinks, triggering a legendary bout of vomiting and diarrhea); and attempts to induce a miscarriage by taking his parents on a super-violent carnival ride called The John Denver Experience. Nothing, however, derails the dreaded sibling-to-be.

Meanwhile, Cartman indeed joins NAMBLA—only it's the other NAMBLA, the North American Man Boy Love Association. The child molesters couldn't be happier about this, and encourage him to get his friends to sign up. Soon Cartman and they boys are all together at a mixer at a local hotel. The boys flee when they finally figure out what's going on. They're pursued by the NAMBLA members, who are in turn chased by the FBI and the members of the North American Marlon Brando Look Alikes, eager to kick the molesters' asses for tarnishing the Brandos' good name. The members of the bad NAMBLA are finally rounded up and carted away. But not before gang-raping Kenny's dad.

Kenny is run over by the ambulance that takes his father to the hospital. Soon afterward his new little brother is born. Not surprisingly he's also named Kenny and seems to have emerged from the womb wearing a tiny orange parka.

MEMORABLE LINES

"God dammit, poor people suck!"
—*Cartman*

"Sorry, I'm not interested in being friends with midgets. Midgets piss me off."
—*Cartman*

"That hits the spot. Makes me forget all about my shattered balls."
—*Kenny's dad*

"Dude! I think these guys mean to have sexual encounters with us!"
—*Stan*

"I got into NAAA-MBLA! And you guys did-n't!"
—*Cartman*

"Alright, alright, I'm sorry I almost got you guys all raped. There."
—*Cartman*

"Why the hell does the FBI keep arresting all my friends?"
—*Cartman*

"You mean you expect me to go out there and let all those horny old men have their way with my fragile person?!"
—*Butters*

BODY COUNT

Kenny, run over by the ambulance that takes his dad away to the hospital after he's gang raped by NAMBLA members.

WHERE DID THE IDEA COME FROM?

The concept was born during a horrific writer's retreat on a bargain-basement cruise to Ensenada, Mexico. The trip, the food, the drinks, and Ensenada all sucked, but at least they got this episode idea out of it.

POP CULTURE REFERENCES

In an attempt to get his mother to miscarry, Kenny talks his parents into riding a theme park attraction called The John Denver Experience. It's a recreation of a plane crash at sea, which is how the real John Denver died.

Cartman's first internet friend, Tony, brings him a couple books of *Kama Sutra*, the ancient Indian guide to unleashing your sexual powers. Chef says he met his would-be wife while reading the same book in "The Succubus" (page 80).

The other NAMBLA—The North American Marlon Brando Look Alikes—is full of people that . . . look like the famous actor Marlon Brando.

POINTLESS OBSERVATIONS

While playing the "Investigative Reports with Bill Curtis" board game, Cartman gives Kyle an "AIDS" card. Cartman actually gives Kyle AIDS in "Tonsil Trouble."

There's a picture of Bill Clinton and Cartman hanging above Cartman's computer.

Garrison has a Freudian slip here, pleading, "I did not want love from a young boy! I like men my own age! AGH! I mean—I like women!!" A few episodes later, he will finally admit to his gayness in "Fourth Grade" (page 132).

Kenny makes his famous "abortion cocktail" for his mother—consisting of vodka, cocoa, and a whole lot of "Pregnant No More" abortion pills. Unfortunately, his dad drinks it. This leads to an equally famous poop-and-puke session by Kenny's father.

After Kenny is killed and a baby Kenny is born, his Dad says, "God, this must be the fiftieth time this has happened." Kenny's Mom corrects him, "Fifty-second." It was indeed the 52nd time Kenny had been killed.

CHARACTER DEBUTS

An important subplot concerns Kenny's attempt to prevent his parents from having another child—an attempt that ultimately fails. The baby is born after Kenny's death, and is named Kenny. He appears to be a reincarnation of his deceased brother, right town to his tiny orange parka.

CELEBRITIES IMPUGNED

At the beginning of the show the boys play the "Investigative Reports with Bill Curtis" board game. (Trey is actually a big fan of Bill Curtis.)

WHAT THE CHILD MOLESTER FROM NAMBLA LEARNED

"Our forefathers came to this country because they believed in an idea. An idea called freedom. They wanted to live in a place where a group couldn't be prosecuted for their beliefs. Where a person can live the way he chooses to live. You see us as being perverted because we're different from you. People are afraid of us because they don't understand. And sometimes it's easier to persecute than to understand. We are human. Most of us didn't even choose to be attracted to young boys. We were born that way. We can't help the way we are, and if you can't understand that, well, then, I guess you'll just have to put us away."

121

CHEROKEE HAIR TAMPONS

Original Air Date: June 28, 2000
Episode No. 407

THE STORY: Kyle is deathly ill and needs a new kidney. His mother insists upon treating his condition using New Age medicine, which she learns about at a new holistic healing shop run by a woman named, Miss Information. Miss Information gets many of her products from two "Native American" men named Carlos Ramirez and Chief Running Pinto (played by Cheech and Chong). Their offerings include the episode's namesake, Cherokee Hair Tampons.

Meanwhile, Mr. Garrison (thanks to his escapades in "Cartman Joins NAMBLA," page 120), has lost his teaching job. He decides to try his hand at writing a romance novel, but an editor at Harlequin states that it's a bit too "gay" for his mostly female audience, since it includes 6,083 references to penises.

Cartman, it turns out, is the town's only viable kidney donor for Kyle, but he refuses to give one unless he gets $10 million. Undaunted, Stan tries to cut a kidney out of Cartman while he sleeps, but is thwarted by a protective device he wears called a Kidney Blocker 2000.

Kyle gets worse, so his mother takes him to Miss Information's store for a consultation with Carlos Ramirez and Chief Running Pinto. The men, aghast at the boy's condition, tell her to take him to a hospital—and further admit that they're Mexican rather than Native American. Kyle gets a kidney from Cartman, who is conned into surrendering one. Mr. Garrison's novel, called *In The Valley of Penises*, is published to great acclaim.

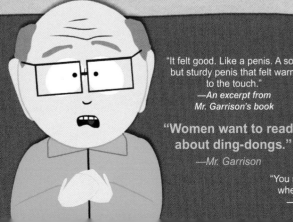

MEMORABLE LINES

"It felt good. Like a penis. A soft, but sturdy penis that felt warm to the touch."
—*An excerpt from Mr. Garrison's book*

"Women want to read about ding-dongs."
—*Mr. Garrison*

"You never care when I die!!"
—*Kenny*

"I just think that taking a woman home and getting some hot poon is about the greatest thing in the world."
—*Mr. Garrison*

"Cartman you are SO going to Hell when you die."
—*Stan*

"Let the wonders and the mysteries of our people, like, change the way you think about tampons."
—*Tommy Chong*

"This is what we in the book publishing business like to call . . . Gay. Really, REALLY gay."
—*Book Publisher*

"I hope it's not too bloody, I'm wearing my favorite pants."
—*Butters*

BODY COUNT

Miss Information, beaten to death by her customers when they learn that Cheech & Chong are Mexicans, rather than Native Americans. And Kenny. A piano drops on his head as he walks away in disgust from Stan, who is crying over Kyle's impending death—something he's never bothered to do during Kenny's endless demises.

WHERE DID THE IDEA COME FROM?

It was a dig on New Age medicine inspired by one of South Park's writers, who announced that she was ridding her body of "toxins" by consuming cayenne pepper and lemon juice. However she couldn't explain what those "toxins" might be, or how cayenne pepper and lemon juice helped.

POP CULTURE REFERENCES

Cartman, when asked if he'll donate a kidney to Kyle, breaks into a joyous song that's just a series of 'No's.' The melody is taken from *Comedy Tonight,* a tune from the musical *A Funny Thing Happened on the Way to the Forum.*

This episode features a live-action commercial for "Cherokee Hair Tampons." Within the commercial, a bloody scene from *The Shining* is referenced.

A townsperson seeks holistic healing from Miss Information's shop, complaining of "a bit of pain in my balls whenever I watch VH1."

POINTLESS OBSERVATIONS

Appearing on *South Park* was the first thing Cheech & Chong had done together in years. Also, this is the first time Cartman's pig Fluffy is seen since "An Elephant Makes Love To A Pig" (page 18).

When Mr. Garrison is told by the school board that he must take a hiatus from teaching, he takes out his "gun and badge" and puts it on the table. This is an homage to what typically happens to people "kicked off the force" in cop dramas.

We learn a bunch of medical stuff about the boys: Kyle is diabetic; Kyle and Cartman are blood type AB Negative (the only two in South Park); and when Cartman laughs too hard, milk shoots out of his nose . . . even if he's not drinking milk. Later, he says it's due to his "crappy kidney," which Kyle winds up getting.

There's a picture of Mr. Garrison's parents hanging in his bedroom. We meet them in "World Wide Recorder Concert" (page 108). In Cartman's hallway, there's a picture of his Grandparents and his cousin Elvin, who are introduced in "Merry Christmas Charlie Manson" (page 68).

Mr. Garrison's penname is Ethan F. Garrison (even though his first name is Herbert); he uses it for his bestselling novel *In the Valley of Penises.*

CHARACTER DEBUTS

Mr. Wyland, the substitute teacher who replaces Mr. Garrison.

Miss Information, an older hippie woman who runs the New Age store.

Chief Running Pinto and Carlos Ramirez, the two "Native Americans" that peddle their goods to Miss Information's store.

WHAT CHIEF RUNNING PINTO LEARNED
"Being in touch with the earth has nothing to do with dying, man."

CHEF GOES NANNERS

Original Air Date: July 5, 2000
Episode No. 408

THE STORY: Chef is pissed about South Park's flag—which prominently features several white stick figures "lynching" a black-looking stick figure—and starts a movement to have it changed. South Park Elementary stages a debate on the issue, with Stan and Kyle on the "keep the flag" team and Cartman on the "change the flag" side. Chef is crushed that the boys would take up for the existing flag.

As the controversy mounts, the debate is turned into a public referendum on how to handle the issue. While conducting research for her team, Wendy finds herself strangely attracted to Cartman (who joined her group just to make her mad). She shares this with a horrified Bebe, who tells her she must do the unthinkable—kiss Cartman to break the sexual tension. This she does, in front of the entire town, during the flag debate.

When the pro-flag team gives its presentation, Chef suddenly realizes that the Stan and Kyle and their friends don't grasp the fact that the people on the flag are different colors, they see them as all the same.

Shortly after, a new South Park flag is unveiled. It's still several stick figures hanging another stick figure, but now their makeup is multiracial and they're all holding hands. Wendy tells Cartman she's relieved that the sexual tension between them is resolved, and that she now feels nothing for him. Cartman laughs it off, then walks away dejectedly.

SOUTH PARK

CHEF

MEMORABLE LINES

"This whole cracker-ass town can kiss my ass!"
—*Chef*

"Last week we decided that we hate blacks and Jews. A LOT."
—*Klan Member*

"Whoaaa, calm down, ho."
—*Cartman*

"All animals kill, and the animals that don't kill are stupid ones like cows and turtles and stuff."
—*Kyle*

"I'm sorry, Chef. Mr. Hat is a racist bastard."
—*Mr. Garrison*

"I never thought I'd have anything in common with you, Cartman."
—*Wendy*

"I'm attracted to Cartman."
—*Wendy*

"Hot shower! Hot shower! Hot shower!"
—*Ku Klux Klan members*

BODY COUNT

Kenny, who meets a truly spectacular end, even by *South Park* standards. After ingesting a pile of antacid tablets (which he mistakes for mints) he drinks a glass of water and explodes. In fact, it's so good, the boys don't even say their famous "You killed Kenny" line; they all just laugh.

Also a Buddhist monk, whom Chef sets on fire as part of his flag protest. During Jimbo and Ned's heart-to-heart with the kids, they gun down a squirrel and a bird (and almost Chris Peterson).

POINTLESS OBSERVATIONS

There's a drawing of Cartman's pig, Fluffy, and Stan's dog, Sparky, on the back wall in Mr. Garrison's classroom.

There have been three class debates prior to this one—"Pro-Choice vs. Cartman," "Pro-Gun Control vs. Cartman," and "People Against the Clubbing of Baby Seals vs. Cartman." Cartman has won them all.

Mr. Hat is in the Ku Klux Klan. Although Mr. Garrison shuns Mr. Hat's racism here, Garrison himself will lead a cloaked charge against Richers in "Here Comes the Neighborhood" (page 170).

DoubleStuff cookies are both Wendy and Cartman's favorite treats.

In Wendy's "nightmare," Cartman is shirtless, riding a white stallion; then the two of them roll around lustfully in a green meadow. It's not quite the same picture in "Breast Cancer Show Ever," where Wendy kicks the shit out of him.

WHERE DID THE IDEA COME FROM?

It was based on a big controversy over whether the state of South Carolina should change its flag, which looks uncomfortably like the old Confederate flag.

BEHIND THE SCENES

The episode was thrown together in an even bigger hurry than usual, because the staff wanted to get out of the office for the Fourth of July weekend.

POP CULTURE REFERENCES

Chef briefly converts to Islam and changes his name to Abdul Mohammed Jabar Rauf Kareem Ali.

While protesting before the Mayor, Chef holds up an actual photo of a monk setting himself on fire—this is the famous, Pulitzer Prize-winning picture of a Buddhist monk performing "self-immolation," or suicide by fire. Part of this picture was used in Rage Against the Machine's self-titled debut album.

Wendy has a poster of Russell Crowe in her bathroom. His head briefly morphs into Cartman's head, which causes her to scream in horror.

When the Klan members dance and play "Who's Got The Silliest Thing On Under Their Robe," an upbeat version of "If You're Happy and You Know It" plays on the organ

WHAT CHEF LEARNED

"All this time I thought those little crackers had turned racist, when actually they were so not racist that they didn't even make a separation of black and white to begin with. All they saw when they looked at that flag was five people."

CHEF

SOMETHING YOU CAN DO WITH YOUR FINGER

Original Air Date: July 12, 2000
Episode No. 409

THE STORY: Cartman, inspired by a dream, believes God wants him to form a boy band and earn $10 million. He quickly puts together a group called "Fingerbang," composed of himself, Kyle, Stan, Kenny and Wendy (who gets in because she can actually sing). Stan's dad becomes furious when he learns of the scheme.

The group puts together their own music video, and uses it to land a gig at the South Park Mall (even though Timmy, the cameraman, captured almost none of their performance). Stan's dad refuses to let his son go, finally revealing that as a kid he was in a world-famous boy band called the "Ghetto Avenue Boys." He enjoyed fame and fortune, only to be abandoned at age 19 when he became "too old." Penniless, he slinked back to South Park and started his life over.

In spite of this, he relents at the last moment and drives Stan to the mall for the Fingerbang show. When Kenny is crushed by an escalator, Stan's dad even steps in as the group's fifth member. Their performance draws tepid applause and earns them $2—after which the boys decide they can't handle celebrity life and elect to sink back into happy obscurity.

MEMORABLE LINES

"Move along, sir."
—*Mall Cop*

"God has finally spoken to me, you guys. And he has told me how I can make $10 million."
—*Cartman*

"I'm gonna fingerbang-bang you into my life."
—*Fingerbang*

"I swear to God, if he ruins this dream of mine I will have his nuts!"
—*Cartman*

"What about her huge friggin' hooters, huh?!"
—*Cartman*

"Well there's plenty of other interesting things you can do. Have you ever tried marijuana?"
—*Randy*

"Once you get girls screaming, you can't sop 'em. They're crazy!"
—*Chef*

"Hell no! I'm not being part of a FOUR member boy band! We'll look stupid!"
—*Kyle*

BODY COUNT
Just Kenny.

BEHIND THE SCENES
This was the first episode in which Matt and Trey decided they could just tell one story per episode, instead of weaving in multiple sub-plots.

POINTLESS OBSERVATIONS
Chef attributes the success of boy bands to canny exploitation of the "Garmlich Effect," a law of physics stating that, "If one girl screams for something, it will make other girls scream. And then, it grows exponentially until all girls within a five-mile radius are screaming." Also, this is the first of a long series of episodes in which Cartman develops various crazy schemes for getting $10 million.

Butters auditions with "Little Bunny Foo Foo," a classic children's rhyme, and Ike follows suit with "It's Bitsy Spider," then the alphabet. Last, Ike sings "Oh Danny Boy," a somber Irish ballad.

Cartman records his "music video" over an old VHS . . . of Mr. Mackey and Cartman's mom in some seriously compromising dominatrix positions. Mackey moans, "Oh, Mrs. Cartman, I've been very bad. Mkay," and then things just get . . . dirty.

Randy's teenage boy band, The Ghetto Avenue Boys, was featured on the cover of *Teen Heat*, a teeny-bopper magazine.

CELEBRITIES IMPUGNED
When Fingerbang approaches the manager of the South Park Mall about performing there, he responds by saying, "Like Tiffany?" Also, during the filming of Fingerbang's video, when Cartman tells a group of girls to scream as if they're seeing Leonardo Di Caprio, they say they don't give a "rat's ass" about him. Instead they pretend they're cheering for Matt Lauer.

WHERE DID THE IDEA COME FROM?
In college Matt and Trey briefly (very briefly) considered forming a band called Fingerbang.

POP CULTURE REFERENCES
The scene in which Stan's dad smashes the china cabinet is an homage to a similar scene in *Star Trek: First Contact*, in which Jean Luc Piccard smashes a display case with a phaser rifle. Also, the piano player used for the auditions for the fifth member of Fingerbang looks a lot like Schroeder from *Peanuts*. He'll reappear briefly (playing piano) in several future episodes.

Fingerbang is a parody of the boy band craze that swept the nation in the late 90s—'N Sync, Backstreet Boys, and 98 Degrees all had chart-topping success when this aired. Stan's dad also speaks about the dark side of boy bands, saying that after their popularity fades, bands like New Kids on the Block and The Osmonds "wander the Earth in disarray."

To create a distraction, Cartman says the mall will be giving away a "free Nissan Sentra" to the first 20 people to buy an orange smoothie. This titillating offer creates a riot.

ORIGINAL SONGS
Wendy wins her audition with her rhyming, upbeat "Mrs. Landers."

There's also the amazing self-titled pop tune, "Fingerbang," performed by the boys. And Randy's pop sensation "You've Got IT," which he recorded as a teen with the Ghetto Avenue Boys.

WHAT CARTMAN LEARNED
"I don't know if I can handle all this fame. I mean, I always thought I'd wanna become famous, but now that I am, I don't know if I like it. I mean, I probably can't even walk through this mall right now without people goin', 'Oh my God, it's the Fingerbang guy! Oh my God!'"

127

DO THE HANDICAPPED GO TO HELL?

Original Air Date: July 19, 2000
Episode No. 410

THE STORY: The boys start taking Sunday school classes after Father Maxi tells them they risk Hell if they don't show up. But their lessons (about confessing their sins and eating the body and blood of Christ) only confuse them. They're also horrified that Timmy can't get into heaven because he's physically unable to confess his sins, and that Kyle won't be allowed in because he's Jewish.

Meanwhile, in Hell itself, Satan is horrified when his ex-lover, Saddam Hussein, returns to disrupt his relationship with his current flame, Chris. The three have a very uncomfortable dinner together, after which Saddam gives Satan his hotel key. Later that evening Satan, torn, stands in front of Saddam's hotel, wondering if he should go in or go home.

Back on earth, the boys rush to church to confess their sins. Kenny is run over by a bus when they cross the street. Terrified that the same fate will be theirs, they arrive at the church and open the confessional only to discover Father Maxi having sex with a woman.

The boys, disillusioned, decide they must take their salvation into their own hands. Cartman becomes a street corner preacher, offering his brand of spirituality to a growing crowd of frightened children.

MEMORABLE LINES

"Jesus wanted us to eat him, but he didn't want us to be cannibals, so he turned himself into crackers and then told people to eat him."
—Stan

"It's a man's obligation to stick his boneration in a woman's separation; this sort of penetration will increase the population of the younger generation."
—Cartman

"Dude, if THIS guy's going to hell, who's gonna save US?!"—Stan

"Oh this guy is SO gonna burn!!"
—Cartman to Father Maxi

"And then this other time . . . I went pee-pee in the Holy Water thing."
—Cartman

"I can't whistle if I eat too many crackers."—Butters

"Yeah, you killed me. So? Where was I gonna go? Detroit?"
—Saddam Hussein

"Satan, that guy is a pussy."
—Saddam

"Screw him! He can't pound your ass like I can!!"
—Saddam

"The guys said that if I don't confess my sins and eat crackers I'm gonna go to hell!"
—Kyle

"No, Chris. You don't understand. Saddam is fucking crazy."
—Satan

BODY COUNT

Kenny gets run over by a bus, but doesn't die. More about that in "Probably" (page 130).

Satan also kills a few demons in an angry rage, but they're probably dead already.

POINTLESS OBSERVATION

Satan owns a collection of Hummel figures.

In his office, Priest Maxi's inbox and outbox are labeled "The Lord Giveth" and "The Lord Taketh."

Cartman baptizes Kyle, Ike, and Timmy with a garden hose (then with a "Wacky Water Weasel"). Shortly after, Cartman and the boys form Kids Against Hell, a religious organization that offers salvation to kids.

CELEBRITIES IMPUGNED

The roster of famous people in hell includes film critic Gene Siskel, George Burns, Frank Sinatra, Dean Martin, Bob Hope, Mao Tse Tung, Jerry Garcia, John F. Kennedy, JFK Jr., Princess Diana, Jeffrey Dahmer, Allen Ginsberg, Michael Landon, Hitler, Tiny Tim and Walter Matthau. Also Conan O'Brien, who isn't dead yet.

CHARACTER DEBUTS

Chris, Satan's kind-hearted, push-over boyfriend. They live together in their River Styx Marina Condominium.

Sister Anne, a kind nun that works at Father Maxi's Church.

We also briefly meet the Pope, who is very, very old.

WHERE DID THE IDEA COME FROM?

Matt and Trey were always intrigued by the idea that, if you strictly interpret the New Testament, babies go to Hell because they lack the mental faculties to accept Jesus. Also, they wanted to feature Satan and Saddam, who hadn't been seen since *South Park: Bigger, Longer & Uncut*. This is the first episode of a two-parter, which concludes with "Probably" (Page 130).

ORIGINAL SONGS

It's Luau Sunday in Hell, and we get the pleasure of dancing along to the Caribbean-themed "Hookie-lau."

POP CULTURE REFERENCES

Ike is reading *Cannery Row* by John Steinbeck—his second Steinbeck novel of the day. Pretty impressive for a 3-year-old.

WHAT CARTMAN LEARNED

"Well, it looks like we're gonna have to save Timmy, Kyle, and everyone else in this town from the angry hand of God ourselves!"

PROBABLY

Original Air Date: July 26, 2000
Episode No. 411

THE STORY: Cartman, disillusioned by events in "Do the Handicapped Go To Hell?" becomes a preacher. Meanwhile, in Hell, Satan has a wild night of sex with his former lover, Saddam Hussein.

Kenny, who was previously struck by a bus, wasn't killed. Instead he'd been dragged all the way to Ensenada, Mexico, where he phones home for help. Cartman takes the call, believing that Kenny is contacting him from beyond the grave. The next day he describes Hell to his followers as a place where "everyone speaks Spanish," and if you drink the water you "pee blood out your ass for seven hours."

A few days later, Stan and Kyle find Cartman rolling around in a vat of $1 bills collected from his followers. He reveals that his "conversion" is just his latest effort to get $10 million. It unravels when Jesus makes an unscheduled appearance at Cartman's church and tells his followers they should live good lives instead of living in fear.

At the same time, Satan goes to heaven to ask God for relationship advice. The Supreme Being calls him a "whiney little bitch" and says he should ditch both his lovers. Saddam is kicked to the curb forever when God agrees to take him into heaven—a place populated with Mormons. As for Cartman, Jesus dispatches him not to Hell, but to someplace worse—Ensenada.

MEMORABLE LINES

"It's time to stop preaching damnation to everyone, sweetie."
—*Cartman's mom*

"Satan, I'm a nineties man. I cry when I need to, I share my feelings, and I keep my mind open about everything."
—*Chris*

"Right here we have a little girl who's very, very ugly. Do you believe he's going to cure your face of the uglies?"
—*Cartman*

"My brain is of a much larger size than you guys's. I couldn't expect you to understand, not until you actually saw the cash flow."
—*Cartman*

"Man, look at that! We went through 14 bottles of vegetable oil!"
—*Saddam Hussein*

"Do not think that you can tempt us with toys and games and powdered donut pancake surprise!"
—*Cartman*

"Right now, all the Jewness is coming out of your body, and being replaced by the spirit of God-a!"
—*Cartman*

WHERE DID THE IDEA COME FROM?

This is the back end of a two-parter. It was split into two episodes at the last minute when Matt and Trey realized they simply had too much material to squeeze into one show.

BODY COUNT

None. Chris and Saddam repeatedly "kill" each other as they battle for Satan's affections. But since they're already dead, none of it really counts. They just resurrect and go at it again. Even Kenny (who everyone thinks is in Hell, but is really in Mexico) survives.

POINTLESS OBSERVATIONS

Among the numerous sex toys strewn about Saddam's hotel room after his night with Satan is an Antonio Banderas blowup doll.

In addition to Powdered Donut Pancake Surprise (a dish she last made in "Cartman Gets an Anal Probe" (page 10)), Cartman's mom has all the boys' favorite toys out—Terrance and Phillip, Chinpoko Mon, Polly Prissypants, Petey the Panda, Mega Man, and everything else. But their love for God is stronger than the temptation of toys.

Timmy walks in this episode . . . very, very briefly.

At the end of this episode, Saddam Hussein is banished to heaven, where he must live with the Mormons. The next time we see him (in "A Ladder to Heaven"), he's building Weapons of Mass Destruction. In Heaven. With the Mormons working for him.

WHAT-THE-FUCK MOMENT

In the *South Park* universe, Mormons are the only people who get into heaven. Yet God Himself professes to be Buddhist.

POP CULTURE REFERENCES

In the midst of the "previously" recap at the start of the episode, there's a brief reference to the famous Happy Days episode in which Fonzie jumps over a shark on water skis. Only in this version he doesn't make it and the shark eats him.

Cartman's over-the-top sermon style is a rip on televangelists who populate television and thrive on monetary donations from viewers.

WHAT JESUS TAUGHT US

"God doesn't want you to spend all your time being afraid of hell, or praising his name. God wants you to spend your time helping others, and living a good, happy life. That's how you live for him."

FOURTH GRADE

Original Air Date: November 8, 2000

Episode No. 412

THE STORY: Freaked out by all the demands that go along with now being in the fourth grade, the boys enlist the help of two college kids (and *Star Trek* nuts) to transport them back to the third grade. To do this, the nerds rig a time machine out of Timmy's wheelchair. The class is set to be transported back to happier times, but instead of opening a time portal it simply takes off at high speed—with Timmy on it. After they discover Timmy's chair will explode if his speed drops below 5 mph, the kids run after Timmy to try to help him.

It's the last straw for the boys' new teacher, Ms. Choksondik. She seeks out how to handle the students from Mr. Garrison, who now lives as a hermit in the mountains. In the process of teaching her how to cope, he has a mystical encounter that helps him to finally accept the fact that he's gay.

In the meantime the police manage to disarm the explosive potential of Timmy's wheelchair, which then actually becomes a working time machine and hurtles him into the past. The class has the *Star Trek* nerds open another time doorway, but Ms. Choksondik prevents their departure by telling them that life is about going forward, not reliving the past.

The time portal belches out Timmy before it closes. He's obviously been all over history, but of course can't say a word about his travels. Mr. Garrison comes down from the mountains, admits to Principal Victoria that he's gay and asks for his job back. He's told the school doesn't hire gay people.

MEMORABLE LINES

"Maybe we can stand like this with our wieners pokin' through the back of our legs ya know, and give her a nice fruit bowl."
—*Butters*

"I don't want to do it if it hurts or if it makes you get all sticky."
—*Butters*

"Suck my balls."
—*Cartman*

"We need to stand up to this new teacher and insert ourselves."—*Stan*

"I'm as gay as a gymnast on shore leave!"
—*Mr. Garrison*

"Oh weak, you guys . . . seriously, weak."
—*Cartman*

"You work and you work for the children and then people start rumors that you're gay even though you love poontang!"
—*Mr. Garrison*

"When a child says 'Suck my balls', you say . . . 'Present them.' "
—*Mr. Garrison*

"You see, Chef, Ms. Choksondik has very large . . . honkers. And she doesn't seem to like wearing a bra."
—*Mr. Mackey*

BODY COUNT

Kenny, dragged to his death while trying to deactivate Timmy's runaway chair. The wheeled cart that he uses to try to effect a rescue is an homage to the one used by Keanu Reeves in *Speed*. After he's killed, Stan simply says, "Who didn't see that coming?"

WHERE DID THE IDEA COME FROM?

Matt and Trey decided to move the boys into fourth grade because it was "just something to do."

POINTLESS OBSERVATIONS

The two nerds who build the time machine argue ceaselessly about how many episodes of the original *Stark Trek* series were filmed—73 or 72. Both are incorrect. There are 79 total episodes.

For their entry into 4th grade, Parker and Stone introduced a totally redone, high-energy, technology-infused opening to the show, complete with Timmy.

Inside the Tree of Insight, Mr. Garrison finally comes face to face with his gay side. From this point forward, he embraces his true self . . . until he gets a vaginoplasty and becomes a woman in "Mr. Garrison's Fancy New Vagina."

CHARACTER DEBUTS

Ms. Choksondik. The boys, somehow missing her name's double entendre, insist on referring to her as "Ms. Makes-me-sick." Every time she lifts her arms, a couple of inches of her enormous, grotesque breasts poke out from the bottom of her shirt. Because of this, little kittens start following her around.

We are also introduced to two *Star Trek* Geeks, who actually are able to build a time machine.

POP CULTURE REFERENCES

Mr. Garrison's novel, *In The Valley of Penises*, is hailed as the greatest homoerotic novel since *Huckleberry Finn*. Also, Cartman says "Ah Ha! Charade you are, teacher!" to Ms. Choksondik, it's his second use of the phrase, which comes from the Pink Floyd song *Pigs (Three Different Ones)*. The first reference was in "Cat Orgy" (page 88). Finally, when Mr. Garrison shouts, "Damn you spirit, haunt me no longer!" he's referencing a line from Dickens' *A Christmas Carol*.

The *Star Trek* Geeks who help the boys time travel are constantly referencing various *Star Trek* quotes and plot lines. Most notably, the line on their shirt reads: "Resistance is futile," a popular catchphrase used by the Borg in the TV show. They also argue over *Battlestar Galactica*, and eventually start a fistfight over it.

Mr. Garrison's ninja-esque teaching of Ms. Choksondik is a nod to Kung Fu movies.

ORIGINAL SONGS

Cartman sings the tearful, heartfelt piano ode to "3rd Grade," which winds up making Clyde cry.

WHAT MS. CHOKSONDIK LEARNED

"Life isn't about going back, it's about going forward. Yes, there are times in our lives that we wish we could relive, but, if we've already lived them perfectly, why live them again? The adventure of life is that there's always something new, new challenges, new experiences. A fun game is a game that gets harder as it goes, so it is with life."

133

TRAPPER KEEPER

Original Air Date: November 15, 2000
Episode No. 413

THE STORY: A grown man who calls himself Bill Cosby shows up on the kids' bus, claiming to be a fourth grader. He shows unusual interest in Cartman's new Dawson's Creek Trapper Keeper Ultra Keeper Futura 2000. It turns out he's really a robot from the future, sent back in time to destroy the Trapper Keeper, which will (thanks to its ability to fuse with other electronic systems) take over the world's computers and launch a war of extermination against humanity.

Cartman reluctantly allows his Trapper Keeper to be destroyed, but then gets his mother to buy another one. It promptly merges with Cartman and becomes a grotesque human/robot hybrid bent on controlling the world. Kyle enters the creature and tries to disable its CPU. He gets some unlikely assistance from Rosie O'Donnell, who makes the creature ill when it consumes her. Kyle manages to deactivate the Trapper Keeper, which disintegrates into a mound of goo. Rosie O'Donnell dies, as does the robot Bill Cosby, who winks out of existence when the timeline changes. Cartman, not surprisingly, survives.

MEMORABLE LINES

"Dude, you can't just ask to be somebody's friend and be their friend. It doesn't work that way. If you want to be my friend, you'll have to pay me."
—Cartman

"Kiss your ass goodbye, fat boy!"
—Stan

"I pooped my pants."
—Ike

"Ooh. Bad pie. Bad pie."
—Trapper Keeper

"So what are you going to do with your crappy robot life now, Bill Cosby?"
—Stan

"Oh Jesus tap dancing Christ."
—Mr. Garrison

"Damn. I thought 4th grade was gonna be different."
—Kyle

"Do you want my heart as well?! You'll find it on the bottom of your shoes."
—Cartman

"Mrs. Crabtree! There's another creepy homeless guy on the bus!"
—Stan

WHERE DID THE IDEA COME FROM?

The show's subplot, in which Ike runs for kindergarten class president, is a commentary on the contested 2000 presidential election. Everything comes down to a girl named Flora, whose ballot is so illegible that Mr. Garrison can't make out who she voted for. "Flora" sounds an awful lot like "Florida."

BODY COUNT

Kenny, smashed against a wall by the Trapper Keeper.

Also Rosie O'Donnell and a guard at the military base are eaten alive by the carnivorous Trapper Keeper monster.

CELEBRITIES IMPUGNED

Rosie O'Donnell, who plays the aunt of Filmore, the kid running against Ike for kindergarten class president. Onlookers repeatedly confuse her with the hideously fleshy and bulbous Cartman/Trapper Keeper hybrid. Also, during the class president controversy Jesse Jackson briefly appears, then just as quickly vanishes when informed that no African American children were involved.

Bill Cosby. His name is adopted by the humanoid robot from the future.

POINTLESS OBSERVATIONS

We saw Ike reading Steinbeck novels in "Do The Handicapped Go to Hell?" (page 128), but we learn here that he's truly "some kind of genius."

When Bill Cosby asks to be his friend, Cartman responds, "I'm not supposed to have male friends that are over thirty. I kind of got screwed on that once." He's referring to when he unwittingly became a poster child for the North American Man Boy Love Association in "Cartman Joins NAMBLA" (page 120).

It's the second time Cartman's house has been destroyed by alien life forms. The first being by Starvin' Marvin's space ship in "Starvin' Marvin in Space" (page 100).

A few episodes earlier, Cartman saves Kyle's life with a kidney transplant in "Cherokee Hair Tampons" (page 122). Here, Kyle returns the favor by saving Cartman's life.

CHARACTER DEBUTS

We meet Mr. Garrison's entire kindergarten class, who appear in several future episodes including "The Wacky Molestation Adventure" (page 142), "Proper Condom Use" (page 160), and "It Hits the Fan" (page 148).

Prominent in this episode is: Filmore, the black-haired kid running against Ike for class president; his friend Quake; and Jenny, the black-haired girl in suspenders.

POP CULTURE REFERENCES

The hideous Cartman/Trapper Keeper hybrid is an homage to a similar biomechanical creature in the Japanese anime classic Akira. Also Kyle's attempt to deactivate the hybrid by entering and disabling its CPU mimics the scene in which Bowman deactivates HAL in 2001: A Space Odyssey.

There are a number of references to the TV drama Dawson's Creek, of which both Kyle and Cartman are apparently huge fans. Pictures of the cast can be seen on Cartman's Trapper Keepers, as well as in the hellish, apocalyptic vision of the future. Cartman also sings the theme song to the show, "I Don't Wanna Wait." He will sing this happy tune again while bludgeoning a Colonial messenger to death in "I'm A Little Bit Country."

The plot of this episode draws directly from The Terminator. Furthermore, Bill Cosby's clothing is reminiscent of the film's main character, Kyle Reese, while his accent (and the fact that he's a robot) are parodies of Arnold Schwarzenegger.

WHAT KYLE LEARNED

"Man, I guess sometimes we let our technology and stuff grow too fast."

HELEN KELLER! THE MUSICAL

Original Air Date: November 22, 2000
Episode No. 414

THE STORY: When the fourth-graders hear that the kindergartners' Thanksgiving play is going to blow their own production of *The Miracle Worker* (with Helen Keller played by Timmy) out of the water, they panic and start making changes. Kyle and Timmy are sent to purchase a turkey that can do tricks, while Cartman brings in a more experienced actor to help with the fourth grader's production. They even change the show into a musical.

But things go bad from the start. Timmy purchases a physically disabled bird, which he names Gobbles. The kids then bring in a professional performing turkey who comes with her own handler. But Timmy won't work with the new turkey—he wants Gobbles—and Timmy is the only one who can play Helen Keller. Cartman decides to kill Gobbles by "accident." But the light he rigs to fall on Gobbles kills Kenny instead.

The handler of the professional turkey comes up with a new plan to get rid of Gobbles. He convinces Timmy that Gobbles will be taken from him and used for hideous experiments unless Timmy lets him go free—which he promptly does. Gobbles is then picked up by a man driving an Uncle Joe's Fresh Turkey truck.

The night of the show, Timmy realizes he's been tricked and leaves to find his pet. Gobbles escaped the butcher shop, only to be cornered by Jimbo and a team of hunters. Timmy intervenes at the last possible moment by jumping in front of the bullet meant for Gobbles. The hunters bring Timmy and Gobbles safely back to the show and gun down the ringer turkey in retribution. The audience goes wild.

Shortly thereafter the kindergartners put on their extremely uninspired play, which lasts approximately 30 seconds.

MEMORABLE LINES

"Helen Keller, Helen Keller, blind as a bat / She can't hear us speak. What's up with that?"
—*Kids' chorus*

"My turkey does not work with other turkeys!!"
—*LeMonde*

"Come on, you blind bitch! Channel your spirit through me!"
—*Cartman*

"Alright, maybe I tried to have Timmy's turkey crushed by a stage light, but I didn't do anything else. I'm not an asshole."
—*Cartman*

"I swore that if I had to see it one more time, I'd put a bullet in my head. But luckily I got really stoned before I came."
—*Principal Victoria*

"Gobbles!!! Timmy!!!"
—*Timmy*

"That's Gobbles, the physically challenged turkey."
—*Cartman*

"We can't be outdone by the kindergartners!"
—*Kyle*

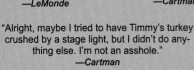

BODY COUNT

Kenny, crushed by a stage light meant for Gobbles. A whole truckload of turkeys at Uncle Joe's Turkey Farm, as well as the ringer turkey, Alinicia, who is gunned down by Jimbo and his hunting buddies.

WHERE DID THE IDEA COME FROM?

Matt and Trey decided that even though Timmy can't talk, they still wanted to make him the center of a big, emotional story.

CELEBRITIES IMPUGNED

While trying to sweat out the lyrics for the show's songs, Cartman fumes about whether Tim Rice had to deal with such distractions while writing *The Phantom of the Opera*. He didn't, in fact, write that (he wrote *Jesus Christ Superstar*).

LeMonde hints that Gobbles could meet an "unfortunate accident," and Cartman laughs, "You mean like Geena Davis getting her own TV show?" He's referring to *The Geena Davis Show*, a sitcom that lasted less than a season.

WHAT-THE-FUCK MOMENT

When Cartman covers his ears and blindfolds himself to try to experience what Helen Keller felt, the images that flash through his mind are perhaps the most disturbing 10 seconds in television history. He sees, in rapid succession, a man on fire, a desiccated mummy, a grisly operation, a mouse eating the brain of a dead mouse, and more. But even worse, when the professional actor who suggested the technique asks if he saw anything useful, Cartman says, "No, just the same old crap I always see when I close my eyes."

CHARACTER DEBUTS

Gobbles the turkey. Originally Matt and Trey planned to use a tiny, physically challenged puppy, but the scene in which Timmy abandoned it was simply "too fucking sad."

Geoffrey Maynard, the "expert" on musical theater who sings most of his dialogue.

LeMonde, the animal trainer, and his show-stealing turkey from Broadway, Alinicia.

POINTLESS OBSERVATIONS

Timmy selecting a handicapped turkey is an homage to Charlie Brown's selection of an unattractive Christmas tree in *A Charlie Brown Christmas*. The same scene was also parodied in the Halloween special "Spookyfish" (page 66). Only that time it concerned a puny-looking gourd that Kenny picked for a pumpkin-carving contest.

Cartman has a poster for Mr. T on his wall. He also has a still photograph of Helen Keller on his desk, which he uses to channel her blind spirit.

POP CULTURE REFERENCES

The tearjerking scene in which Timmy abandons Gobbles is an homage to a similar moment in the 1997 movie *Air Bud*. Also, the death of the turkeys at the slaughterhouse mimics the human euthanasia scene in *Soylent Green*.

Geoffrey Maynard, the expert on musical theater, is an homage to the character Jean Valjean of *Les Miserables*.

When Gobbles is about to get shot by Jimbo, Timmy jumps in front of the turkey in a super slo-mo shot yelling, "Gobbblllleeess!!" This is a classic action movie scene, where the hero takes a bullet for their friend (and only winds up with a flesh wound).

ORIGINAL SONGS

The fourth graders perform a number of songs for their Helen Keller Musical, the most notable being the fast paced "1800's Alabama," and big show-ending number "Water, Helen."

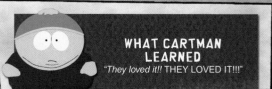

WHAT CARTMAN LEARNED

"They loved it!! THEY LOVED IT!!!"

WHAT TIMMY LEARNED

"Gobbles!!"

PIP

Original Air Date: November 29, 2000
Episode 405

THE STORY: This episode tells the story of Pip's life before he came to South Park—a life that bears a striking resemblance to the plot of Charles Dickens' novel *Great Expectations*. A poor, orphaned blacksmith's apprentice from the village of Dratfordshire Upon Topsmart, he takes a job at the Havesham estate as a playmate for Estella, the daughter of Ms. Havesham. Estella verbally and physically abuses Pip, who falls in love with her.

An unknown benefactor gives Pip the cash to travel to London to become a gentleman. Afterward he returns to the Havesham estate, where Ms. Havesham tells him that he should let Estella know how he feels about her. Pip does this, only to discover that the love of his life now has a 17-year-old boyfriend named Steve.

Devastated, Pip discovers that Ms. Havesham intentionally broke his heart, because she uses the tears of brokenhearted males to power her "Genesis Device," which will allow her to meld her soul with Estella's body, restoring her youth. Pip is then attacked by robot monkeys and barely escapes with his life.

Pip returns with reinforcements, confronting Ms. Havesham just as she's about to activate her Genesis Device, powered solely by the tears of Estella's numerous ex-boyfriends. He pulls Estella free of the machine, turning Ms. Havesham into a pile of ashes. Estella expresses her passion for her "small-testicled love," and the two embrace. The narrator assures us they live happily ever after. Which, of course, is not the case.

MEMORABLE LINES

"Stop dreaming about me you slow-witted rectal belch!"
—*Estella*

"Pip spent the next several months learning how to be a gentleman. He was taught fencing and marksmanship, and he was shown how to dance and eat box."
—*Narrator*

"We're going to play a little game called 'Smack the Blond Boy in the Head with a Large Log.'"
—*Estella*

"And the story ends, Pip, with me suggesting that one should never pull out their wee wee and check it for scabs whilst at the table."
—*Pocket*

"Oh, hello! Why, you look like an escaped convict."
—*Pip*

"Not so fast you ugly, ancient bitch!!"
—*Pip*

"Oh, what a gay time we shall have, and I do mean gay as in festive, not as in penetration of the bum."—*Pocket* "As for you, Pip, my robot monkeys should take care of you!"
—*Ms. Havesham*

"Right-o!"—*Pip*

BODY COUNT

The kind-hearted Escaped Convict has his face melted off by Miss Havesham's acid-goo saliva. Shortly after, Ms. Havesham is vaporized by the Genesis Device. Also, 25 baby bunnies have their necks broken by Estella before she finally tires of it. Everyone else lives happily ever after. Well . . . except for Pocket, who dies of Hepatitis B.

WHERE DID THE IDEA COME FROM?

For years Matt and Trey had toyed with the idea of doing a *Great Expectations* adaptation. Their version sticks pretty close to the spirit of the book—until the end, when the robot monkeys and Genesis Device are deployed.

POINTLESS OBSERVATION

This is the first episode in which Kyle, Stan, Cartman and Kenny do not appear.

Vivaldi's string masterpiece "Spring" from *The Four Seasons* plays over the opening and closing credits.

Over the course of the episode, Joe (the blacksmith) makes a metal firepoker, a metal orange, a metal newspaper, and a pair of metal fuzzy dice. Ironically, it's in the metal newspaper that they find Ms. Havesham's want ad.

BEHIND THE SCENES

A live-action introduction by Malcolm McDowell (who identifies himself only as "an English person") was added so that viewers understood up-front that they wouldn't be seeing any of the regular *South Park* characters. But this worked out great, because McDowell shared plenty of awesome anecdotes about Stanley Kubrick and the making of *A Clockwork Orange*.

CHARACTER DEBUTS

Mrs. Joe, Pip's mean older sister, and Joe, the blacksmith.

Estella, the young blond girl whom Pip falls in love with.

Miss Havesham, the mean old bitch with a broken heart.

Pocket, Pip's young roommate and friend, as well as the Escaped Convict, whom is indebted to Pip for his kindness.

CELEBRITIES IMPUGNED

For some reason former British Prime Minister Tony Blair is identified as the king of England.

POP CULTURE REFERENCES

The Genesis Device is the name of a machine pivotal to the plot of *Star Trek II: The Wrath of Kahn*.

WHAT PIP LEARNED

"Well, I've certainly learned a lot. That being a gentleman doesn't mean learning to dance, or proper table manners. It means being a gentle man. Gentle to everyone."

FAT CAMP

Original Air Date: December 6, 2000
Episode 415

THE STORY: Cartman is shipped off to Hopeful Hills Children's Weight Management Center to lose a few pounds. Instead of following the program, he hires a kid from a nearby drug rehab center to go home and pretend to be a slimmed-down version of himself. The kid smuggles junk food to him, which he sells to the other camp inmates.

Meanwhile, Kenny (egged on by Stan and Kyle) becomes a celebrity by doing hideously disgusting stunts, including eating dog poop and consuming his own vomit. Soon he gets his own TV show, *The Krazy Kenny Show*. It features him performing "crazy" acts for cash, like washing his hair in battery acid and giving his grandfather a full-body sensual massage. He even gets his own pay-per-view special, on which he plans to crawl into Ms. Crabtree's uterus and stay there for six hours.

However he's arrested for prostitution (specifically, for giving Howard Stern a "BJ" for $10) and can't make the show.

Stan and Kyle unmask the fake Cartman and force him to stand in for Kenny on TV. The boy is crushed to death by Ms. Crabtree's uterus, at roughly the same time that Cartman's junk food racket is uncovered at the fat camp. All the kids are given another chance to lose weight honestly—except for Cartman, who is sent home.

MEMORABLE LINES

"Oh, sweetie. . . . Those were all just lies. You're just fat."
—*Cartman's mom*

"I feel great! I haven't had this much attention paid to my kootch since I was 16!"
—*Ms. Crabtree*

"I told you I was a tight virgin flower!"
—*Ms. Crabtree*

"You know, Kyle, there was a time when your fat jokes would have gotten to me, but now I'm totally slim and totally happy."
—*Cartman*

"Dangnabit, children, how come every time you come in here, you gotta be asking me some question I shouldn't be answerin'?!"
—*Chef*

"Oh no, kids! It's glutinous fat!"
—*Rick the fat camp buy*

"Will somebody put this retard out of his misery?"
—*Cartman*

"Well I'm pissed off Rick! How are you?"
—*Cartman*

"They've kinda killed Kenny's look-alike. You bastards!"
—*Kyle*

"Mr. Candy Bar doesn't judge you, Chad. Mr. Candy Bar likes you just the way you are."
—*Cartman*

BODY COUNT

Cartman's skinny double (dressed as Kenny) gets crushed by Ms. Crabtree's uterus. So does another unnamed child, who slides out at the last minute. Also, an endangered manatee is bludgeoned to death by Ms. Choksondik, so it can be dissected and properly understood.

CELEBRITIES IMPUGNED

When Chef sings a song to the children explaining what prostitutes do, James Taylor for some reason joins him. During an appearance on *The Howard Stern Show* Kenny, Tom Green and Johnny Knoxville are each offered $50,000 go give Stern oral sex. After all three agree—and continually drop their price to get the "honor"—Kenny finally "wins" by agreeing to fellate the shock jock for $10.

Butters has an R. Kelly thermos, which Kenny uses to scoop up vomit. We will get to actually meet R. Kelly in "Trapped in the Closet."

WHERE DID THE IDEA COME FROM?

The story about Kenny doing disgusting stunts was inspired by the popularity of programs such as *Jackass* and *The Tom Green Show*. It was also written around the same time many *South Park* staff members were accepting money from other *South Park* staff members to do disgusting things.

CHARACTER DEBUTS

Rick and Susan, the energetic Fat Camp counselors, as well as a bunch of Fat Camp kids.

The Skinny Eric Cartman, and Kenny's grandfather (who receives a sensual massage at the hands of his grandson) also make single-episode cameos.

POINTLESS OBSERVATIONS

The infamous Antonio Banderas love doll, first seen in "Korn's Groovy Pirate Adventure" (page 94), sits behind Howard Stern when Kenny visits his show.

A lot of people come together for Cartman's intervention: Dr. Doctor, Mrs. Cartman, Mr. Mackey, Mr. Garrison. Stan's Mom and Dad, and Kyle's Mom and Dad. All of whom helped pay to send him to fat camp, except for Mr. Garrison who "just wanted to see the look on his face" when they told him.

Cartman mentions, "When I was in prison, we used to sneak stuff in by hiding it up our ass." This colon-smuggling happened in "Cartman's Silly Hate Crime" (page 114), where he snuck in a variety of goods, including Disneyland.

There's a scene featuring college students at the University of Colorado in this episode. Both Stone and Parker went to college there.

POP CULTURE REFERENCES

A scene in which the boys dissect endangered manatees in order to "understand" them is an allusion to the Japanese whaling industry, which regularly makes the case that it wants to kill whales in order to "understand" and "protect" them.

Cartman hums "You'll Never Find Another Love Like Mine" by Michael Buble while he's making a Toaster Pastry Chocolate Mix Butter Bar.

ORIGINAL SONGS

Chef and James Taylor jam out to the very informative, acoustic guitar duet "Prostitute."

WHAT THE CARTMAN IMPOSTER LEARNED

"We set Kenny up to further and further himself each time, having to always outdo himself. Now he's in jail for being a whore. And perhaps, just perhaps, we are to blame." (This out-of-character show of empathy was what led Kyle to unmask the fake Cartman.)

THE WACKY MOLESTATION ADVENTURE

Original Air Date: December 13, 2000
Episode 416

THE STORY: Kyle is upset when his parents won't let him go to the "Raging Pussies" concert with all the other boys, and angrily wishes he didn't have any parents. Cartman suggests he call the police and claim they're "molestering" him. Kyle does it, and his parents are immediately carted off to prison. The arrangement looks so appealing that soon every child in South Park accuses an adult of "molestering." The grownups are all hauled away, leaving the town in the hands of the kids.

Sometime later a couple named Mark and Linda are passing through South Park when their car breaks down. The town has become a desolate, post-nuclear-family wasteland divided into two warring factions—one led by Cartman (Smiley Town),

the other by Stan and Kyle (Treasure Cove). Their main disagreement is over how to worship The Provider—a 20-foot-tall statue of former Denver Broncos quarterback, John Elway.

The out-of-towners convince the kids that the "birth givers" (their parents) from "the before time" are necessary evils. They're also stunned to learn that the grownups have only been gone 10 days. The kids agree to tell the police they were lying about the "molestering." The parents return, but intense therapy while in prison has convinced them that they did, indeed, molest their children. They promise not to do it again. Then the boys wander off to build a snow igloo.

MEMORABLE LINES

"OUTLANDER!! WE HAVE YOUR WOMAN!!!"
—*Mayor Cartman*

"I'm gonna be sacrificed to the Provider!!"
—*Butters*

"Having no parents is awesome!"
—*Stan*

"You can go to the Raging Pussies concert if you clean out the garage, shovel the driveway, and bring democracy to Cuba."
—*Kyle's mom*

"When I wanted to get rid of my mom's last boyfriend, I just called the police and said he was molestering me, and I haven't seen him for three months."
—*Cartman*

"Parents can be pretty cruel sometimes, dude. They get off on it."
—*Stan*

"Snow igloos kick ass."
—*Cartman*

"Be careful, Mark! They'll make you disappear with the M word!!"
—*Linda*

BODY COUNT

Kenny, whose corpse lies at the feet of the town's 20-foot-tall statue of John Elway. There's also a couple other dead kids at the base of the statue. Butters, although more than willing, narrowly avoids being sacrificed to The Provider.

POINTLESS OBSERVATIONS

Craig dresses up as an astronaut and plays Spaceman. Mark calls him "Spaceman Spiff," a reference to a similar character in the comic strip *Calvin and Hobbes*.

After Castro decides to make Cuba into a democracy and allow American tourists, the newscaster reports that "plans can finally resume for Knott's Berry Farm, Cuba." Knott's Berry Farm is a popular theme park located in California.

When parents are being rounded up, Chef is one of two half-naked men escorted out of the house with Cartman's mom.

BEHIND THE SCENES

Originally Matt and Trey planned to have Cartman build a huge shield that blocked the sun from the side of town he didn't control. But at the last moment they discovered that *The Simpsons* had already done something similar.

CHARACTER DEBUTS

Butters' parents, who in light of their somewhat cavalier attitude toward his physical and emotional well-being in coming episodes, seem very concerned about him in this show.

POP CULTURE REFERENCES

The episode borrows from the movies *Children of the Corn*, *Mad Max: Beyond Thunderdome* and *Logan's Run*. Also the episode "Miri" from the original *Star Trek* series.

Bob Seger's "Old Time Rock n Roll" blasts during the child molestering montage. The first scene, where Kyle slides into the living room in his underwear, is taken directly from the classic Tom Cruise film *Risky Business*.

Outside of the mayor's office in Smiley Town is a huge blow-up King Kong replica, complete with an airplane in its grips.

When the Prison Counselor is trying to speak with all the parents about their uncontrollable child-molesting urges, he pulls out a life-sized black-and-white cutout of Jerry Mathers as "the Beaver" (from *Leave it to Beaver*). The Counselor also uses the phrase "Help me, help you," which is a famous quote from the movie *Jerry Maguire*.

ORIGINAL SONGS

Kyle sings to bring democracy to Cuba with his song "One Wish." It's so powerful, it single-handedly causes Fidel Castro to make Cuba democratic.

WHAT STAN LEARNED
"Things were a lot better with our parents around."

A VERY CRAPPY CHRISTMAS

Original Air Date: December 20, 2000
Episode No. 417

THE STORY: Concerned that South Park lacks the spirit of Christmas, the boys descend into the sewers to consult with Mr. Hankey. They find him living in a small cottage with his wife, Autumn, and three kids, the nuggets (Cornwallis, Amber and Simon). Mr. Hankey sends his kids to the surface to spread holiday cheer, but to no avail.

Undaunted, the boys decide to make their own animated holiday special and show it at the local, abandoned drive-in. They get $300 in seed money from the mayor for the project, which they call *The Spirit of Christmas*.

The animation process turns out to be a night-mare. Cartman quits, forcing Stan to dub his dialogue. And when the movie is finally shown, the film snaps in the projector. But Mr. Hankey, at first depressed over the disaster, finds a way to fix the film and bring the townspeople back to watch it.

The production teaches everyone that commercialism is the true meaning of Christmas, prompting them to rush out to buy presents. The mayor asks the boys if they'd like to make their own show and do 100 more episodes, to which Stan replies, "Are you kidding? I think we'd rather stab ourselves in the head."

MEMORABLE LINES

"We got so caught up in the little things of Christmas like love and family . . . that we almost forgot that it's buying things that makes our economy thrive."
—*Ms. Choksondik*

"That is the sprit of Christmas. Commercialism. Because that's what makes our country work!"
—*Randy Marsh*

"We're just pieces of crap. Christmas isn't for us."
—*Mr. Hankey's son, Cornwallis*

"How come everyone in cartoons has such big heads?"
—*Stan*

"Kyle, I have a full day of watching TV tomorrow, I don't have time to go on a poo hunt right now, okay?"
—*Cartman*

"We're just gonna have to face that the commercialism has been sucked out of Christmas."
—*Stan*

"You're the smartest piece of crap since Albert Poodinger!"
—*Mr. Hankey*

"Goddammit it's Christmas and we're gonna be a happy family around the tree!"
—*Mr. Hankey's wife, Autumn*

"Hey! Merry Christmas, asshole!"
—*Cartman*

"Hey, you boys . . . you boys wanna bet me I won't take off my clothes?"
—*Mr. Hankey's wife, Autumn*

POINTLESS OBSERVATIONS

As the boys discuss whether to make an animated film, scenes from *A Charlie Brown Christmas* can be seen on the TV in the background . . . including a scene of Snoopy beating a naked Charlie Brown in the face with a board.

When Butters makes construction paper cut-outs of the boys, Cartman complains that he's been made too fat, and Kyle says, "They kind of look like us. I mean, Stan's got blue eyes and I've got a sharper nose."

The little nuggets all sing "Good King Wenceslas" while trying to spread Christmas cheer. Cartman is dressed up as Santa, while Kyle, Kenny, and Stan are dressed as reindeer. Even with all these festive costumes, no one cares.

Mr. Hankey's wife Autumn has fake boobs—they're made of silicorn.

In the Drive-In projection booth, there's a picture of Barbara Streisand hanging on the wall. We first meet her in "Mecha-Streisand" (page 32).

BODY COUNT

Kenny, run over by a car.

WHERE DID THE IDEA COME FROM?

The show references *The Spirit of Christmas*, a 1995 video short that was one of the precursors to *South Park*. According to Matt and Trey, the problems the boys faced in making their film are exactly the same as the ones they had.

CHARACTER DEBUTS

Mr. Hankey's wife, Autumn, and their three little nuggets, Cornwallis, Amber and Simon. Autumn is an alcoholic who constantly complains about Mr. Hankey's impotence, while Simon is "slow" because he was born with a peanut in his head.

POP CULTURE REFERENCES

The boys decide to make their own Christmas special after watching *A Charlie Brown Christmas* and deciding that they . . . or anyone, for that matter . . . could do better. Also, Mr. Hankey sings an "inspirational" song called *The Circle of Poo* that's based on the Lion King number, *The Circle of Life*. Finally, the song *Even A Miracle Needs A Hand* is taken from an old 1974 Rankin-Bass special called *Twas the Night Before Christmas*. If you look closely, you can briefly see Kyle's face switch to the animation style from that 1974 special.

CELEBRITIES IMPUGNED

A poll on the TV news states that 38 percent of respondents were tired of Christmas, 5 percent were indifferent, and 57 percent said they would kick Bon Jovi square in the balls if given the opportunity.

ORIGINAL SONGS

The tribal, poop-filled song "The Circle of Poo" (sung by Mr. Hankey and Cornwalis) teaches us all the critical importance of poop.

BEHIND THE SCENES

Actual snippets from *The Spirit of Christmas* are shown during the episode, though the original soundtrack (lifted without permission from various CDs) had to be changed. Also, Cartman's voice was so different in the old video that they invented the idea of Stan impersonating him to explain it.

WHAT STAN'S CHARACTER IN THE FILM LEARNED

"It doesn't matter if you're Christian or Jewish or atheist or Hindu. Christmas is about one very important thing. Presents."

SEASON

5

IT HITS THE FAN

Original Air Date: June 20, 2001
Episode 502

THE STORY: The entire country freaks out when the HBC TV show *Cop Drama* uses the word "shit" uncensored. Suddenly everyone (including South Park's children, along with their parents and teachers) starts dropping the S bomb. At the same time a mysterious disease, which causes its victims to puke up their intestines, sweeps the land.

Kyle and the boys, with Chef's help, discover that the plague is triggered by excessive use of the word "shit"—which is referred to in ancient texts as a "word of curse." The more it's used, the worse things will get. And it's about to be used a lot more, because HBC plans an evening of live, shit-laden shows called "Must Shit TV."

Chef and the boys travel to Hollywood to talk the HBC executives out of their plans. But their attempt is preempted by an ancient warrior from the Royal Order of Standards and Practices. He storms the network's boardroom, attempting to use an ancient runestone to expose one of execs as "Gelden," an evil dragon that will be resurrected by excessive swearing and lay waste to the world. Instead he's shot to pieces by security, crashes through a window and lands on the sidewalk at the boys' feet. He gives them his rune- stone before he dies, but doesn't explain how to use it.

In order to divine the ancient relic's purpose, Kenny, Kyle, Cartman, Stan and Chef head for the nearest repository of wizards and ancient wisdom—The Excalibur Hotel and Casino in Las Vegas. There, a wizard explains that the Runestone of Undoing has the power to send Gelden back to the underworld.

The Knights attack the studio during Must Shit TV, but too late to prevent the dragon's appearance. Just then Chef and the boys arrive and use the runestone to drive the demon back into the underworld. Having learned his lesson, the President of HBC vows never to use the word "shit" again. Kenny vomits up his intestines and dies.

MEMORABLE LINES

"Yeah, they've taken all the fun out of shit." —*Cartman*

"They can't say 'shit' on television!" —*Stan*

"I'm very proud of you, children. Let's all go home and find a nice white woman to make love to." —*Chef*

"Oh, Kyle, you are so full of Mee Krob." —*Cartman*

"Tonight . . . On Cop Drama. . . On TV. . . They're gonna say. . . Shit." —*Cartman*

"Jeez, you're a little irritable, Ky What's the matter? You got some sa in your vagina —*Cartr*

"Hey, there, shitty shitty fag fag / Shitty shitty fag fag, how do you do?" —*Mr. Garrison*

"If that sand in your vagina doesn't get released, you could become a walking time bomb!" —*Cartman*

BODY COUNT

Numerous townspeople fall victim to the black plague and vomit out their intestines (including Kenny). An HBC Exec is decapitated by the red-haired Knight of Standards and Practices—immediately after, the Knight is shot to death by HBC security guards. Geldon the Dragon raises hell and kills a number of people in the studio audience, before being relinquished back into the depths of the earth.

Drew Carey and Mimi (from *The Drew Carey Show*) are both hacked to pieces by the Knights.

POINTLESS OBSERVATIONS

In addition to saying "shit," Mr. Garrison constantly uses the word "fag"—which isn't bleeped when he utters it because he's gay. When straight characters attempt to use the word, they're bleeped—except for Jimbo. "Guess we learned something new about you, Jimbo, you freakin' fag!" Mr. Garrison says. "You wanna make out or something?"

Butters shows his first signs of rebellion here, as he's seen graffiti-ing his name on the side of a building. He'll fully embrace his dark side in "Professor Chaos."

The HBC Television Network makes its *South Park* debut. HBC can be seen in many future episodes, providing both news and programming to the boys.

Chef and Principal Victoria are in bed together, watching *Cop Drama*.

WHERE DID THE IDEA COME FROM?

Originally Matt and Trey considered saying "shit" just once, then promoting it as some sort of "landmark television event." Comedy Central wasn't interested. However, when they suggested saying it maybe 200 times in one show, the brass was intrigued.

POP CULTURE REFERENCES

The phrase Must Shit TV is a pretty obvious twist on NBC's old Must See TV Thursday-night lineup.

Kyle has four tickets to see *The Lion King* musical, but no one wants to see it with him. Instead, they watch *Cop Drama*.

Cartman shares his hypothesis about Kyle's irritability by reading from a Nancy Drew novel, "Nancy goes to the beach and gets sand trapped in her shoe. This could explain how Kyle got it in his vagina."

CHARACTER DEBUT

HBC Network Executives, the marketing geniuses behind the whole "shit" phenomenon.

CELEBRITIES IMPUGNED

When the boys ask Chef what the Black Death might be, he replies, "LaToya Jackson, children." Also, the program singled out for abuse on Must Shit TV night is a parody of *The Drew Carey Show*.

OBSCENITY WATCH

The word "shit" is uttered exactly 162 times. Even Timmy manages to squeeze one out. Cartman, disheartened that the word has lost its potency, decides to say other things, such as "Mee Krob" (or "meecrob," as it's spelled in the anient book of Runestones). He explains that it's ." . . the stuff you get as an appetizer at Thai food restaurants. Meecrob is way grosser than shit, dude. I'd scarf down a whole wet bucket full of shit before I ate another plate of meecrob."

WHAT KYLE LEARNED

"Swearing can be fun, but doing it all the time causes a lot of problems."

CRIPPLE FIGHT

Original Air Date: June 27, 2001
Episode No. 503

THE STORY: Kenny, Cartman, Stan and Timmy join the State Mountain Scouts of America. Their troop leader is Big Gay Al. At their first scout meeting, they meet another disabled boy named, "Jimmy"— a new scout whose motivational stand-up comedy routine makes him an instant hit. "He's the coolest kid with disabilities in the world," Butters raves. Timmy, however, is not so enthusiastic.

The boys' parents aren't thrilled about leaving their kids with Big Gay Al. They complain to the State Mountain Scout's leadership, who boot him because they don't allow openly homosexual members. He's replaced at the next meeting by the macho-looking Mr. Grazier. "Now the first activity for this evening will be . . . naked pictures," Grazier announces.

The boys protest in downtown South Park to have Big Gay Al reinstated. Jimmy does his stand-up routine. When Timmy refuses to help him with

a joke by putting on a stupid-looking purple hat, the two move their argument to a dumpster-filled alley to slug it out. The bloody cripple fight draws a huge crowd, which reporters mistake for a show of support for gays in scouting. The case gets national exposure. Attorney Gloria Allred agrees to represent Big Gay Al. The Colorado Supreme Court finds in his favor, orders his reinstatement and has the scout "elders" placed in stocks. But Al refuses to rejoin and asks that the scout leaders be released. "If I'm free to express myself, then the scouts have to be free to express themselves, too," he says.

Mr. Grazier is arrested by the FBI and discovered to be a notorious pedophile named "Mr. Slippyfist." Jimmy and Timmy call a truce. Or at least, Jimmy does. Timmy Photoshops his nemesis' head onto a picture of two naked men embracing, and gets him thrown out of the scouts.

MEMORABLE LINES

"My mom says God had a plan for everyone, I guess I was plan B."
—Jimmy

"Get your big gay ass off the couch and come be our scout master again."
—Cartman

"I'm super, thanks for asking!"
—Big Gay Al

"Was your dad in scouts, Cartman? Oh yeah, you don't have a dad!"
—Stan

"If you work hard at it, maybe you could be as handiCAPABLE as me."
—Jimmy

"Cripple fight!"
—Cartman

"Wow, what a great audience."
—Jimmy

"Stanley, you call your friend an asshole this instant!"
—Stan's Dad

"Well, you know what I say about kids. They're all pink on the inside."
—Mr. Grazier

BODY COUNT

Kenny, carried away by a giant eagle as he stands on the steps of the Colorado Supreme Court, celebrating Big Gay Al's legal victory.

WHERE DID THE IDEA COME FROM?

Matt and Trey spotted a news story about a gay Boy Scout leader who got kicked out of the program. It came along none too soon, because they had only a week to prepare their next episode and no ideas.

CHARACTER DEBUT

Jimmy, a disabled kid who enjoys performing stand-up comedy. It's implied that he's from out of town, but in later episodes he becomes one of the boys' classmates. Marc, Big Gay Al's friend and pianist. He can actually be seen tickling the ivory in "Mr. Hankey's Christmas Classics" (page 104), but he gets a proper introduction here.

POINTLESS OBSERVATIONS

During their climactic fight, both Jimmy and Timmy seem able, briefly, to stand unassisted.

This is the first time we've seen Big Gay Al since his 1st season debut in "Big Gay Al's Big Gay Boat Ride" (page 16).

Priest Maxi speaks about how he himself "went through a homosexual phase" (and apparently had sex with a man named Peterson, among others). The boys also caught him committing sins with a female in "Do the Handicapped Go to Hell?" (page 128).

In an attempt to get him killed, Timmy gives Jimmy an orange parka—Kenny's orange parka. As Jimmy walks away, he narrowly avoids being killed by: a falling safe, a car crash, a giant eagle, Jimbo and Ned's gunfire, a flamethrower, a stampede of cows, and a falling space shuttle. The giant eagle eventually succeeds, scooping up the real Kenny at the end of the episode.

As a young scout, Big Gay Al attended Camp White Swallow and got medals for his achievements in 'Rope Tying' and 'Skin Diving'.

Timmy's wheelchair is a Lil' Run-About model.

Even though they're clearly Jewish, Kyle's dad and mom can be seen sitting in the Catholic Church when Cartman yells, "Cripple fight!."

POP CULTURE REFERENCE

The spectacular fight scene is an homage to a brutal combat sequence from the 1988 science fiction film *They Live*, in which professional wrestler "Rowdy" Roddy Piper and Keith David pummel each other in an alley. In "Cripple Fight," Jimmy wants Timmy to put on a stupid hat. In *They Live*, Piper wants David to put on a pair of alien-detecting sunglasses.

CELEBRITIES IMPUGNED

Gloria Allred, a real-life celebrity lawyer who comes off sounding like a shrill egomaniac. There's also a Steven Spielberg cameo, in which he also comes off sounding like a shrill egomaniac.

WHAT STAN'S DAD LEARNED

"Just because somebody's gay doesn't mean they're going to molest children. Straight people do that too."

SUPER BEST FRIENDS

Original Air Date: July 4, 2001
Episode No. 504

THE STORY: Magician David Blaine comes to town, enthralling everyone with his tricks and inviting them to enroll in his David Blaine Workshop at the Center for Magic. The boys attend, and are persuaded to join a Blaine-centered religion called Blainetology. Stan realizes something's wrong and escapes, but Kyle (along with Butters, Cartman, Kenny and others) stays behind.

Jesus, at Stan's urging, confronts Blaine during a Denver show, but is blown away by the magician's tricks. Deciding he can't defeat Blaine on his own, Jesus calls in the Super Best Friends—a "superhero" team composed of Buddha, Moses, Muhammad, Lao Tse, Joseph Smith, Krishna and Sea-Man.

They confront Blaine in Washington, D. C., where he's ordered his followers to drown themselves in the Reflecting Pool in front of the Lincoln Memorial—a protest against the government's refusal to give his church "tax-exempt" status. Kyle (who tried to escape from the cult but was betrayed by Cartman) has been imprisoned inside a plastic bubble.

Blaine uses his magic to make the giant stone Abraham Lincoln monument come to life, but the Super Best Friends counterattack with a giant stone John Wilkes Booth . . . which shoots Lincoln in the back of the head. Blaine flees and his still-surviving followers abandon him. Stan and Kyle reunite, then repeatedly and savagely kick Cartman in the crotch.

MEMORABLE LINES

"We've gotta stop that oversized Abraham Lincoln!"
—*Jesus*

"More than friends, young boy, we are Super Best Friends. With the desire to fight for justice."
—*Muhammad*

"I had no idea how unhappy I was until today!"
—*Kyle*

"Don't call Mr. Blaine a gaywad! He's a brilliant man."
—*Kyle*

"Blainetology is for everyone. There are Blainetologists who are Catholics, Buddhists . . . why even Kyle here is a Goddamned Jew."
—*Cartman*

"Oh, don't worry, I have a few more miracles up my sleeve!"
—*Jesus*

"We all believe in the power of good over evil. Except for Buddha, of course, who doesn't believe in evil."
—*Joseph Smith*

"I don't want to die either. I haven't even gotten my pubes yet."
—*Cartman*

"I don't think I'm very happy. I always fall asleep to the sound of my own screams."
—*Butters*

"Did you hear that guys?! We're finally gonna die!!"
—*Cartman*

"Jesus Christ!"
—*Jesus*

BODY COUNT

Kenny, who drowns himself in the Reflecting Pool. Countless Blainetologists commit suicide by drowning themselves as well. Furthermore, a bunch of cult members are killed by the giant stone Abraham Lincoln—who is, in turn, assassinated by a giant stone John Wilkes Booth.

POINTLESS OBSERVATIONS

Moses looks just like he did in "Jewbilee" (page 92). Which is to say, he looks like the Master Control Program from *Tron*.

The David Blaine workshop advertises "Free punch and pie!" in its flyer. This incentive was also used in the movie *South Park: Bigger, Longer & Uncut*, to entice kids to come join Terrance and Phillip's cause.

This is the first (and only) time we see all the kids with shaved heads. Without their signature winter hats and/or hair, they all pretty much look the same (well, except Cartman). It gets so confusing, Stan actually forgets who he is for a second, "Oh, wait . . . who am I again?"

Kyle and Stan play a little "Marco Polo" game in the Reflecting Pool, with Stan calling out "Oh my god. They killed Kenny!" and Kyle finishing "You bastards!". Stan uses it to pinpoint Kyle's location and save his life.

CELEBRITIES IMPUGNED

Well, David Blaine, who's portrayed as some sort of insane cultist. The real Blaine called the *South Park* offices after the episode aired and said that people were actually asking him for his Blainetology book. For the record, there's no such thing.

When Kyle tries to wake up Cartman, he screams out from his sleep "No Paula Poundstone, leave me alone!!"

POP CULTURE REFERENCES

A couple of David Blaine's actual TV specials are referenced in this episode, including his *Frozen in Time* primetime spectacular (referred to as "the miracle of being frozen in ice at Times Square").

When this aired, George W. Bush had just been sworn into office, and Parker and Stone's live action TV show *That's My Bush* had just debuted on Comedy Central. As the Blainetologists start killing themselves in D.C., we actually see the whole cast of *That's My Bush* animated *South Park*-style—from George W. right down to Larry, the wacky next-door neighbor.

CHARACTER DEBUTS

The Super Best Friends—including Muhammad. His appearance caused nary a ripple, which is strange because during "Cartoon Wars," Comedy Central absolutely refused to show him, out of fear of a backlash from Muslims.

George Bush, and his clan of Presidential cronies.

SUPERHERO REFERENCES

The Super Best Friends are a takeoff of DC Comics' famous superhero team: *Justice League of America*, which featured Superman, Wonder Woman, and Batman, among others. The character of Sea-Man is an allusion to Aquaman, who was also in the League. More specifically, this episode parodies the popular 1970s cartoon *Super Friends*, which was an animated adaptation of *Justice League*.

WHAT STAN LEARNED

"You don't need David Blaine to tell you how to live. See, cults are dangerous because they promise you hope, happiness and maybe even an afterlife. But in return they demand you pay money. Any religion that requires you to pay money in order to move up and learn its tenets is wrong. See, all religions have something valuable to teach, but just like the Super Best Friends learned, it requires a little bit of them all."

153

SCOTT TENORMAN MUST DIE

Original Air Date: July 11, 2001
Episode No. 501

THE STORY: Cartman announces to the boys that he has gotten his first pubic hair. He bought them from an eighth grader named Scott Tenorman for $16.12. Cartman vows revenge when he finds out you don't buy pubes, you grow them yourself. He decides to get Tenorman's favorite band, Radiohead, to come to town for a chili festival, then have a specially trained pony bite off his penis. He brings Stan and Kyle in on the scheme, and they promptly rat him out.

Tenorman convinces his parents to take the penis-biting pony, located at Farmer Denkins' ranch, to an animal shelter. In their absence he makes a batch of chili that's filled with pubic hair from all the boys in town.

At the chili festival Tenorman gets Cartman to try a bowl of the "pube chili," while he eats some of the chili Cartman prepared. Afterward, Cartman reveals that he knew Tenorman would give him a serving of pube chili, and that he switched it with food Chef brought. Then Cartman reveals that the chili he gave Tenorman is made from the bodies of his own dead parents, who were gunned down by Farmer Denkins when they tried to take the pony. It seems that Cartman knew that Kyle and Stan would betray him. That's why he revealed a portion of his plan to them.

Tenorman breaks down and starts crying just as the band Radiohead arrives. They mock him for being a baby. Cartman triumphantly licks the tears off his enemy's face.

MEMORABLE LINES

"Do you like it? Do you like it Scott? I call it . . . Mr. and Mrs. Tenorman chili."
—*Cartman*

"Didn't you hear the letter? This poor kid has cancer. In his ass."
—*Thom from Radiohead*

"You're not from the IRS! You glued my pubes onto your face!"
—*Scott Tenorman*

"You gonna cry all day, cry baby?"
—*Colin from Radiohead*

"Now dance little piggy. Dance and oink for me!"
—*Scott Tenorman*

"Come on, pony, bite the wiener. Bite it."
—*Cartman*

"Cartman, you are so God damned stupid, it's unbelievable."
—*Stan*

"That asshole! That big, smelly, ass-sniffin' asshole! I'm gonna get him!"
—*Cartman*

"Cartman, you don't buy pubes, you grow them yourself!"
—*Kyle*

"Oh, the tears of unfathomable sadness!"
—*Cartman*

BODY COUNT

Scott Tenorman's parents, and of course Kenny, who laughs himself to death while watching a videotape of Cartman begging Tenorman for his $16.12 back.

POINTLESS OBSERVATIONS

This is the second time Cartman has "achieved" manhood before all the other boys. The first being when he got his "period" in "Are You There God? It's Me, Jesus" (page 106).

When Mr. Tenorman yells at Ned and Jimbo for spying on his wife, a number of South Park males burst out of the bushes in various disguises, including Stan's dad (in a fake eyeglass/mustache combo), Kyle's dad (in a rainbow afro and clown nose), and Kenny's dad (with a paper bag over his head).

WHERE DID THE IDEA COME FROM?

Originally this episode was conceived as something that could be done in a hurry but might not turn out very well. Instead it became the darkest, most infamous of all *South Park* tales.

WHAT-THE-FUCK MOMENT

In the midst of consuming his bowl of chili, Tenorman discovers his mother's wedding ring—with his mother's finger still in it.

POP CULTURE REFERENCES

When envisioning an appropriate punishment for Scott Tenorman, Cartma first describes a scene from the film *Hannibal*. His later tasting of Tenorman's tears is also from the movie. Also, when he tries to enlist other kids to help him take down Scott Tenorman, Cartman gives a version of Mel Gibson's inspiring pre-battle speech from *Braveheart*.

Cartman, posing as an IRS agent, introduces himself as Kris Kristofferson—the name of a popular country singer-songwriter, known for the hit song "Me and Bobby McGee."

International rock gods Radiohead play an integral part in this episode. Scott Tenorman has posters of them on his wall, and Cartman and Ned even sing a bit of one of their early hits, "Creep." Also, in a failed attempt at revenge, Cartman dubs over an MTV News interview with the band.

CHARACTER DEBUTS

Scott Tenorman, an eighth grader with red hair and freckles. The Ticket Cashier at the movie theater is also briefly introduced. He can be seen again in a bunch of future episodes, including "The Passion of the Jew."

BEHIND THE SCENES

Tenorman has red hair, so his pubes should also be red. However they had to make them black, so that when Cartman carried them around they wouldn't get lost against his red jacket.

CELEBRITIES IMPUGNED

Cartman tries to distract Scott Tenorman by telling him, "Courtney Love is in South Park! She's all drunk and spreading her legs and showing her poonaner to everybody!"

WHAT KYLE LEARNED

"Dude, I think it might be best for us to never piss Cartman off again."

TERRANCE AND PHILLIP: BEHIND THE BLOW

Original Air Date: July 18, 2001
Episode No. 505

THE STORY: The boys get tickets for a live Terrance and Phillip show in Denver, but then learn that they're supposed to help that night with preparations for Friday's Earth Day Brainwashing Festival. In order to see the show, they tell the Earth Day organizers they'll get Terrance and Phillip to perform at their event.

However only Terrance—a fat, out-of-shape Terrance—appears at the Denver show. Afterward the boys learn that the comedy team has broken up, with Phillip now performing Canadian Shakespeare in Toronto. In a bid to reunite the two, they travel to Canada and get Phillip to sign on for an Earth Day appearance, without telling him that Terrance will be there too.

When Terrance and Phillip meet on the big day they instantly get mad and refuse to perform together. The boys instead offer a taped *Behind the Blow* documentary about the two during the live event. Upon seeing this, the Earth Day organizers go berserk and start chasing Stan, Kyle, Cartman and Kenny around with a meat cleaver. But after watching the television special, Terrance and Phillip reconcile and agree to perform together. The Earth Day organizers spare the boys' lives.

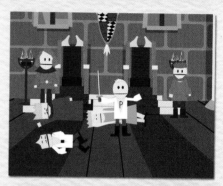

MEMORABLE LINES

"Oh, Kyle, you just made a huge withdrawal at the First Bank of Lies."
—*Cartman*

"Republicans are ruining the Earth."
—*Earth Day President*

"Look, if you don't come and do the show, I'll make you eat your parents!"—*Cartman*

"I don't think we're female groupies or random sluts."
—*Stan*

"Why don't you go eat some more pudding you fat ass drug addict!"
—*Phillip*

"Nothing is more important than the environment, boys . . . not even your lives"
—*Earth Day President*

"Well, in that case, I'd say you four boys are up Fart Creek without a paddle."
—*Terrance*

"Excuse me, is this where the Earth Day crap is happening?"
—*Phillip*

WHERE DID THE IDEA COME FROM?

The plot was hatched while the show's writing trust was sitting in a restaurant in Hawaii.

BODY COUNT

Kenny, who's killed bit by bit over the course of the show. Initially, an Earth Day operative cuts off his left hand when it looks as if Terrance and Phillip won't show. After the comedy duo refuses to perform, he chops off Kenny's other hand. Later, both his legs are hacked off, leaving a bloody stump. When Terrance and Phillip finally get back together, Cartman rolls over Kenny's limbless body towards the stage, "Look, Kenny! Everything turned out OK!!"

POP CULTURE REFERENCES

One of Terrance and Phillip's "classic" sketches is a takeoff on Abbott and Costello's famous "Who's On First" routine.

The TV show *E! True Hollywood Stories*, best known for it's biographical portrayal of celebrity downfalls—is parodied throughout as *Behind the Blow*. Punky Brewster—the cute little freckled girl from an 80s sitcom of the same name—has her own *Behind the Blow*, where it's revealed: "She learned that the price of fame can be pleasing sixty-five men at once in a dark, dirty alley."

The Earth Day spokespeople all use the "Jedi Mind Trick" from *Star Wars*, waving their hand magically and stating an order they want to be followed. Kyle also uses it to convince Terrance and Phillip to do the Earth Day show.

Phillip performs in the Canadian Shakespeare Company's performance of *Hamlet*. It actually stays pretty true to the classic play, if it were translated into Canadian.

In their biopic, Terrance and Phillip are shown throughout entertainment history: on *The Ed Sullivan Show*, *Sonny and Cher*, *Donnie and Marie*, and *The Tonight Show with Johnny Carson*; meeting with former president Gerald Ford and *Playboy* bunnies; and on the cover of *The Times* and *Teen Heat* (a magazine Randy also headlined in "Something You Can Do with Your Finger" (page 126). They even had their own *Star Trek*-esque Saturday Morning cartoon, for which they supplied the voices.

Clips of past *South Park* adventures are shown, corresponding with T&P's two feature films: *Not Without My Anus,* from the Season 2 episode of the same name (page 38), and *Asses of Fire* which was featured in *South Park: Bigger, Longer, & Uncut*.

CELEBRITIES IMPUGNED

Sonny and Cher, who are portrayed as brain-dead idiots during a vintage Terrance and Phillip appearance on a 1974 edition of *The Sonny & Cher Comedy Hour*.

POINTLESS OBSERVATIONS

The documentary *Terrance and Phillip: Behind the Blow* provides a trove of information about the duo. Among a great many other things, we learn that the war between Canada and the United States sparked by the comedy duo cost 8 million lives (we see this carnage in *Bigger, Longer & Uncut*); that their appearance on *The Donnie and Marie Show* won them the Nobel Peace Prize; and that their film *Not Without My Anus* caused enraged viewers to burn down the TV network's headquarters when it unexpectedly aired instead of the *John Schneider Variety Hour*. Finally, their full names are Terrance Henry Stoot and Phillip Niles Argyle.

Terrance and Phillip have the adage "Crapper Sweet Crapper" hanging in their bathroom. That sign also hangs in Kenny's bathroom, as we see in "Cartman Joins NAMBLA" (page 120).

Cartman threatens to make Phillip eat his parents if he doesn't agree to do the Earth Day Show. Stan even says, "He'll do it, dude." If you still don't believe him, watch "Scott Tenorman Must Die" (page 154).

Terrance and Phillip are responsible for the "birth of Canadian comedy"—an event that happened live on the *Ed Sullivan Show*.

ORIGINAL SONGS

A young Terrance and Phillip perform a fast-paced Canadian ditty "Chicken and Ham."

WHAT TERRANCE AND PHILLIP LEARNED

"You know, Phillip and I have learned an important lesson: That when you go through a lot with somebody, you can't let trite things come between you."

To which Phillip responds: "That's right, Terrance. You should only let trite things come between your asscheeks."

CARTMANLAND

Original Air Date: July 25, 2001
Episode 506

THE STORY: Cartman's grandmother dies, leaving him with a dream come true . . . one million dollars. He uses the cash to buy his own amusement park, which he names Cartmanland. He won't let anyone in but himself. This turn of events causes Kyle (who at the same time develops an infected hemorrhoid) to question the existence of a God who would allow someone like Cartman to be so happy.

But Cartman has problems of his own with his new amusement park. To raise cash to keep the park running he has to admit more and more paying customers each day. It seems that his policy of not letting anyone in has sparked public interest. People line up for blocks, clamoring for tickets. Cartman is hailed as a financial genius. Kyle, confined to the hospital by his crippling hemorrhoid problems, sees this news and immediately takes a turn for the worse.

Meanwhile Cartman, disgusted by the crowds, sells the park back to its original owners for $1 million—half of which is immediately taken by the IRS, and the other half is seized to pay damages for the death of Kenny (who was killed on a ride). Kyle, at death's door, is taken to the park to see Cartman grieving over the loss of his million dollars AND the amusement park. The sight causes him to rally, his hemorrhoid goes into remission and his faith in God is restored.

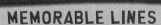

MEMORABLE LINES

"Why couldn't the funeral have been on a school day?"
—*Cartman*

"We'll be back as soon as Kyle's hemorrhoid is better!"
—*Stan*

"Kenny?! He dies all the time!"
—*Cartman*

"To my grandson, Eric, you were always my favorite fat little man. My perfect round little pudding piler."
—*Grandma Cartman's Will*

"Eric is the primary benefactor of my estate, since it is likely the rest of you would spend the money on crack."
—*Grandma Cartman's Will*

"Oh, God, do you have to embarrass me even in death, Grandma?"
—*Cartman*

"You made Kyle lose his faith in God you fat asshole!"
—*Stan*

"Amazing. Eric Cartman is surely the financial genius of our time."
—*Money Man*

"I have a hemorrhoid, and Cartman has his own theme park."
—*Kyle*

BODY COUNT

Kenny, impaled through the head by a pipe while on the Mine Shaft Ride at Cartmanland.

WHERE DID THE IDEA COME FROM?

Matt and Trey almost didn't do this concept because the idea of Cartman buying an amusement park seemed lame. But the idea of Cartman buying a park *and refusing to let anyone in* proved golden.

POINTLESS OBSERVATIONS

Kyle's questioning of God's existence seems a bit hypocritical, given that he actually met the Supreme Being in "Are You There God? It's Me, Jesus" (page 106). Also, the security guard Cartman hires is the mall cop from "Something You Can Do with Your Finger" (page 126).

We meet all of Cartman's relatives, shown briefly here at his Grandma's funeral, in "Merry Christmas Charlie Manson!" (page 68).

Stan tries to sneak into Cartmanland under the alias Mike Gayner.

Cartman's "You Can't Come Technique" is hailed as a marketing breakthrough, and immediately implemented by stores and businesses across the country.

CELEBRITIES IMPUGNED

Stan and Kyle use a firecracker to blow up a doll in a car—a doll they pretend is Jennifer Lopez. They make the doll plead for its life by saying, "I promise I'll never make another album or movie!" Also filmmaker Michael Bay. At the height of his existential funk, Kyle cries out, "Job has all his children killed, and Michael Bay gets to keep making movies. There isn't a God."

POP CULTURE REFERENCES

Cartman's prolonged rant about theme park lines is taken from *How the Grinch Stole Christmas*, when the Grinch goes into an equally impassioned tirade about noise.

The story of Job from *The Bible* is reenacted in *South Park* fashion here. It's actually a pretty depressing story.

WHAT KYLE LEARNED
"You are up there."

PROPER CONDOM USE

Original Air Date: August 1, 2001
Episode No. 507

THE STORY: When the fourth graders start beating off their dogs (in the mistaken belief that they're "milking" them), their parents demand they receive sex education. The fourth-grade girls are instructed by Ms. Choksondik (who despises sex) and the boys are taught by Mr. Mackey (who hasn't had sex since he was 19).

The girls are soon convinced that the boys have to wear condoms at all times to prevent disease transmission. So the boys buy some and start wearing them. When this gets back to the parents, they decide that sex education should begin even younger—in kindergarten. We are then treated to the spectacle of Mr. Garrison demonstrating to the kindergarten class how to put on a condom—by using one's mouth. Then he and the little kids review sexual positions.

The boys discover from Mr. Mackey that they don't have to wear condoms all the time—only during sex. Feeling that the girls are the source of all disease, they square off against them in an epic after-school battle involving flamethrowers and tricked-out cars.

Meanwhile, Mr. Mackey and Ms. Choksondik develop a sexual relationship. But their love making is broken up by the huge explosions from the kids' battlefield. Soon the town's adults break things up. Chef scolds the parents for not taking responsibility for teaching their own kids about sex. It's decided that, just perhaps, grade school isn't the best place to be introduced to the mysteries of sex.

MEMORABLE LINES

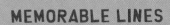

"It's very simple children. The right time to start having sex is 17."
—*Chef*

"I don't think ol' Mackey knows a hymen from a hysterectomy."
—*Chef*

"You think that sex is about fun and games and love? Wrong! Sex is about disease!"
—*Ms. Choksondik*

"I'm pretty sure I took the penis and I. . .what the hell did I do with the damn thing?"
—*Mr. Mackey*

"I want you, m'kay."
—*Mr. Mackey*

"Dumbass, you can only milk a dog once every few hours."
—*Cartman*

"Stay away from us, bastards! We don't want to get pregnant!!"
—*Wendy*

"No we can't do fingerpaints! You kids wanna get herpes?! How about a nice bucket of AIDS?!"
—*Mr. Garrison*

"Beating off the dog is not appropriate when we have company!"
—*Stan's dad*

"Oh geez, I don't wanna get the AIDS, fellas!"
—*Butters*

"Come on, dog! RED ROCKET!"
—*Cartman*

CHEF

BODY COUNT

The epic battle between girls and boys leaves a couple children injured, but only one dead: Kenny, who has his head sliced in half by a boomerang.

RANDOM OBSERVATIONS

The Parent's Book Club is discussing the Steinbeck novel *Cannery Row*. Ike was reading the same novel in "Do The Handicapped Go to Hell?" (page 128).

"For Maximus Protection" the boys buy some *Gladiator 'Lil Mini's* condoms. Kenny will purchase some *Big Mamba* condoms in "The Ring," although his pharmacist is a lot more supportive.

Mrs. Choksondik is a virgin. And Mr. Mackey's nickname in college was: 'That guy with the really big head'.

As the credits roll, we don't hear the typical outro. Instead, we are treated to more of Mr. Garrison's kindergarten lecture on sexual positions.

WHAT-THE-FUCK MOMENTS

This episode contains not one, but two, classic scenes that are almost impossible to watch without cringing: Cartman masturbating a dog to climax, and Mr. Mackey and Ms. Choksondik having sex.

POP CULTURE REFERENCES

When Butters, wearing a hockey mask, tells the girls in their fort to "just walk away," he's mimicking the character Humungus from *The Road Warrior*. This famous Mel Gibson film will also be referenced many times in future episodes, including "Good Times with Weapons" and "Eat, Pray, Queef."

CELEBRITIES IMPUGNED

Stan and Kyle torture a doll with a magnifying glass, pretending that it's Jennifer Lopez. As the doll melts, Stan shouts, "Scream for me, bitch!" They torture the same J-Lo doll in the previous episode, "Cartmanland" (page 158), only that time, it was with fireworks.

WHERE DID THE IDEA COME FROM?

Trey and Matt were channeling some of their anger over the STD scares of the 1980s, which they feel marred their own teenage sex lives.

CHEF

WHAT CHEF LEARNED

"Sex is emotional and spiritual. It needs to be taught by the family. I know it can be hard, parents, but if you leave it up to the schools to teach sex to kids, you don't know who they're learning it from. It could be from someone who doesn't know, someone who has a bad opinion of it, or even a complete pervert."

TOWELIE

Original Air Date: August 8, 2001
Episode No. 508

THE STORY: The boys' new 2001 Okama Game-Sphere is stolen by mysterious operatives seeking an intelligent towel that's wandering around South Park, asking people if they want to get high. The boys are told that if they want their Game-Sphere back they should bring the towel (called Towelie) to a gas station outside town. A gunfight breaks out and the boys and Towelie escape in a military truck.

It turns out there are two factions battling over Towelie—a group of space aliens masquerading as executives for a company called Tynacorp, and a group of disaffected former Tynacorp employees masquerading as a unit of the U.S. Army.

None of them matter to the kids, they just want their GameSphere back.

A huge battle at Tynacorp headquarters ensues. The building blows up, leaving the boys suspended over a vat of acid, hanging onto Towelie for dear life. A more advanced Evil Towel (called the GS-401) offers Towelie a joint if he'll drop the kids.

Making a supreme effort, Towelie manages to take a hit off the joint, then hoist the kids to safety. The Evil Towel falls into the acid and disintegrates. The boys recover their GameSphere and take it home to play, while Towelie gets monumentally high.

MEMORABLE LINES

"Hold on, let me get high. . .THEN I'll remember where it is!"
—*Towelie*

"Oh man, I have no idea what's goin' on."
—*Towelie*

"I've been out wandering around on my own for the past few weeks, you know, helping people out with towel safety and proper towel use. It's important."
—*Towelie*

"Well I'm through playing hide and seek! We've got no other choice! Prepare to blow up all of Colorado!"
—*Army Commander*

"Dude, he's in there punishing my toilet."
—*Stan*

"We shouldn't have this many responsibilities! We're children!"
—*Cartman*

"Don't forget to bring a towel!"
—*Towelie*

"You wanna get high?"
—*Towelie*

BODY COUNT

Countless military personnel, Tynacorp henchman, and scientists are killed in the bloody battle to recapture Towelie. Even Commander Thomas and Tynacorp's head scientist/alien, Zytar, are killed in the final showdown. Kenny and the Evil Towel are both incinerated when they fall into the vat of acid. And every towel within a 100-mile radius of South Park is shot to pieces.

POP CULTURE REFERENCES

The scene in which Towelie encounters failed, cloned versions of himself is taken from a similar moment in the movie *Alien Resurrection*.

There's also an alien hidden in one of the test tube towels behind Commander Thomas. Furthermore, the scene with the boys hanging onto the catwalk over a vat of molten lava is borrowed from *Aliens 3*.

When Commander Thomas and his army forces are searching for the missing Towel, one of the Marines suggests that maybe the boys are "telepathically linked to the towel. Like E.T."

While trying to remember the code to the security system, Towelie gets high and plays the famous disco jam "Funkytown" on the key pad.

CHARACTER DEBUTS

Towelie (aka Smart Towel RG400), an absorbent, stoner towel that befriends the boys. Also, his rival, the Evil Towel (aka the GS-401). We are also introduced to Commander Thomas on the military side, and the head Tynacorp scientist, Zytar, who turns out to be an alien in a wheelchair.

POINTLESS OBSERVATIONS

Throughout the episode, the *Popeye* theme plays when Towelie takes a hit off a joint, just as it did when Popeye ate spinach.

Even though Cartman and the boys bought tampons and got their "periods" in "Are You There God? It's Me, Jesus" (page 106), they still have no idea what a period actually is.

We see a live action commercial for Towelie products in this episode. "I Love Towelie" and "I Hate Towelie" t-shirts, as well as a Towelie Towel complete with push-button catchphrases. Not since the debut of Mr. Hankey in "Mr. Hankey, the Christmas Poo" (page 26) have we seen a new character get such immediate product placement.

The boys are pretty daring in this episode: Stan drives a car, with Kenny operating the gas and brake. Also, all four boys (and Towelie) jump out of a plane and parachute onto a military base.

JAPANESE CULTURE REFERENCES

The Okama GameSphere is a reference to the Nintendo Gamecube. The word "okama" means "gay" in Japanese.

WHERE DID THE IDEA COME FROM?

The show was a conscious attempt to create the worst, lamest character ever.

BEHIND THE SCENES

The Evil Towel (aka the GS-401) doesn't actually have a name in the episode, but in the script—and to people who worked on the show—he is called Gary the Evil Towel.

WHAT CARTMAN LEARNED

"You are the worst character ever, Towelie."

163

OSAMA BIN LADEN HAS FARTY PANTS

Original Air Date: November 7, 2001
Episode No. 509

THE STORY: When the boys each send $1 to Afghan children, Stan inexplicably gets a goat in return. Unable to keep it, he gets Kyle, Kenny and Cartman to help him smuggle it onto a military transport heading back to Afghanistan—which takes off while they're still aboard. Soon they're in Afghanistan, where they personally take the goat to its owners—four boys who look exactly like them, and happen to despise Americans. They sent the goat out of honor, because they couldn't take a dollar without giving something in return.

The boys are then captured and taken to Osama bin Laden, who makes a videotape of the four and their goat. The tape reaches the West, where the goat is mistaken for Stevie Nicks. Thinking she's been captured by the Taliban, American forces immediately attack bin Laden's headquarters. As the battle rages the Afghan boys sneak in and rescue Stan, Kyle and Kenny. Cartman stays behind to take care of bin Laden.

Kenny is killed during the escape—as is the Afghan boy who looks just like him. Meanwhile, in a takeoff on the various "battles of wits" between Bugs Bunny and Elmer Fudd, Cartman tortures and humiliates bin Laden, who is then finished off with a bullet to the head by an American soldier.

The show ends with the goat, backed by Fleetwood Mac, doing a USO concert. The two sets of boys decide that, one day, perhaps the American kids can grow to hate Afghanistan as much as the Afghans hate America.

MEMORABLE LINES

"It's an Afghanistan goat, so it can't stay here or else it will choke on the sweet air of freedom."
—*Cartman*

"Dude, don't call me a Canadian!"
—*Cartman*

"A flippity flappity floop! Jihad! Jihad!"
—*Osama bin Laden*

"Stan, if you're finished having your tearful goodbye with the goat, we'd like to go now, please."
—*Cartman*

"Terrorists is the craziest peoples!"
—*Osama bin Laden*

"So am I to understand there's been a 'Towelie Ban'?"
—*Towelie*

"Hey look! An infidel!!"
—*Cartman*

"Stanley, your mom's a little freaked out right now, why don't you go play with your big brown package from Afghanistan outside."
—*Stan's dad*

"Go America. Go Broncos."
—*Kyle*

"Remember when life used to be simple and cool?"
—*Kyle*

BODY COUNT

Kenny, Kenny's Afghan counterpart, numerous Taliban fighters and of course, Osama bin Laden. There's also the American Soldier who, upon smelling Cartman's fart, vomits and falls dead on the spot.

CELEBRITIES IMPUGNED

Stevie Nicks, who apparently is indistinguishable from an Afghan goat. Upon seeing the goat, soldiers swoon over her, saying "she looks great." The goat, backed up by Fleetwood Mac, perform an awful rendition of their hit "Edge of Seventeen."

While bin Laden is trying to woo a camel, Cartman holds up a series of insulting picture signs: a picture of shit and a head; a picture of a jack and an ass; and a picture of Barbara Streisand.

POINTLESS OBSERVATIONS

n the middle of the episode Towelie suddenly drops in unannounced. His sole role is to introduce a gag about how the kids don't want him around, and that there's been a "Towelie ban."

At the time this aired, there was a huge anthrax and small pox scare going on. The boys all wear gas masks at the bus stop in an effort to combat this.

All Kenny has in his backpack is pornos: *Hotties, Juicy, Whoppers*.

We can see Stan's address clearly on the letter he sends to the Afghan kids: Stan Marsh, 2001 Bonanza Street, South Park CO 80439. In "Jakovasaurs" (page 82), we saw Cartman's address: 21208 E. Bonanza Circle, South Park, CO.

Agent Johnson tests for diseases by French kissing the goat.

He dressed up as a Vietnamese prostitute in "Cow Days" (page 62) and an undercover-cop prostitute in "Chickenlover" (page 42), but here, Cartman tries to woo Osama bin Laden by dressing up as a Muslim woman. Osama goes for the camel instead.

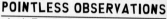

CHARACTER DEBUTS

Osama bin Laden, and the Afghan versions of Kenny, Stan, Cartman, and Kyle.

POP CULTURE REFERENCES

Cartman refers to Afghans as "Jawas," the tiny, robed aliens from *Star Wars*. He also, incorrectly, calls them "Sand People," a title reserved for the Tusken Raiders.

After getting into an Afghan "taxi" (which is just an engineless car pulled by a mule), Cartman says, "God what is this, the freakin' *Flintstones*?"

The series of scenes in which Cartman taunts Osama bin Laden is a parody of the antics of Bugs Bunny outwitting Elmer Fudd, from the iconic *Looney Tunes* cartoons. The signs that Cartman holds up, the music cues, the big smooch he gives him, the dynamite finish—all parody popular elements of the show.

While arguing over which country is better, the Afghan kid yells, "It's better than a civilization that spends its time watching millionaires walk down the red carpet at the Emmys." Stan's dumbfounded, "He's got us there, dude."

WHERE DID THE IDEA COME FROM?

The episode reflected a general consensus that *South Park* had to talk about 9/11, which happened only a few weeks before this show aired.

WHAT STAN LEARNED

"America may have some problems, but it's our home. Our team. And if you don't wanna root for your team, then you should get the hell out of the stadium."

HOW TO EAT WITH YOUR BUTT

Original Air Date: November 14, 2001
Episode No. 510

THE STORY: Kenny poses for a class photo with his butt sticking out of his parka instead of his face. Cartman takes the joke a step further by convincing a local milk company that the picture is of a missing child. The company promptly plasters the shot on all their milk cartons. Incredibly, a Wisconsin couple with butts for heads (an ailment they refer to as "torsonic polarity syndrome") sees the photo and, thinking it might be of their missing son, contacts the milk company.

When the butt-faced couple meets Cartman face-to-ass, he blows a "funny fuse." Having seen the funniest thing he's ever likely to see, his sense of humor overloads and he's no longer able to laugh at anything else.

Meanwhile, Steven and Marsha Thompson (the butt-faced people) use the Dairy Gold Milk Company's computer database to find for their real son—who turns out to be actor Ben Affleck. When Cartman suggests that they call him "Ben Assfleck" from now on, the other kids notice that he laughs at his own joke. Stan and Kyle theorize that the real reason he couldn't laugh was because he felt guilty about the prank. But when things turned out for the best, his sense of humor returned.

A moment later Kenny is run over by a motorcycle and killed. Cartman finds this absolutely hilarious.

POINTLESS OBSERVATIONS

This is the first time that Kyle takes his hat off, revealing a massive orange/red Jew-fro.

From Cartman's house, Kenny lives "about 4 houses away, on the bad side of town."

This is the first of many times we see Butters grounded by his parents. This time it's for "making a funny face" in his school pictures. In fact, his silly faces are so out of control, his parents make him wear a paper bag over his head.

Gross Out Comedy 8 is playing at the theater. This is not to be confused with *Fisting Firemen 9* from "Butters Very Own Episode" (page 174). In the theater, Cartman is confronted by Mark, the drummer from Lords of the Underworld (seen in "Cat Orgy" (page 88) and "Timmy 2000" (page 116)).

This is the first time we've seen Jimmy since his introduction in "Cripple Fight" (page 150). He performs some jokes one-on-one for Cartman, but they don't go over well.

CHARACTER DEBUTS

Steven and Marsha Thompson, the butt-faced couple. And Ben Affleck, who appears again (and falls in love) in "Fat Butt and Pancake Head."

BODY COUNT
Just Kenny.

POP CULTURE REFERENCES

Whenever a question is asked of the milk company's computer, it replies with "Working," just like the library computer on *Star Trek*. Also, Mr. Mackey tells Cartman that if he truly feels he's lost his sense of humor, he could always become a writer for the TV show *Friends*.

CELEBRITIES IMPUGNED

Ben Affleck, who apparently was fathered by two people with asses for faces. His actual photo is used, and is lovingly squeezed between his two full-cheeked parents during their reunion.

WHERE DID THE IDEA COME FROM?

In high school Trey drew a comic strip about two people with butts for heads.

WHAT STAN LEARNED
"Wow . . . Cartman actually felt bad for somebody and couldn't laugh at them."

167

THE ENTITY

Original Air Date: November 21, 2001
Episode No. 511

THE STORY: Frustrated over the hassles of airline travel, Mr. Garrison develops a revolutionary new form of transportation called the "IT." The device travels 200 mph and gets 300 miles per gallon. The only drawback is the controls—one stick for each hand, another for the mouth and a fourth inserted in the anus. However there's a general consensus that it's still more pleasant than dealing with the airlines. Millions are sold.

Meanwhile, Kyle's cousin (also named Kyle) comes for an extended visit. He's a whining pain in the butt, breathes heavy, wears gigantic glasses, and suffers from every food allergy and respiratory ailment known to humanity. Even worse,

Kyle's mom insists on referring to the visitor as "Kyle," and to her own son as "Kyle 2." The boys try various ways to run him out of town, including putting him in a box and stuffing it onto a plane bound for Antarctica. But he keeps coming back.

Mr. Garrison's IT is a huge success—until the government, concerned that the device will bankrupt the airlines, outlaws its manufacture, sale and use. Ironically this causes Kyle's cousin to pack up and leave town. He invested in the IT project and received a $5 million bailout check, which he plans to use to help his family. Before he departs he tells "Kyle 2" that he and his friends are a bunch of redneck douche bags.

MEMORABLE LINES

"Gentlemen, imagine being able to travel safely at incredibly fast speeds, and not having to go to the stupid fartface airports!"
—*Mr. Garrison*

"Oh Jesus, why don't you just cut off my balls?"
—*Cartman*

"I mean, I'm a Jew and he's making me hate Jews!"
—*Kyle*

"Boy, that Enrique Iglesias can sure gyrate his hot ass around."
—*Mr. Hat*

"You people are all just such hick, jock rednecks. . . It's like you're right out of a stereotype catalog."
—*Kyle's Cousin Kyle*

"Kyle, this is Cartman. He's my sort of friend-ish."
—*Kyle*

"Good job, Jew!"
—*Cartman*

"So then couldn't I just order one that works WITHOUT going in and out of my ass and mouth?"
—*Stan's dad*

BODY COUNT

Kenny, gunned down at the airport when security guards find him carrying a pair of nail clippers.

WHERE DID THE IDEA COME FROM?

The episode lampoons both post-9/11 airport security measures and the hype surrounding the Segway, which was supposed to "revolutionize travel." Matt and Trey purchased one for the *South Park* offices, then broke it while taking it off some jumps.

POINTLESS OBSERVATIONS

Mr. Garrison says he possesses a master's degree in mechanical engineering from Denver Community College.

Running list of Kyle's Cousin Kyle's ailments: Asthma, degenerative problem with his intestinal lining, polyps on the back of his hands, a fear of splinters, poor eyesight, and extreme sensitivity to dry air and cold temperatures. For this reason, Kyle offers Cartman $40 to not rip on his cousin, but Cartman doesn't even make it through one period of school without breaking.

CHARACTER DEBUTS

Kyle's cousin Kyle. A hypoallergenic, annoying relative from Connecticut. He will make another appearance in "The Losing Edge."

POP CULTURE REFERENCES

In the commercial for the IT, there's a shot of two old ladies at the Grand Canyon. When asked how they got there, they yell "Hoveround!!" This is a parody of the popular Hoveround commercials for power wheelchairs.

CELEBRITIES IMPUGNED

Enrique Iglesias, whose ass-gyrating TV performance inspires Mr. Garrison to use gyroscopes on his new personal conveyance. Also John Travolta, who does a graphic commercial plugging the IT.

The top minds and investors in America gather for Garrison's presentation of the IT: Steve Forbes, Steve Jobs, Ted Turner, Donald Trump, Bill Gates, and. . .Yasmine Bleeth, who's dirty, sniffling, and has a rubber tube tied around her arm.

WHAT KYLE LEARNED

"Sometimes people have trouble fitting in at school and . . . and um . . . let's see, what did I learn about? What did I learn about today?"

...COMES THE NEIGHBORHOOD

Date: November 28, 2001

...512

THE STORY: When the other kids make fun of Token because his family is rich, he decides to attract more wealthy people to town by placing an ad in *Forbes* magazine touting South Park as the next Aspen.

To his delight, rich celebrities (all of whom happen to be black) take notice and move in. But the locals aren't happy about South Park being overrun by "those types." And by "those types" they mean the "rich." Tensions between the "richers" and the townies hit the boiling point when a mob led by Mr. Garrison burns a "lower-case T" (for "time to leave") on Kobe Bryant's lawn. The "richers" retaliate by organizing a Million Millionaire March.

Meanwhile, Token discovers he doesn't fit in with the newcomers either. Feeling like he doesn't fit in anywhere, he gives up on human friends, and moves in with the lions at the zoo. But this soon gets old. He realizes he likes his old, poor South Park friends best, even if he doesn't quite fit in. The kids take him back, telling him they'll never again mock him for his wealth. Instead, they'll call him a pussy for being so emotional about his hurt feelings.

In a last ditch effort to drive out the "richers," the townsfolk dress up in white sheets and pretend to be ghosts. This does the trick. The newcomers flee the town.

MEMORABLE LINES

"Hey look, these pants are only five bucks apiece. They must really suck."—*Token*

"There goes the neighborhood."
—*Jimbo*

"It looks like it will be a great turnout, as some of the millionaires also paid several thousand Mexicans to march for them."
—*News Reporter*

"Your mother is a chemist for a pharmaceutical company, whereas your friend Eric Cartman's mother is a crack whore. One pays more than the other."
—*Token's dad*

"Maybe you didn't see the sign out front. This bar is for people living below their means ONLY!"
—*Barkeep*

"What's in the huge box, richer? Your checkbook?"
—*Garrison*

"For my project I made a pencil taped to a pen. In this way we see the duality of writing devices that occur in nature."
—*Cartman*

"I do believe this town is HAINTED!"
—*Rich Guy*

BODY COUNT

Just Kenny, though we don't know how. Toward the end of the episode we see his badly beaten body, but what happened to him isn't explained.

WHERE DID THE IDEA COME FROM?

The show is about racism, sort of, though it's cast as a battle between rich and poor—right until the very end, when Mr. Garrison blurts out the front half of a racial slur before being cut off by the show's credits. Some people consider it smart and ironic, but Trey and Matt aren't so sure. "It seems to be smart, but I don't think it is very smart," Matt says.

POP CULTURE REFERENCES

When Token brings over a DVD of *The Lion King* for the boys to watch (not realizing none have DVD players), Cartman offers to "take this disk up to the Enterprise and see if Captain Kirk can decrypt it." Also, the lion that leads the pride in which Token tries to live is named Azlaan, after the "Great Lion" character Aslan from *The Lion, the Witch and the Wardrobe*.

Token's clothes are from Armani Exchange, an expensive Italian clothing store. The boys' clothes are from J-Mart (a spoof of K-Mart), where Token eventually shops to try and fit in. While in J-Mart, there's a line of home goods called "Bertha Stewart," a parody of Martha Stewart's home décor line. We'll see more of Stewart in "Red Hot Catholic Love" and "Eat, Prey, Queef."

Token has an autographed Barry Bonds baseball bat.

The Million Millionaire March is a parody of the Million Man March, a mass political demonstration put on by African American men in 1995.

CHARACTER DEBUTS

Azlaan the lion, who seems unusually interested in practical jokes. Also Oprah Winfrey (who will be seen again in "A Million Litte Fibers").

POINTLESS OBSERVATIONS

When Token's parents visit the local discount store, Kyle's mom wonders why they bother when they can afford to shop at Cherry Creek—a real Denver-area shopping mall.

After getting a check minus on his presentation, Cartman says to Ms. Choksondik, "I'll make you eat your parents." This is the second time he's used that threat (the first being in "Behind the Blow" (page 156)).

While the rich kids play polo, the boys play their own game . . . "I'll kick you in the nuts."

ORIGINAL SONGS

Token has his singing debut with the somber "Send More Rich Kids To My Town." Snoop Dogg also lays down some smooth beats with the snippet "Girl Who Had An Inny."

CELEBRITIES IMPUGNED

Pretty much every A-list African American television, music, movie and/or sports star (along with their kids, who come off as snooty and over-privileged). More specifically, we see: Will Smith, Snoop Dogg, Oprah Winfrey, Kobe Bryant, Bill Cosby, and Puff Daddy's kids (named P. Diddy Mini, Pidi Poofy Bite Size, and Puff A Diddy Daddy Puffy Fun Size)

WHAT TOKEN LEARNED

"You see, even though kids at South Park make fun of me, I still like hanging around them more than snobby rich kids or lions. Even though I may be different from them, I still like my old friends best."

171

KENNY DIES

Original Air Date: December 5, 2001
Episode No. 513

THE STORY: Cartman discovers a crashed truck carrying aborted human fetuses and tries to sell them to various research labs, only to have his plan derailed when Congress bans stem cell research. But when the boys are informed that Kenny has been diagnosed with a terminal disease and will soon die, Cartman—in an uncharacteristically dramatic, emotional encounter—vows to find a cure for him. He then breaks down at the hospital and cries in Kyle's arms.

Cartman goes to Washington to address a joint session of Congress. His impassioned singing of Asia's song "Heat of the Moment" convinces the legislators to change their minds and repeal the ban. But it comes too late. When Stan (who hasn't been able to summon the courage to visit Kenny) finally turns up at the hospital, he finds that his friend just died.

Stan is despondent at Kenny's funeral, until Cartman suddenly bursts in and tells them to come outside to see a "miracle." It turns out he only wanted the ban repealed so that he could use the stem cells (which can regenerate other types of cells) to clone his own Shakey's Pizza. Kyle immediately begins to savagely pummel Cartman, while Stan, relieved, realizes he wasn't Kenny's worst friend after all.

MEMORABLE LINES

"No! This can't happen! Kenny can't die! Kenny can't die!"
—*Stan*

"I'm just like the fetuses, Chuck—I wasn't born yesterday either."
—*Cartman*

"Aw man, here we go again! Use the Jew as a scapegoat."
—*Kyle*

"There's a pretty brave kid fighting for his life in the hospital right now, Doctor. . .I'm gonna go get him some bigger boxing gloves."
—*Cartman*

"These are primo fetuses Randy, I wouldn't jerk you around."
—*Cartman*

"Alright Cartman, what's so important that you had to pull us away from lighting cow crap on fire?"
—*Kyle*

"Oh, you're breaking my balls."
—*Cartman*

WHERE DID THE IDEA COME FROM?

Trey and Matt were sick of thinking of new ways to kill Kenny every week and wanted to dispose of him permanently.

BODY COUNT

Kenny. Also, the driver of the feuts truck, who crashes off a cliff to avoid a deer in the road.

CHARACTER DEPARTURES

Kenny. And this time, he stays dead for more than a year.

POINTLESS OBSERVATIONS

On a couple of occasions the boys amuse themselves by setting fresh piles of cow manure on fire.

The show opens with a doctor about to give a woman an abortion. The same woman can be seen getting an abortion in "Woodland Critter Christmas," only that time, the doctor gets some help from three lion cubs.

Cartman stumbles upon 33 aborted fetuses, which he tries to sell through telemarketing. After the ban on stem cells kills his customer base, he tries selling them as "succulent shrimp from the West Indies."

This is Kenny's second funeral, the first being in "Spontaneous Combustion" (page 78). And it's not his last—he gets another peaceful send off in "The Ring."

CELEBRITIES IMPUGNED

Madonna, whom Kenny calls (via Kyle's translation) "an old anorexic whore who wore out her welcome years ago, and that now she suddenly speaks with a British accent and she thinks she can play guitar and she should go fuck herself."

POP CULTURE REFERENCES

Cartman begins his speech before Congress by saying, "I love Kenny McCormick, and I want you to love him too." This is lifted from the movie *Brian's Song*, when Gale Sayers makes a speech on behalf of Brian Piccolo.

Unplanned Parenthood is a rip on Planned Parenthood, an organization that tries to promote sexual health and education. During the opening scene where the doctor is prepping his patient for her abortion, a laugh track is heard between lines of dialogue. We then cut to the TV and see it's from *The Benny Hill Show*.

Willie Nelson's classic traveling tune "On the Road Again" plays over the montage of fetuses being packed up and shipped away. When Cartman rolls up on the overturned fetus truck, he's humming "My Baby Takes the Morning Train" by Sheena Easton. Lastly, when Cartman gives an impassioned speech to Congress, he seals the deal with a timeless song: "Heat of the Moment" by Asia.

Cartman says he learned about stem cells on *3-2-1 Contact*, an educational science show that ran on PBS in the 80s.

Shakey's Pizza, the ultimate object of Cartman's desire, is a popular pizza chain.

WHAT CHEF LEARNED

"If you want to make a baby cry, first you give it a lollipop. Then you take it away. If you never give it a lollipop to begin with, then it would have nothing to cry about. That's like God, who gives us life and love and help just so that he can tear it all away and make us cry, so he can drink the sweet milk of our tears. You see, it's our tears, Stan, that give God his great power."

BUTTERS' VERY OWN EPISODE

Original Air Date: December 12, 2001
Episode No. 514

THE STORY: Butters' parents' anniversary is right around the corner. Wanting to see what present her husband is getting her, Butters' mom asks Butters to follow his dad around town. Butters does this, and reports back to his mother that his dad had spent the evening seeing a movie (*Fisting Fireman 9*), and then going to the gym (a place called the "White Swallow Spa").

Butters doesn't understand the implications of his father's actions, but his mom does, and immediately has a psychotic breakdown. First she drives Butters to a lake and rolls the car into the water with her son still in the front seat. Then she goes home to hang herself. But before she does, her husband comes home, apologizes, and says he still loves her and wants to change his ways.

Then they decide cover up their son's mur-der by saying their car was carjacked by "some Puerto Rican guy" with Butters inside. But Butters isn't dead. The car floated miles downstream be-fore hitting some rocks, allowing him to get out in the middle of nowhere. Then, slowly—driven on by the fact that his parents had planned to take him to eat at Bennigan's—he makes his way back to South Park.

He gets home in time to surprise them on their anniversary. After regaining their composure, they tell Butters he has to say that a Puerto Ri-can man dropped him off. Taken aback, Butters gives an impassioned speech about how lying is wrong. It affects his parents so deeply that they call a press conference and admit that not only was his dad having random sex with strange men, but his mom actually tried to kill him. This of course horrifies Butters, but on the bright side he still gets his dinner at Bennigan's.

MEMORABLE LINES

"It looks like the car is fillin' up with water. Yeah, I think maybe now might be a good time to come back inside the car and drive, mom."
—Butters

"He went in there and wrestled with all kinds of guys. He wasn't too good though. This one black guy had him pinned down for fifteen minutes straight!"
—Butters

"Sometimes telling a little white lie is okay. Like, for instance, when you catch your father jacking off in a gay men's bath house."
—Butters' dad

"I could use some God-damned poontang myself right now."
—Butters

"Wow dude, your dad's a perv and your mom tried to kill you."*—Stan*

"I ain't grounded, am I?"*—Butters*

"Inspector Butters is on the case, ma'am!"*—Butters*

"Paint. . . Must paint. . . Everything clean. Everything new . . ."
—Butters' mom

BODY COUNT
Nobody.

WHERE DID THE IDEA COME FROM?
After killing off Kenny "Kenny Dies" (page 172) in the previous episode, Matt and Trey did an entire show about Butters to "introduce" him as Kenny's replacement.

POINTLESS OBSERVATIONS
This particular episode is treated as if it really was a show about Butters. It even has its own intro and theme music. A similar approach was taken with "Starvin' Marvin in Space" (page 100). Also, a headline on a newspaper being read by Butters' dad says "Towelie Ban Lifted." It refers to a joke in "Osama bin Laden Has Farty Pants" (page 164).

This won't be the last time that Butters' parents think their son is dead and resort to drastic measures. In "Marjorine," they actually try to bring him back from the dead.

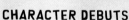

CHARACTER DEBUTS
This is the first time we get a really good look at Butters' parents, Chris and Linda. The Old Gas Station Worker is also introduced. We see him again in "Asspen" and "Marjorine," and each time, he dispenses some spooky, mythical knowledge about the areas around South Park.

POP CULTURE REFERENCES
While walking along a deserted road, Butters is for some reason targeted by a three-dot laser site that's exactly like the one used by the aliens in the *Predator* movies.

In Butters' theme song, there's a picture of Butters and Broncos quarterback John Elway. A line in the song also mentions, "He loves John Elway."

Butters' dad's cozy, wholesome office is an homage to Beaver's dad's home office in *Leave It to Beaver*.

"Jingle Bell Rock" plays on the radio while Butters' mom sends her son and car into the lake.

Bennigan's, a now-bankrupt family restaurant chain, is the driving force behind Butters getting home. He loves the eatery, a love that he will mention again in the future.

The Butters case attracts the attention of John and Patsy Ramsey, O.J. Simpson, and Congressman Gary Condit—all people involved in famous murder cases. They initiate the Stotches into their support group with the chant "One of us! One of us! Gooble Gobble! Gooble Gobble!." This is a parody of the classic horror movie *Freaks*.

ORIGINAL SONGS
Butters gets royal treatment in this episode, with his very own campy theme song for *The Butters Show*.

WHAT BUTTERS LEARNED
"I really wish I didn't know that stuff. I guess I learned that sometimes, lying can be for the best. Yup."

THE SOUTH PARK
EPISODE GUIDE

VOLUME 1   SEASONS 1 - 5